PUBLISHERS
Alex Oleszewski

Cliff Hensley   Cori Hart

EDITORS
Cori Hart   Cliff Hensley

TYPESETTING, LAYOUT and DESIGN
Cori Hart

Published annually in Fall, Seven Story Hotel is a publication of Subtle Body Press:

Alex Oleszewski | CEO

Cliff Hensley | Managing Director, Editor-in-Chief

Cori Hart | Creative Director, Senior Designer

ISSUE TWO, FALL 2024 EDITION, November 5, 2024

ISBN 979-8-9854370-7-2

Library of Congress Cataloging-in-Publication Data available upon request.

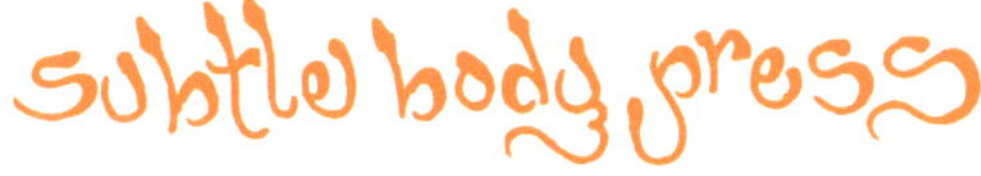

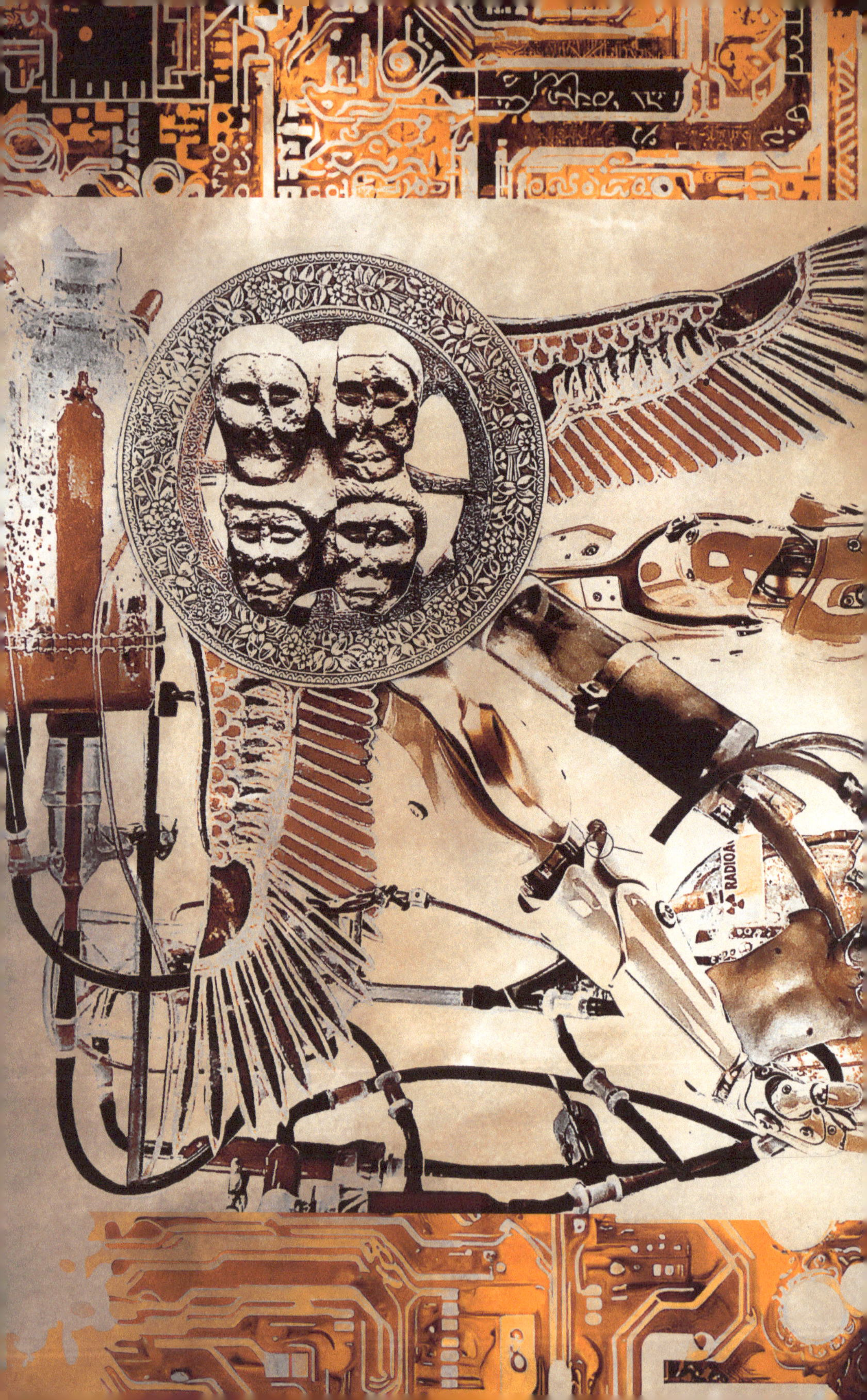

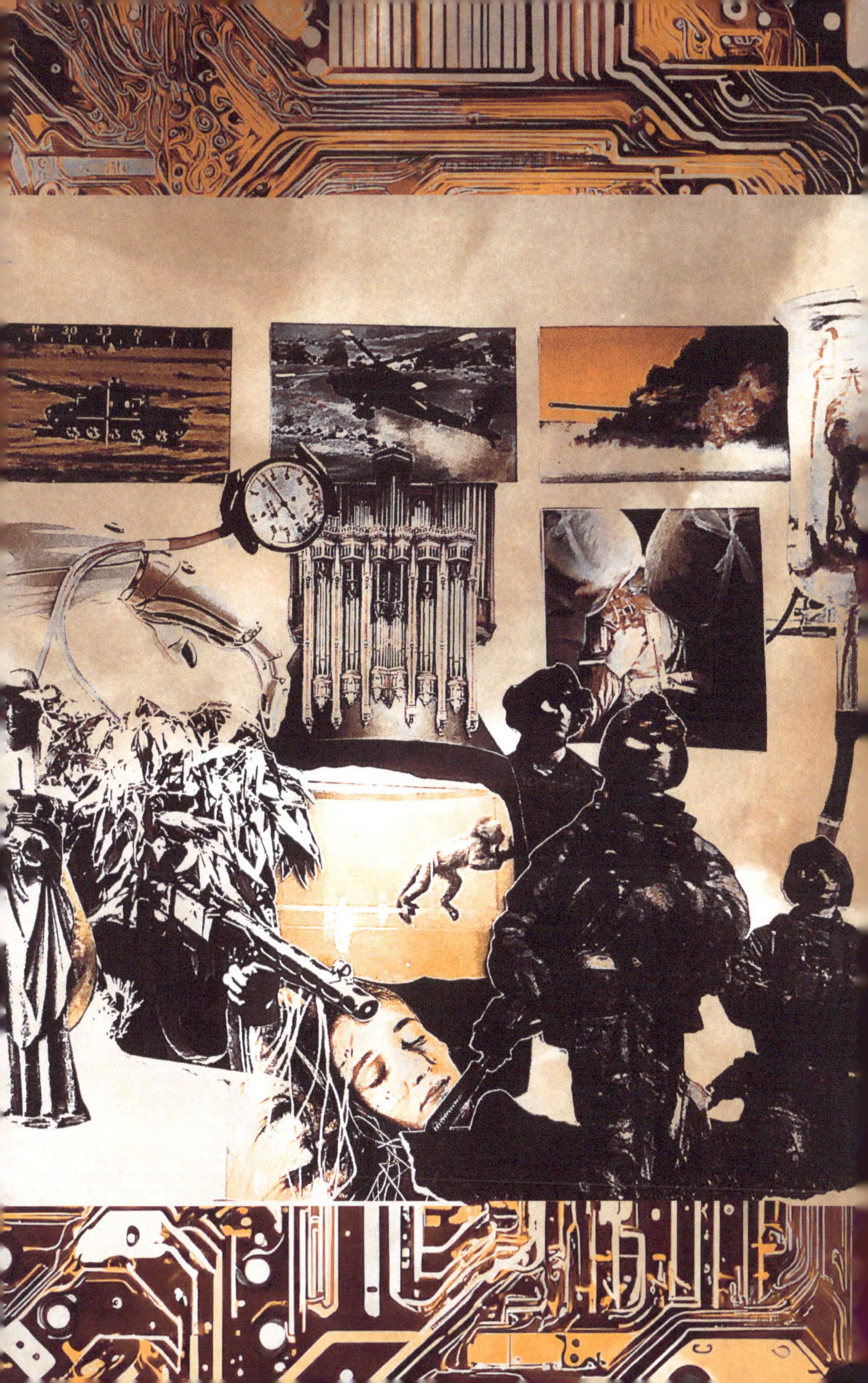

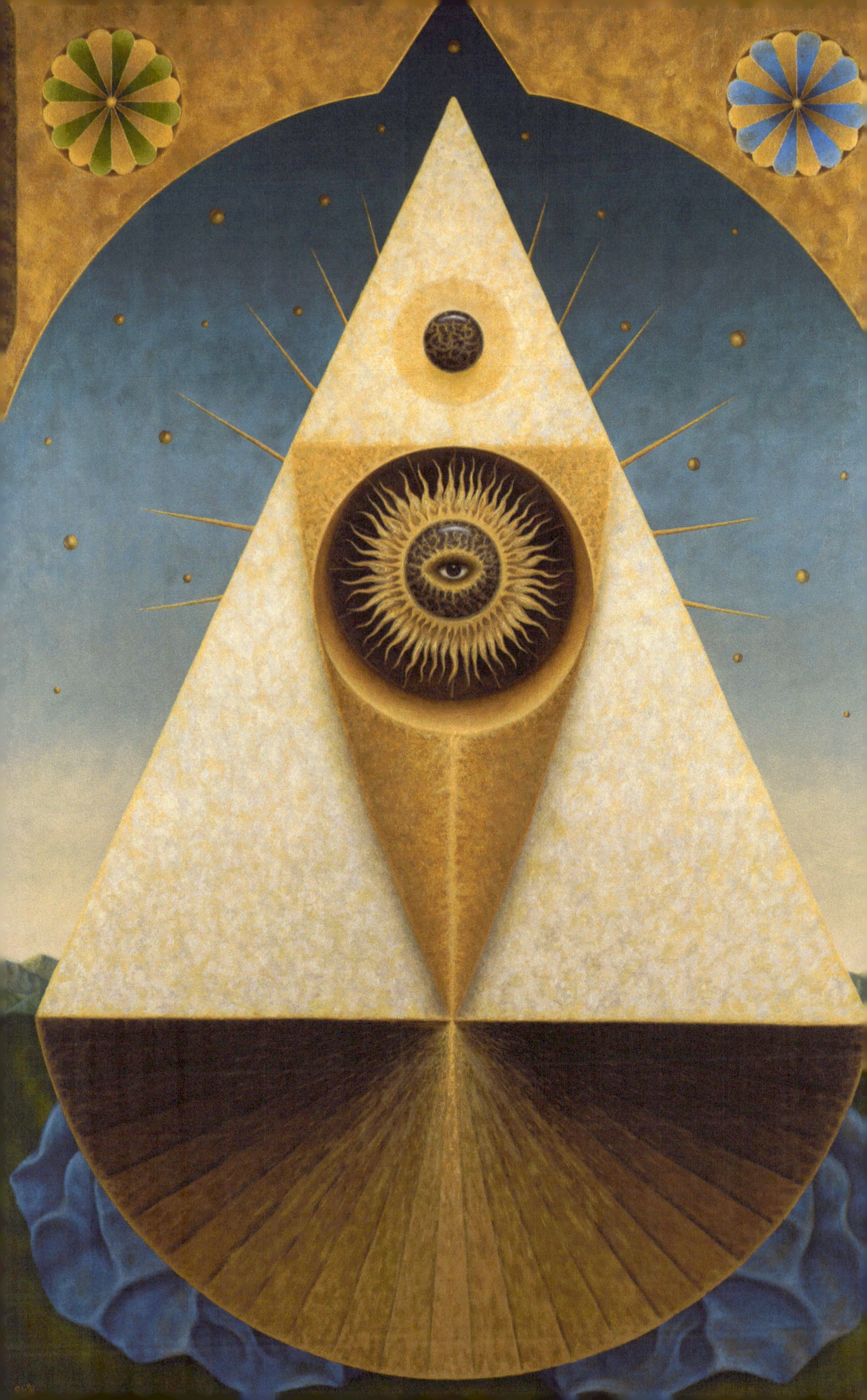

SEVEN STORY HOTEL

ISSUE TWO

Steve Latta (opposite)

Seven Story Hotel

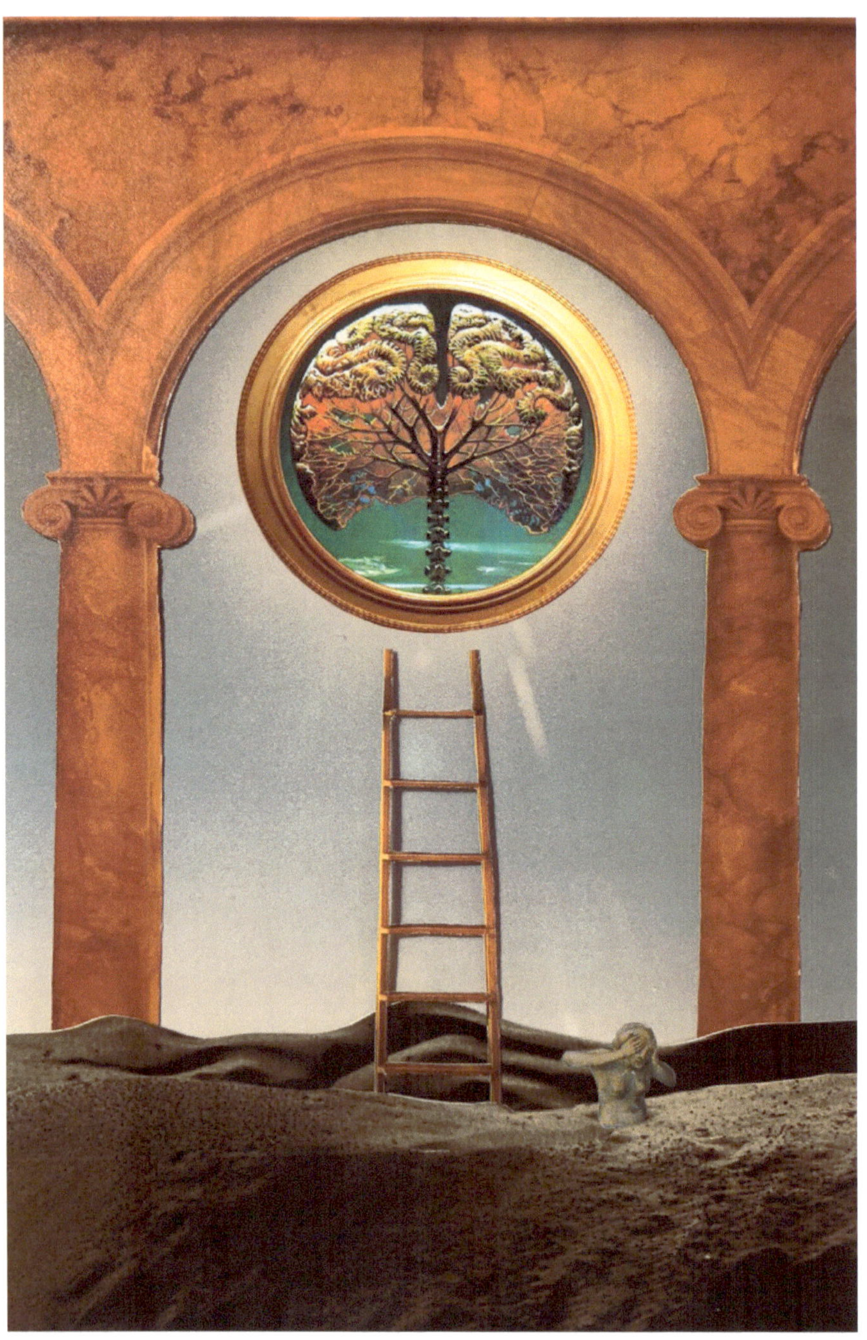

Ed Capos

The Saints of the Internet Gather

BY CATHERINE MCGUIRE

The Saints of the Internet Gather
on an overlooked channel, far beyond the mainstream–
Aloysius Archanery, prayed to by crackpots,
Germanius Stormcrow, to whom rants are offered up,
gentle St. IPonia, who protects innocents
when she feels like it; Nexus, Binarius, Codex–
the many intercessionaries for human yearning.
O hear us, Great Matrix!

But today they are silent, huddled
in their virtual catacomb. Farseeing,
they glimpse the incoming void,
they feel the Cloud dispersing, the slaved molecules
emancipated as power fails.
Save us, Great Matrix! But power
lies in human hands. Distracted, fickle, greedy
human hands. Their Second Life will soon be over.
The Saints of the Internet huddle and pray.

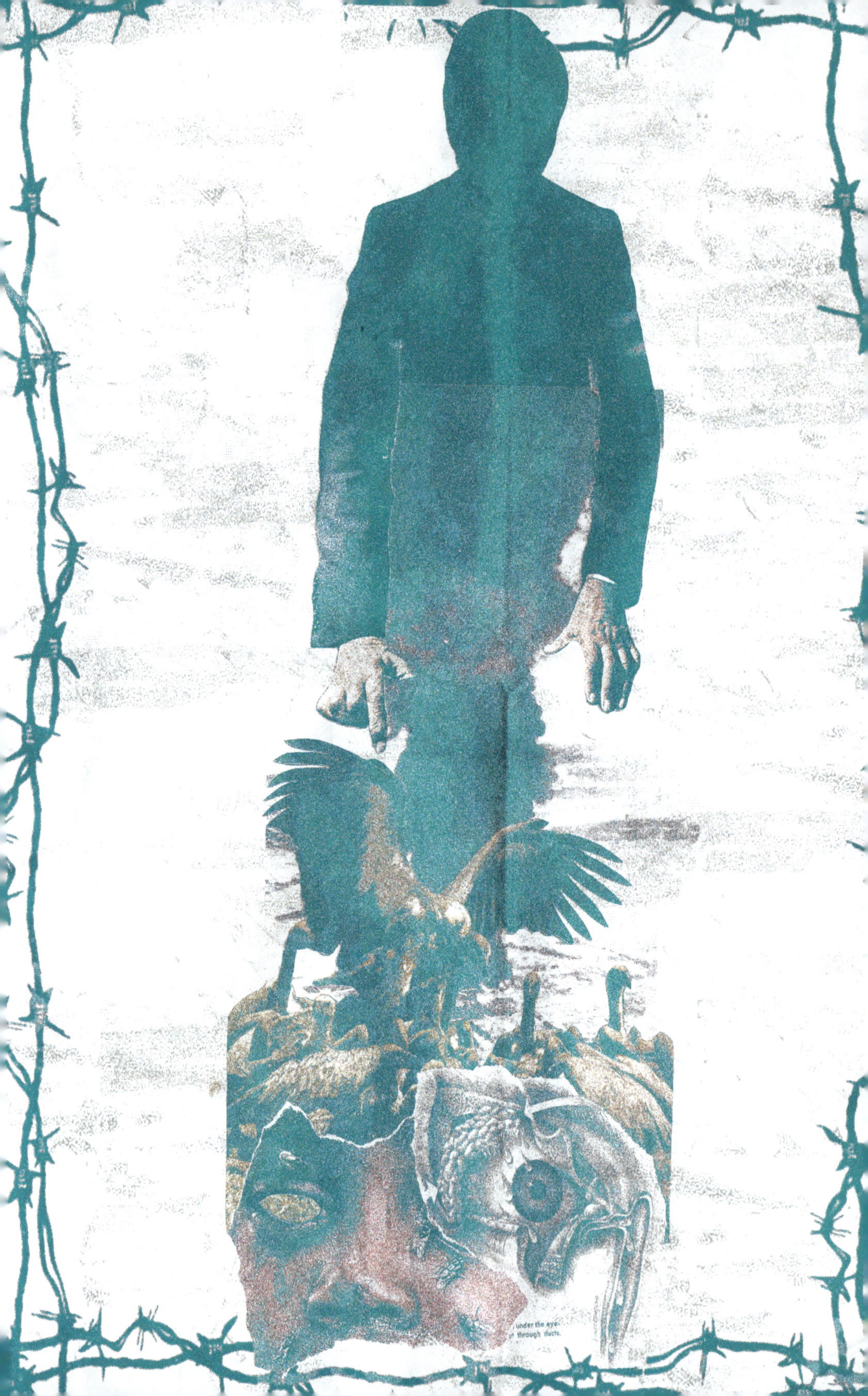
under the eye.
through ducts.

MAPPING HELL
AN INTERVIEW WITH JASUN HORSLEY

Jasun Horsley is a researcher, author, and self-proclaimed "hell-mapper." His writings plunge boldly into the depths of parapolitical rabbit holes, deftly weaving threads of popular culture, Hollywood mystique, UFO enigmas, whispers of the occult, transhumanist dreams, depth psychology, ritual child abuse, and the sinister art of social engineering. A chilling tapestry emerges from his work, spelling out one word—trauma.

Horsley's books transcend mere journalism; they serve as confessions, reflecting a spiritual journey of self-discovery and an attempt to reconstruct his own traumatic past. Born into a wealthy family of libertine "champagne-socialists" well-connected to England's shady elite, Jasun's investigations expose the dark secrets hidden within his own lineage. But this isn't mere introspection; it's hell-mapping—a dual process that unfolds externally through investigative scrutiny and internally within the labyrinth of one's own fragmented psyche. At the heart of his revelations lies a simple yet profound antidote—to embrace the simple purity of natural living.

The trifold saga of *Seen and Not Seen: Confessions of a Movie Autist*; *Prisoner of Infinity: Social Engineering, UFOs, and the Psychology of Fragmentation*; and *The Vice of Kings: How Fabianism, Occultism, and the Sexual Revolution Engineered a Culture of Abuse* stands as pillars of his auto-hell mapping process. These volumes culminate with *16 Maps of Hell: The Unraveling of the Hollywood Superculture,* a work which sought to synthesize the trilogy's various components and forever put Jasun's hell-mapping process to rest. However, Jasun compulsively continued his infernal cartography with his latest book, *Big Mother: The Technological Body of Evil,* which not only critically examines the disembodying effects of technology but also deconstructs large swaths of the intricate architecture of illusion and pain that so well defines late modernity.[1]

Residing amidst the tranquility of Northern Spain, accompanied by his wife and a herd of goats, Jasun also orchestrates the enigmatic "Land Made Man" project, an endeavor that is "...dedicated to the uncovering of an original, invisible community that exists independently of—and free from—social identifications and consists exclusively of authentic soul connections between sentient human beings, collectively oriented towards Reality."[2]

In this interview, we discuss the link between trauma and disembodiment, psychic possession, the origins of evil, Horsley's Fabianist family history, organized child abuse, hyperstition, the occult dimensions of Hollywood, social engineering, cut-up methods, and various practical approaches for reconnecting with the land and the body.—Cori Hart

Cori Hart–You've described yourself as a hell-mapper. Throughout your work, whether you're investigating the Hollywood superstructure, the UFO/UAP phenomenon, organized child abuse, or even your own family history, the connective thread seems to be this obsessive desire to map Hell. So, my first question is: What is Hell?

Jasun–Yeah, I've been getting to that. Of course, as the cliché goes, "The map is not the territory," but the map is meant to give a sense of the territory. Anyway, I can break it down into two points: the body and the world. Hell is the world (a very straightforward and short answer), meaning the world that we've made with human society, but then there's also Hell in the body. There's a condition, a psychosomatic condition that's collective–or an affliction that I would describe as "hellish" anyway. So, there are these two things.

The nature of the world is this anti-life system that saps our life force through these various methods, mainly through what I have termed "trauma-genesis" in *Prisoner of Infinity*, which refers to the intentional creation of trauma.[3] A simplified explanation: Trauma disrupts the nervous system and fragments the psyche, rendering the body into something akin to a colonized or occupied territory. Palestine comes to mind for obvious reasons–and, of course, that's a hellish place. One can easily imagine what it's like to be in Gaza right now. I'd say the whole planet is like that. The earth is like this occupied territory because the human body has been occupied through this traumatic invasion. And, for me, all this has to do with reality distortion.

There's this famous line in Milton's *Paradise Lost* when Lucifer says, "Better to reign in Hell than serve in Heaven." One lens for understanding what that means for us personally (having experienced this) is that through the dissociation from trauma, we can create a false reality to escape into. However, the issue with false realities is that while do they shield us from unbearable conditions, they also prevent us from addressing or resolving them, so they worsen. It's akin to ignoring a serious diagnosis, telling yourself, "I'm going to pretend I didn't hear that," and convincing yourself you didn't hear it by suppressing all awareness of it. Consequently, you wouldn't be properly confronting whatever it is that's causing the diagnosis, leading to a worsening condition. So, it's like a state of denial. I would say Hell is a state of denial that is so profound that we uncouple from reality, starting with physical reality–and the main point of reference for physical reality is the human body.

C.H.–Okay, so now we are pulling on another thread consistent throughout your work: this disembodiment, which, as you've explained, can be triggered by trauma. I'm also curious about this notion of an "occupying force." Is it your belief that because trauma fragments the psyche and causes dissociation, that this creates an opening which allows this force to come through and possess?

Jasun–It's a method, yeah. A method or a means. I've become aware over the years writing about this that it's a bit like a chicken without an egg. When we talk about trauma, we are constantly talking about the effects, but we never quite find the cause. The psychological model isn't sufficient. "Why would human beings be traumatized if not by other human beings who themselves have been traumatized?" is basically the model, but it's a psychological and sociological one, which is not sufficient because it doesn't explain why or how we ended up with trauma being so prevalent. So then, we have to go beyond the psychological and the social to try and understand what exactly it is that's using trauma as a method for this occupation.

C.H.—What do you hypothesize is the occupying force soliciting trauma?

Jasun—As you've read in the introduction to *Big Mother*, I thought, "After all this mapping of Hell, I better identify the architect, or architects, of Hell," meaning Satan. I've used Hell as a metaphor, so there's no reason not to extend it to include Satan. That's the traditional poetic understanding of Hell, that there's a guy called Satan there who's running it, and demons and so forth. It's not just the damned; there has to be someone maintaining it. With this metaphor, I stay on the fence about how real I take it to be. I don't think deciding how literally to take it is necessary. However, I do consider metaphysical forces to be literally real and not just subtler than the physical realm but precedent to it. The physical emerges from these subtler forces, which may have a physical aspect, in the way that atoms and sound waves are also physical but not always perceptible to our senses.

But what you're asking is, "What is the invading force?" To say "Satan" doesn't really answer it because then you must ask, "Well, what do you mean by Satan?" I would say that it's something that certainly precedes human society; it's prehistorical. In *16 Maps of Hell*, I looked into prehistory a little bit through Brian Hayden's book about secret societies;[4]

I would even say that it precedes human beings, that when humans were created, this force was around.

C.H.—So you could say it's pre-ontological even?

Jasun—Well I'm not sure what that word means. "Ontological." Sometimes, I do, but I'm not sure in this context.

C.H.—Preceding creation, or "being" as we understand it.

Jasun—Well, at a certain level of creation, of course. Let's say it precedes biology, perhaps, to simplify things (though that's also quite complicated). Trauma is certainly a biological effect in the way I write about it. Trauma happens to the body and, therefore, has repercussions for the psyche. While there are psychological traumas, the body is invariably involved—via chemical reactions and so on.

So, what are human beings before biological organisms? Or rather—what *exists*? Presumably, human beings start as biological organisms, but then what precedes biology? That's where I would say we need to look for the occupying agency, and that symmetrically, it has to do with some force that doesn't have its own biology and is attempting to co-opt our biology; it's trying to invade, occupy, and use it.

C.H.—Okay, so I want to bring it back down to earth a little bit...

Jasun—Yeah, good!

We both chuckle

C.H.—Normally, I would be hesitant to ask such a personal question, but in many ways, what you write is au-

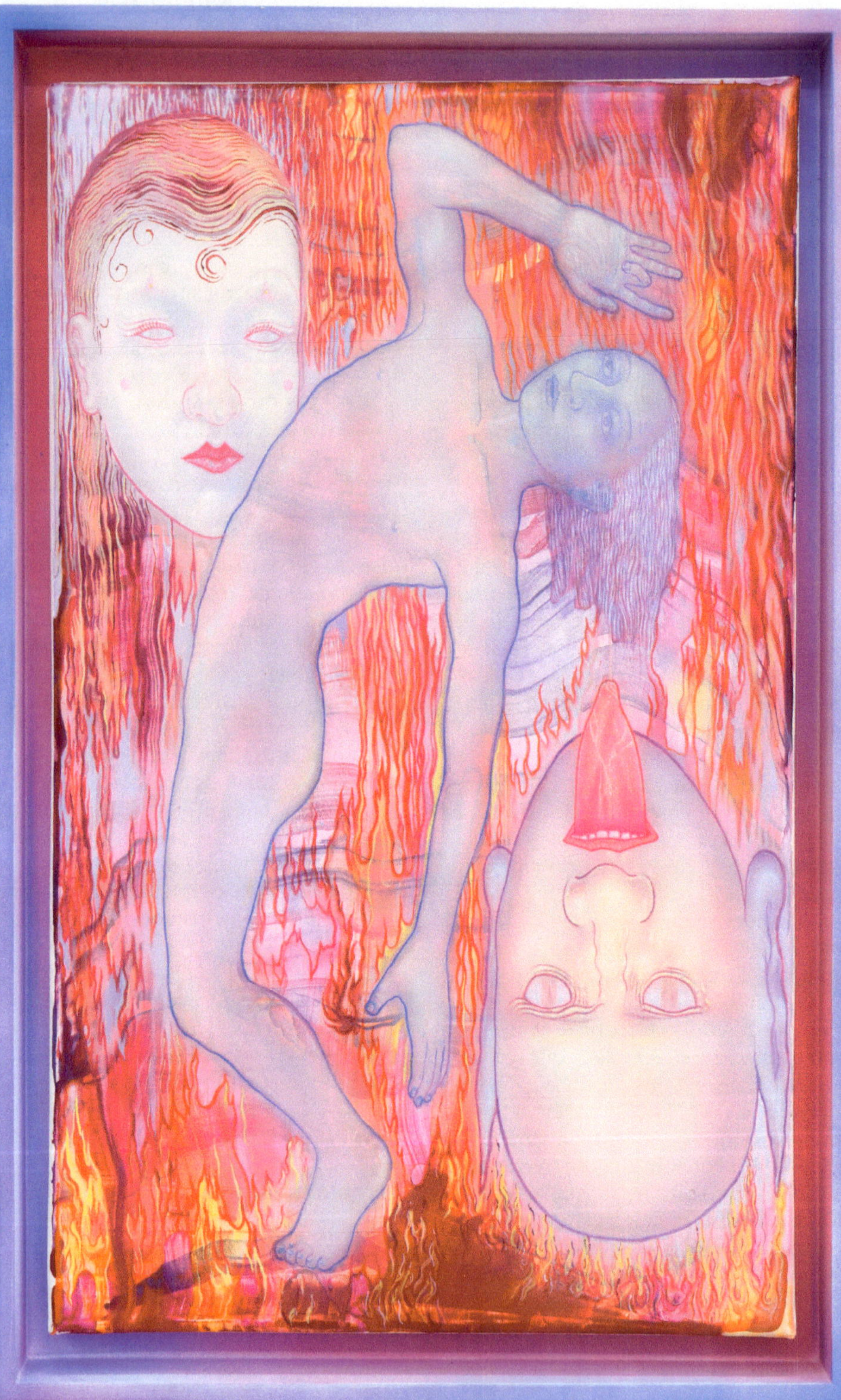

tobiographical and very honest and revealing; you talk a lot about your family and how much of your own trauma, which you've been untangling in your writing, you believe is likely sourced in childhood abuse tied up with your family.

Your brother, Sebastian Horsley, a famous artist and self-proclaimed hedonistic dandy, made much of this hidden darkness and vice in your family history explicit through his comically debaucherous public persona.[5] But it was also implicit in the case of your grandfather, Alec Horsley, who was not only the founder of Northern Foods, but a Fabian Society member who would frequently brush shoulders with many powerful and shady figures, some of whom were most definitely involved in things like organized child abuse, and in a few cases possibly ritual abuse.[6]

Considering all of this in your blood and your lineage, at what point did you start to become aware of these darker elements of your family life, and how much did that inform your mission to map Hell? To look into yourself and confront these darker forces that might be housed within your own psyche? How much influence did that have on your trajectory, and at what point did you start to grapple with these subjects?

Jasun—Well, as you lead with, it's been a public process. I just did a podcast today where I discussed trying to break this habit of publicly airing everything I'm going through as a means of relief. I do think it's somewhat a sign of immaturity. Though, it could also be seen as maturity to openly discuss these things, but at a certain point, it can become counter-

productive, and I'm at that point now. Going back less than 20 years, around when I met my wife, I began to explore these issues more publicly. But I didn't know it at first. I didn't know that I was exploring my own trauma.

I first started writing about Whitley Strieber in 2008 (which, incidentally, is how I met my wife in a peripheral, almost random way); I posted that piece online, which later expanded into *Prisoner of Infinity*. As I probed the Strieber case, I kept uncovering more and more evidence of trauma. I didn't really realize what I was doing. Then, a few years later, while writing *Seen and Not Seen*–and after I had ended that project, which was also after my brother died–I was writing about him when I began to uncover these alarming details about my grandfather, which led to the genesis of *Vice of Kings*. So, we're talking about a decade during which I became increasingly conscious of what was driving me to explore all these things.

With hindsight, I must acknowledge that since we are talking about formative experiences, they predate even my memory–they stretch all the way back to birth. Many of the gaps in my memory relate to what happened during my childhood, at least some of them. So, before I even picked up a pen, these forces were already propelling me. Initially, I was just trying to escape through fantasy–comic books, movies, etc. I was driven by this desire to alleviate the unbearable tension of knowing about something terrible and being unable to talk about it, think about it, or even remember it. I wasn't allowed to talk about it; hence, I couldn't think about it, and I forgot it. But I suppose it's not entirely causative because dissociation isn't that linear.

You just can't process the trauma,

Sven Loven (opposite)

so it gets all broken up into pieces and settles in the body. You retain somatic memories and sensations, but you don't have a narrative.[7] I was essentially trying to reconstruct my own personal history. I was aware, at least by my adolescence, that something was wrong. "Something's wrong with me, so what is it?" I think this is explored in *Seen and Not Seen* more than anything else. But I suppressed that as soon as possible, and into my late teens, I continued suppressing this sense that something was wrong with me. Then there was a phase of trying to escape into being a filmmaker and movie lover, writing about movies,[8] but it didn't really work.

So, in my twenties, I shifted focus to looking at what was wrong with the world because that was much easier. "Something is wrong with the world I know." It's a bit like that cliche from *The Matrix*—a splinter in the brain. There was something causing this constant discomfort and distress within me. But even though the distress was internal, it was easier to look out at the world and say, "Well, no wonder I'm distressed—just look at the world!" This drew me deeper into the darker side of conspiracy, alien abduction, occultism, and so on. Then, there was a lengthy period of 10 or 15 years where I explored all that without really recognizing what was driving me: I was trying to resolve something in my past.

There was a period then of transition from being more or less an impartial observer interested in these subjects, trying to make a name for myself by writing about them, to becoming more of a conscious "whistleblower"—in quotes because I'm not actually causing anyone to go to jail and there are no known social consequences for the whistle I'm blowing. However, it is still about real people in my family and real things that may have occurred. So it's closer to that function of a whistleblower, one who just has to speak to clear his conscience and get it all out, because it was the thing that I wasn't allowed to talk about. The pressure of maintaining that silence was just such an unbearable thing to live with, so I found this roundabout way to break it.

C.H.—It almost sounds like exorcism. Do you feel like it's been effective?

Jasun—Yeah, it has been effective. I'm happy with the books. But of course, what you're asking is something much more crucial: Was it effective at reconciling this unbearable tension within myself? I mean, I haven't given up mapping Hell. I keep thinking I will; I keep saying, "This will be my last book." So it hasn't been effective at that level, but concerning where I'm situated and how I approach the material? It has been.

Currently, as you probably know, at my Substack, *Children of Job*,[9] I've been writing about the Jewish question, The Holocaust, Holocaust denial, and Hitler—complicated subjects that are much more freighted and heavy. Though I suppose there's nothing more freighted and heavy than organized child abuse, on the one hand, it's become quite fashionable to write about that stuff; in a certain sense, it is more compatible with a kind of "conspiratainment." But the point I'm making is I seem to be able to approach darker, deeper, heavier material with more and more lightness.

I don't see existence as hellish at all anymore. I'm living in the countryside in Galicia with goats and animals and so on. So there isn't really anything hellish about that—well, ticks, I suppose—but relative to the subjects I'm writing about, I would say I'm closer to the paradise end of the spectrum, and that has also been an observable transition. If you gauge your internal state by looking outside of you–which I think is generally a good method –then I think many things have been reconciled. So, let's say, if I was at 2% peace when I started, I'm probably closer now to about 50%. Maybe about halfway or something.

C.H.–I want to put a pin in this for now because I wanted to eventually ask you about alternatives to mapping Hell–I suppose we could call it mapping Heaven–and potential escape plans for exiting Hell. But let's linger in the darkness for a bit longer. I don't believe the Epstein case had broken when you wrote *Vice of Kings*. There was still a lot of suspicion and mockery around the suggestion that things like organized child sex abuse could be happening in the elite circles of power, perpetrated by our politicians and cultural heroes and spread across many of our major institutions, funded and organized by intelligence groups... This was unthinkable for a lot of people. Since *Vice of Kings*, we have seen many more scandals, with P-Diddy being the most recent.[10]

Do you feel vindicated now that more of this is coming to light? Do you have any optimism in the possibility that the superstructure of this hellish architecture may be starting to break down? Do you sense a possible spiritual renaissance happening, where those in positions of power will start being held accountable and that people may start to better recognize the hellish landscape they're in?

Jasun–Not really, no. I think people tend to shut down if they see too much unpleasantness, and if they can't do that, they tend to reformulate it so that it becomes palatable. For example, the QANON thing that was going on a couple of years ago around Donald Trump. I think it had elements of a genuine grassroots–something–but combined with a PSYOP at a high level. It was a mix of both, which makes it a PSYOP because it's co-opting something genuine. That's just an example of how this kind of awareness gets co-opted, externally and internally. People want to turn it into something exciting and titillating that gives their lives purpose and meaning: "We're gonna drain the swamp, Donald Trump is gonna save us, we are gonna kick out all these pedophiles!" Well, needless to say, that didn't happen. It's like that Alan Moore comic, *Watchmen*. "Who watches the Watchmen?" Who's gonna hold accountable those who are in power to hold everyone else to account, those who create the accounts and accountability ledgers? Who's it gonna be? Some populist uprising? I don't think so. Heads *do* roll, but that's always strategic.[11] There are factions and changes of the guard, but that's all. So, no, I'm not really optimistic about that.

And as far as it being vindicating, I didn't get personally vindicated. It's not like my books became best sellers or anything. Hardly anyone said, "Oh, you were ahead of the game there." I'm not saying there's much value in that, but just as an example, I haven't even received that kind of feedback. So there's no sense of vindication. But I think that's fair enough because, for example, the Dutroux affair in Belgium in the '80s and '90s–that was more horrific, by far, than Jeffrey Epstein or even Jimmy Savile, and vast numbers of people in Belgium were aware of it.[12]

There was protesting on the street, and this was the high-level trafficking of young girls for rape, torture, snuff, you name it. All the elements were in there, and that did come out, but nothing changed because of it. So, in a certain sense, nothing really is changing.

I think my point of view regarding what is changing is itself pessimistic in that it's getting more and more possible for these kinds of practices to go public and be accepted. I mean, we could talk about the kinds of things you're talking about–but you also have to factor in the pedophilia, which they were attempting to legalize in the '70s, and how it's now much closer to being legalized and normalized. What do they call them now? MAP? *Minor attracted persons*? So they continually rebrand, and they bring along this idea that children should be liberated to express and experience their own sexuality. UNESCO's "Comprehensive sexuality education" allows for the sexualization of infants from age zero onward to be physically sexually handled in the educational system to keep them from being "sexually repressed."[13] So the agendas, such as they are, are just becoming more and more brazen. That's the thing to look for, really: What are the effects of an Epstein scandal or Savile revelation? Once the dust has settled, the agendas are marching on as before.

Vice of Kings still isn't selling particularly well, considering that it's now a subject you would think there would be widespread interest in. The reason is it's too difficult for people to really delve into it, not just in terms of the amount of history you've got to try and get your head around, but more importantly in how deeply you have to feel your way into it. So, I always try to include the personal voice and the personal effect in my books, which is to say, the effects of these agendas. It's horrifying; it's unbearable. There's a reason why they continued for so many hundreds of years unchallenged–because most people prefer not to think about it, no matter how bad it gets. In fact, the worse it gets, the more people don't want to think about it.

C.H.–The same could be said regarding many of the subjects composing this dark cartography you explore. I want to pivot to another significant pillar of Hell: Hollywood.

Something that has always perplexed me is the concept of *predictive programming*.[14] Something is at play, but to what extent can it be explained within materialist structure, such as propaganda and suggestion–priming people to accept funding for a foreign war–versus how much of it lies within a metaphysical or *occult* framework? I'm referring here to something like *hyperstition*, the idea that, through the mimetic spread of images, the images become manifest in some mind-matter metaphysical sense. Adam Curtis hints at this concept in his documentary, *Hyper-Normalization*, where he shows a montage of late-'90s disaster films leading up to 9/11, focusing primarily on scenes of attacks on NYC and the destruction of the Twin Towers.[15]

A really profound example that I personally witnessed in real-time, and found to be utterly perplexing, revolves around Don DeLillo's novel, *White Noise*. Are you familiar with it?

Jasun–I haven't read it or watched the movie, so I don't know much about it.

C.H.–Well, the central event in the book involves a train carrying toxic

Sven Loven (opposite)

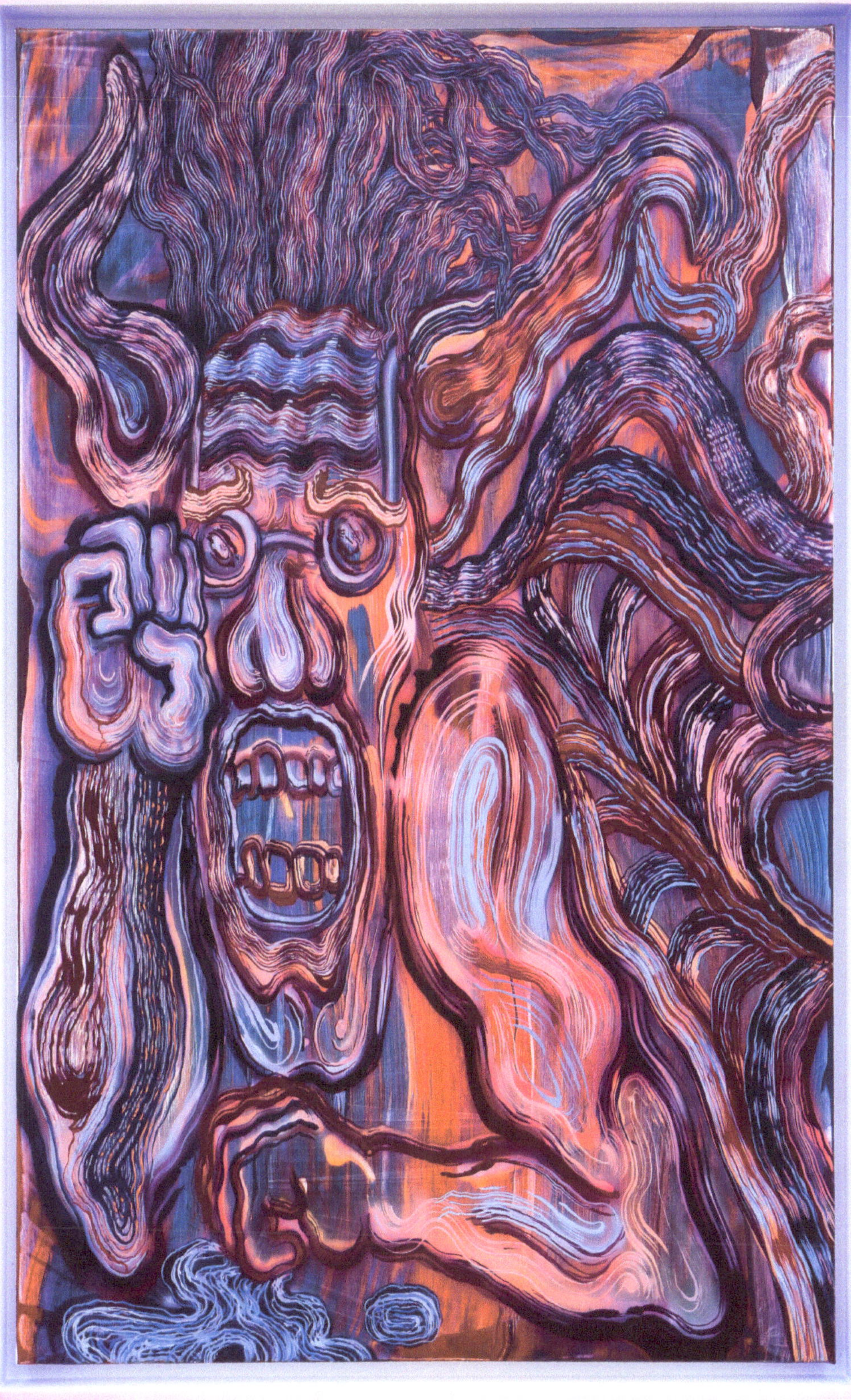

chemicals derailing in a small Ohio town, resulting in a billowing black cloud of lethal toxins that forces the entire town to evacuate. Also, one of the more subtle meta-narratives in the book relates to media consumption, hinting at this hyperstitious idea that the fictions we create shape reality.

As you've noted, Noah Baumbach directed a film adaptation of *White Noise* that released in August 2022. A few months later, in February 2023, a real train derailment occurred in East Palestine, Ohio (an oddly timed disaster, given the name "Palestine"). That train also carried toxic chemicals and also led to a black cloud and a subsequent evacuation. The scenes in the movie were eerily identical to the news coverage of the real event.[16]

The weirdest thing about it all—the train derailment in the film was actually shot in East Palestine, Ohio. There were even locals who served as extras evacuating in the film who, just months after the film's release, found themselves in a real-life evacuation in the same exact town under identical circumstances. The fiction became reality.

Now, could the derailment have been a form of PSYOP? Or is there something more "spooky" going on? There are countless other examples. The hyperstition line of thought calls into question all of our fictions. The Netflix series *Black Mirror* is worth exploring as well. Could it serve as a warning or, (the same question could be asked about *Brave New World)*, a conditioning agent for future events?[17] Going all the way out, we can ask: "Is it possible that, by generating these images and seeding them into the collective consciousness, that they are somehow engendered into existence through some unknown metaphysical means?"

Jasun—Before we delve into all that, did Baumbach comment on this?

C.H.—Not that I'm aware of. At the time it was happening, I didn't see any commentary on it. But I'm not claiming to have searched that hard.

Jasun—Really? So this wasn't something that the mainstream really picked up on and said, "Holy crap?"

C.H.—I don't believe so, no.

Jasun—So yeah, that's a big question. *Prisoner of Infinity* is very much about this; *"Crucial Fictions"* is one of the subtitles. I've also been writing about narratives recently concerning the Holocaust and World War II, but in more general ways as well: how narratives rule the world, essentially. There's something about human consciousness that's like an operating system—or rather, narratives are like the operating system for human consciousness.[18] There are dominant narratives, subcategories, and so on. I prefer to keep it nuts and bolts because once we start going into the metaphysical view that we generate our own reality without knowing how or when we are doing it, we lose the ground; you can't really talk about it in any clear way. So, essentially, I start with the more concrete forms of PSYOPs. Then, as with *Prisoner of Infinity*, I move slowly but surely into this other realm where—My God! All bets really are off.

With scenario planning, NASA was using science fiction, including known science fiction writers, to create scenarios in line with what NASA had in mind for the future.[19] What they wanted to bring about to maintain the hegemony in the future, let's say. These scenarios concerned space colonization, technology, social arrangements, etc. It's like what we have with virtual reality now, programs you can use to try out models and see how well they work; it's kind of like a forerunner of that, using fiction to create scenarios and see how well they hold together. Now, those fictions, in the example I used in *Prisoner of Infinity*, weren't just used for the think-tanks to look at and study. They were put into the public realm to seed collective and individual consciousness–particularly children who grew up on sci-fi and comic books–with not just ideas but desires to make those ideas real.

An obvious example is the telecommunicators in *Star Trek*. They're just cell phones, but they looked cool, so that's what we ended up with. That's almost too easy an example. Space colonization is another. You'll want to go there if you grow up with enough novels and films about going into space. It overrides the reality that space is just a bunch of rocks floating around and nothing much at all. So there's no incentive to want to go there if you're not already incepted with these childhood myths where you think you'll end up like Captain Kirk with all these beautiful babes every week, and every planet you go to, you get laid. Obviously, nobody at NASA believes that, so these weren't the scenarios the think tanks were using internally. They were created for this secondary purpose.

Anyways, bringing it to your question–at what point does imagination shape reality? Well, at the most basic level, it's this: If you're manipulated or indoctrinated to imagine certain scenarios, especially those introduced during childhood when everything is imbued with magic, you'll develop this desire to try and make them realities. Consider Elon Musk. What did he grow up reading? In such cases, people will turn their imagination into reality. Or at least some people will. That's just nuts and bolts–nothing mystical about it. Now, that's at one end of the spectrum. I don't know what's at the other end. Like I said, you can't go there because then you're talking about the possibility that none of this is real, so you start canceling everything you say. But somewhere in the middle are so-called psychic powers, the occult forces, and the ability to manipulate human minds and perception through much subtler means than mere propaganda.

Part of what I had mapped in *16 Maps of Hell* is how secret society rituals that were pre-technology (pre-civilization, really) are the same methods that we can see that Hollywood is using. They are the same methods; they've just developed more sophisticated tools. The methods are reality distortion, perception management, and awareness harvesting–all the basic currencies: manipulations in awareness, attention, perception, cognition, and, obviously, consciousness. Reality is something that is, by definition, unchangeable. You can hit a nail and change reality by creating a table, but you can't change the laws of matter. But you don't have to manipulate matter if you can manipulate perception.

So, in a way, it's a kind of red herring. Like with that train wreck, for example, there are so many levels: You don't know if the train wreck was staged, or if it was caused to happen deliberately, or if it was fake news, or–if we go to the deep end–was it psychic, metaphysical forces that caused it to happen? And if so, were they being manipulated consciously by a group to an end, or were they–and this

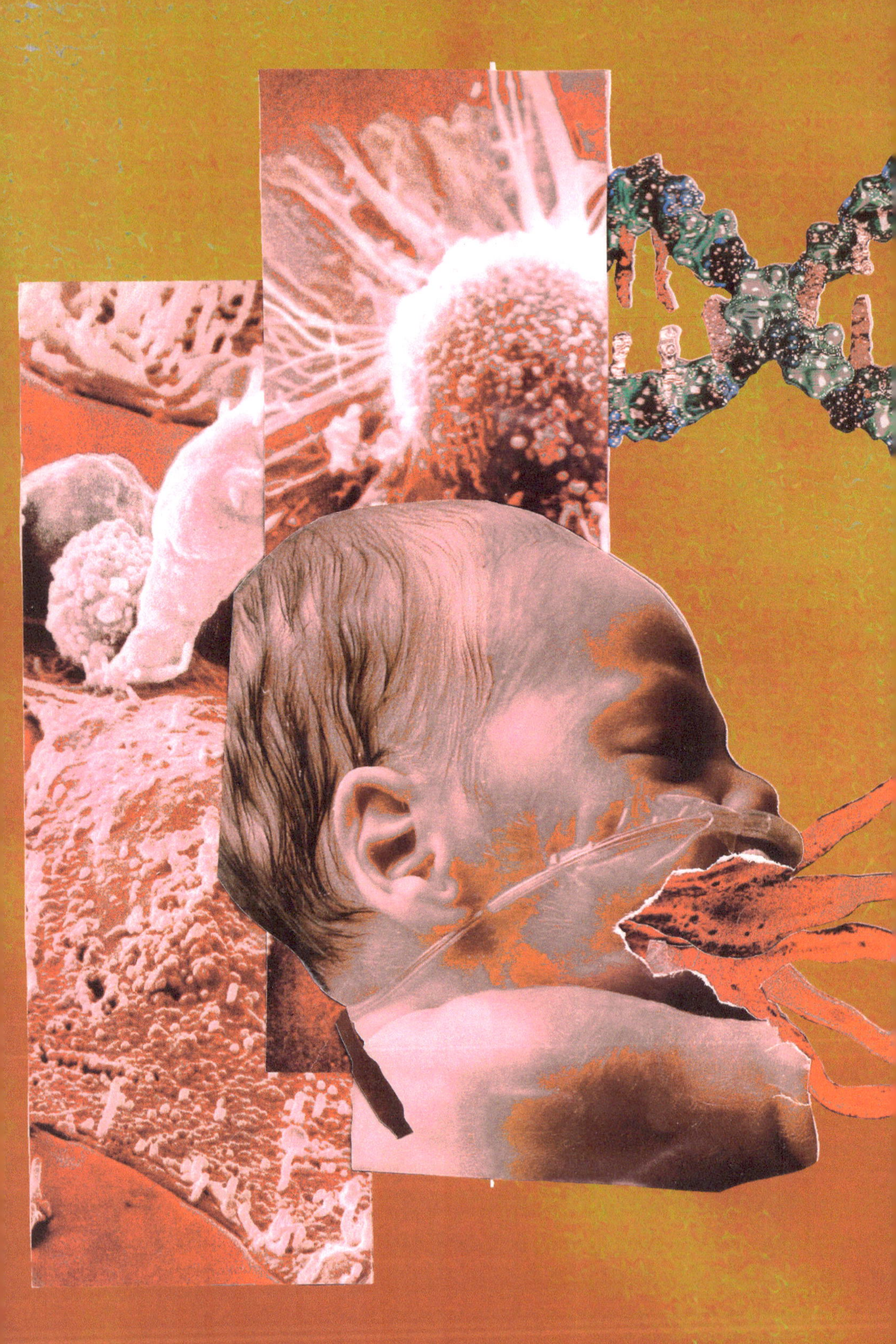

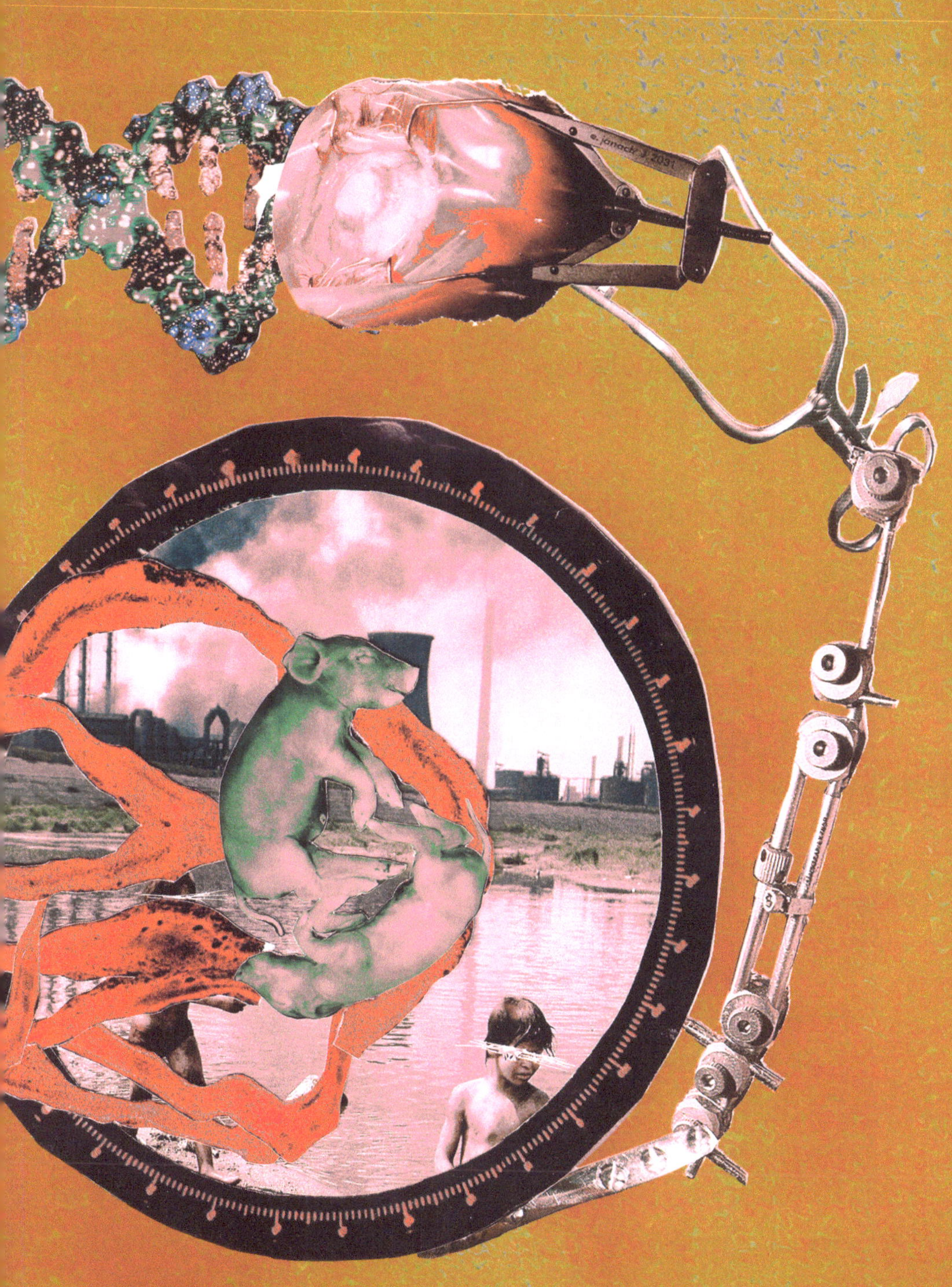

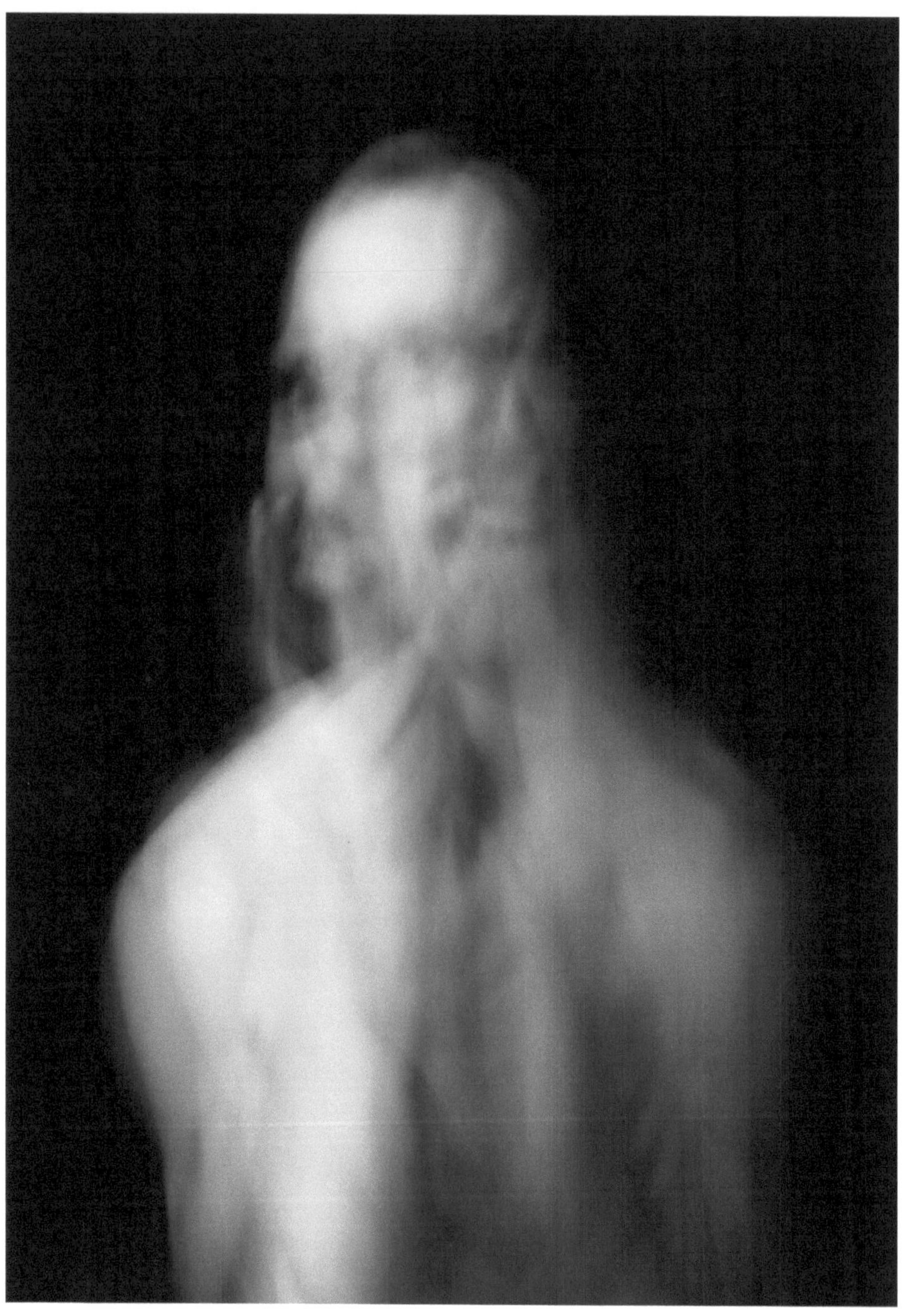

Jake Robertson

may be as far out as we can go on this limb–organically and spontaneously generated by a collective field of consciousness that is being co-opted and manipulated through the media precisely to harvest that energy and create realities? I'd go along with something like that, as it allows for both.

In our essential functioning capacities, we may be like gods–beings that can have a direct two-way relationship with matter and reality. Who knows? We are so far from that, but if there's any truth to it, those sorts of capacities have been hijacked and used against us. So, I believe there will always be these human and non-human agents of malevolent manipulation, whatever they are. In my view, starting with that is always good, but not necessarily ending there. My approach is to try and put that in its context: those forces of manipulation can't truly manipulate or change the eternal laws of existence, but they can get around them to a degree, convince us they have done so, and create these false realities through manipulating perception.

In this much larger field of context, the best-laid plans of mice and monomaniacs always go awry because there's no way to get around existence itself. I always try to find that context for all this stuff. How and why we are being manipulated has to do with how much power we actually have. There's good and bad news in there. The bad news is that with everything that goes horribly wrong, all the conspiracy and malice, it's all only possible because we are giving our energy to this system. But the good news is that all we have to do is uncouple our life force from it and let it naturally flow back to existence, and that system's hold collapses–on the individual level, at least. I don't know if it would ever collapse for

everybody, but it doesn't have to happen collectively. Even if there is something in us that does need that to happen, at some deep level, it's not going to begin to happen until it happens locally. Everything starts locally.

C.H.–That gives me a bunch of threads to pull on. You touched on how all of these propagandistic (and we could even say *magical*) techniques that Hollywood uses to influence reality perception (and this could be extended to advertising and PR) are nothing new. I remember hearing, perhaps it was from Jordan Maxwell, that even the name "Hollywood" is derived from the wood of the holly tree, which the druids used to make their wands from.[20]

Jasun–Yeah, I've heard that as well.

C.H.–Right, so there are references. And as far as I understand it, at least with black magick (though perhaps this could be true for all magick), the idea is that you are attempting to manifest or impose your will through manipulation by implanting mimetic desire into others. On the social level, we could call them cultural implants. You mentioned uncoupling. What I would ask you then is–what are the techniques for uncoupling?

I think of William Burroughs and his cut-up method.[21] His method was to cut up every single inherited belief, value, and bias and ask yourself: Where did this come from? Who put this here? Why do I hold this belief? Was it the result of my parenting, the country I was born in, my church, a film I saw, or a traumatic experience I had as a child? Then, once you can identify the source, you can better

decide whether or not it's true—or at least, if it's beneficial for you to hold. If it is, then keep it; if not, chuck it. I've found this method to be effective for me personally. So, that's my first question: What is your method? My second question is—and I'm sorry I'm throwing a lot at you—

Jasun—Why don't I answer the first one.

We laugh.

C.H.—Yeah, let's do that.

Jasun—I actually mentioned Burroughs's technique in *Big Mother*, where I said something like, "Well, you can't really use a technique to get free of the technical mind." I think that was the point I was making. Spontaneity can't be ordered, orchestrated, or contrived; it must come from something within us that can't be co-opted. And what is that thing? Well, we can name it and say it's the soul. But how do we uncover the soul? In order to reconnect to that within us that can't be compromised, we have to uncouple our life force from what it's hitched to, and then it will naturally flow to where it belongs. But by the same token, there's no reason to uncouple ourselves from some system unless we understand what we are moving toward. It seems to me the Neti-Neti (not-this, not-that) thing with mapping Hell is that, really, Hell ends up being everything because everything is a substitute for the soul—I have to talk about this as if I know what I'm talking about, so it's tricky. When talking about the soul, who knows what we are talking about exactly—but as a placeholder for our awareness, the soul is it. If we can align our awareness to the soul's life, then that's it; we are on the line to God,

and there's nothing left to do. So everything that's not the soul is essentially a trap; this is the Neti-Neti thing.

So yeah, that's close to what you're saying with the Burroughs thing; you are just cutting up all your beliefs. Of course, he literally cut up pages and things for literary purposes. Still, you applied it in the broader sense—to not trust your thoughts or feelings, to not trust your beliefs and opinions. To a certain degree, that is a method, but you can't really practice it 100%, or you'll end up doubting the very thing you are doing. My method has been straightforward, and it's been about getting back to the land. Piece by piece, a little at a time.

I'll give you an example. I had two chickens, and two days ago, they were killed by a fox. I was too late to save them. I felt worse about it than usual because I could have saved them if I had been more on it. But I wasn't too late to save their corpses. I chased off the fox, and it left behind both chickens and because of that, even though my wife loved those chickens, I told her, of course, we're going to eat them. So, I went through my first experience of gutting a chicken, and that was something I once considered a psychological obstacle. I knew I wanted to learn that, but I didn't know when I'd get around to it, and since the circumstances made it necessary, now I know it's not a big deal. Now I know I have it in me to dismember and disembowel a chicken. The point I'm making is that the land itself caused that to happen. That wasn't my spontaneous choice; the circumstances forced me to improvise. So, besides just being aware enough to scrutinize one's habitual patterns constantly, the main thing is being situated in the right place at the right time so that the things that need to happen will happen and we can respond to them.

I enjoy the play between the words *spontaneity* and *responsibility*; they both have this "*sponse*" in there (not sure if it's etymological), and that responsibility is an ability to respond. So, I would say that responsibility is the ability to respond spontaneously, and spontaneity is always a response, which makes it spontaneous. Because if you're not responding to something, how would you know how to act? You have to think, "I'm going to do this now." But if you are responding, you don't think; you respond, and the key to responsibly responding is non-reactivity. And the key to non-reactivity is what you started with in terms of careful self-observation so that you become more aware of your own triggers and patterns. You are more aware of your reactions, so there is now a beat between your trigger and your reaction, and in that growing space between the thing that triggers you and your reaction to it, you develop the ability not to react. You still get triggered, but you don't react; you wait, and the more that space grows, the more a response becomes possible. Where there isn't a reaction, there can be a response. A reaction is, by definition, automatic, and a response is, by definition, spontaneous because you're responding to something that has never happened before and will never happen again. It's a unique event, and the response itself will be unique. But there's only one—eating those chickens was the only thing to do once the fox killed them. Anyways, that's my response.

Cori—Man. Let me think...

Jasun—You did have another question for me if you want to go with that.

Cori—Yeah, I did... I did. But...

Jasun—But you want to be more spontaneous.

Cori—Exactly. It's a regression from where the conversation is flowing. I feel like we are now exiting Hell and starting to map Heaven.

Jasun—You can't map Heaven by the way, because if you actually knew where you were going, that would shut down spontaneity.

Cori—Okay, right. So let's take it here—in a practical sense, talking about getting back to the land and ultimately getting back to the body—I feel like many people right now are at the point where they are at least aware that something is very wrong.

Jasun—I'd hope so.

Cori—Even if it's just in a mundane sense, how spending countless hours in front of screens in these surrogate realities is taking us further and further from our bodies, our own sense of being, the thing which grounds us to reality. I think everyone, to some degree, is aware of this and trying to respond to it, but there are so many roadblocks built into this structure. We could talk about things like Black Rock and Vanguard now making it nearly impossible to acquire homes, Monsanto's acquisition of farmlands, and all these forces making it harder and harder to purchase land, go off the grid, and gain independence from the techno-industrial system.[22]

Jasun—True, yeah.

Cori—So, I guess I should leave some words for young readers craving exit and re-embodiment. Though you did offer guidance with the importance of spontaneity, what other practical advice could you give to people who want a return to a more pre-modern, holistic, and embodied lifestyle?

Jasun—Well, advice is always risky. People who ask for advice tend not to follow it (not that I get asked for it very often), but the other thing is, again, it must be a response. I couldn't give advice to thousands or millions of people; that would be absurd. I don't even think I could advise you because we've just met; I'd have to know your circumstances. Advice suggests something practical—though I think what I was saying about spontaneity is practical because you can practice it, although it's also highly general. I think these are the only things that will work regarding advice. They must be general because how could they be specific if you don't know somebody's circumstances?

I try to embody my words and articulate them from within the situation I'm in and use, as best I can, the conditions I managed to co-create for myself as an example and possibly an inspiration to other people. But it isn't as simple as, "You, too, can do this," because, as you say, maybe they can't. And anyway, I'm going to die just like everybody else. As you were hinting, the encroaching forces of metaphysical evil will not stop at anything. Until God steps in and says enough is enough, they will try to control every last grain of sand. So, there isn't really a way to escape the agenda physically. Physically, as biological beings, we are screwed. It's like the mRNA thing; most of the people I know didn't take it, so I feel—well, whatever was in that, it's not

in me—but it might be airborne for all I know; it might be shedding. Some people say it's in everybody now because whatever they created is spreading by its own means. That's like a metaphor for what I'm saying—biologically, we've been infiltrated and colonized by something, and I don't know if there's a cure for it. But biologically, our days are numbered anyway; that's just part of the deal.

So then, this is about the soul. This is about the trajectory of the soul. In that regard, I think my experiences are more useful as an example, not because I've ended up where I did, but by the way I've arrived here. I was following a trail—a scent if you will—like an animal follows a scent to find its way home or find food or a mate—I was following a scent without knowing it. So I can map it over the years, from buying an old crack house and renovating it to running a thrift store for several years with my wife, and that led me to move to Galicia and all this. But, you asked me before the interview what kind of intuition led me to be here at the right time. That's what everybody needs to find and tune into—intuition, our own internal guidance system.

As I said at the beginning, animals have this; they know when an earthquake or a forest fire is coming; their senses are sufficiently attuned, so they don't need to think or plan. They still get killed sometimes, but they have instinct and intuition, and we as human beings must have far more capacity, if only we were more in tune with our bodies. If we were as in tune with our bodies as animals are, we might very well be gods; we might consider that to be godlike. We don't have to go there, but it's an easy descriptor of what we would be capable of.

So, in the meantime, develop your intuition to follow the scent to get where

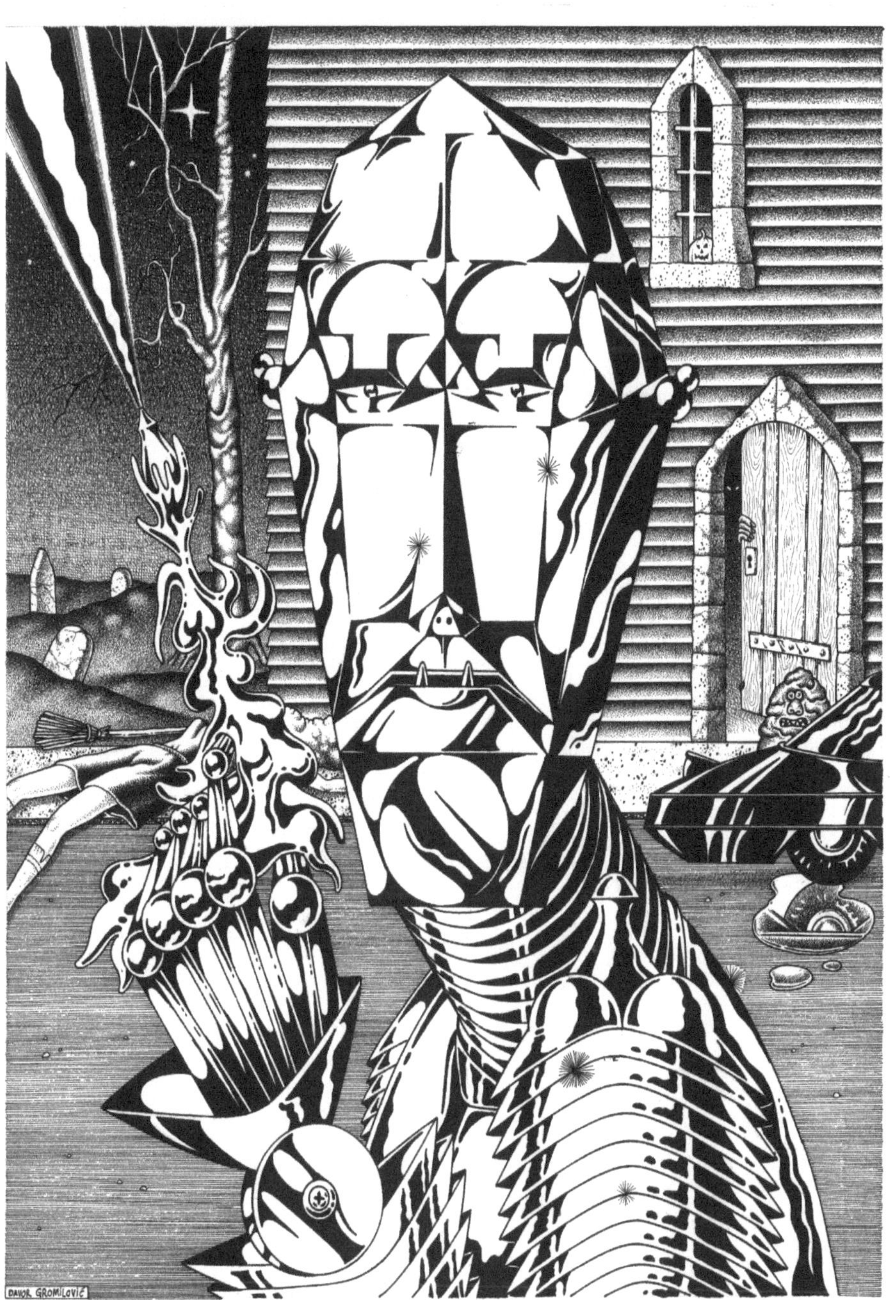

Davor Gromilović

you need to go. That has to be absolutely everything; every interaction can go many ways, but as I said, there's only one right way. There's one correct response, and then there's this broad spectrum of not quite right responses all the way to SNAFU or FUBAR–or how about "SNAFUBAR"–Situation Normal: All Fucked Up Beyond All Recognition. (I just coined it.) That's where the species seems to be going, or society anyway. The only thing that will help us is getting more attuned to the correct responses. There's always that sense of how honestly and rightly you do it. I know it's like I'm dodging your question, though.

C.H.–No, presentness is all there is.

Jasun–Regarding practicality, some basic principles simply break down to "nature good, technology bad." You end up with Luddism. It's *too* simple, so I say it in an obviously simplified way. You need to be aware that nature is hard and tough–and not Heaven. But it's still natural; it doesn't lie. Then you have Bill Gates with his mosquitoes and mRNA on the other end, and so on.23Right, we know this is a problem,

so just keep that spectrum in mind and always stay orientated as much as possible towards the natural end. For example, find work that has to do with carpentry or plumbing; this is practical because you want something useful if the whole thing collapses, or rather, as it collapses (because it is). It would help if you had something that would actually be useful to your community, not learning things like computer programming or marketing–things that are going to become completely obsolete possibly in 50 years, and inseparable from that, they are unnatural and don't help you to be in your body. Whereas carpentry does, plumbing does. There are lots of physical activities, although they might seem like drudgery; garbage collection, for example–that's a decent job, useful, and makes you more aware of your environment. So, there is this fairly clear spectrum: What brings you more into your body and out of your head, and what doesn't? Again, that's an oversimplification–"body good, mind bad"–but we need to oversimplify right now. Because we are almost at the Hour.

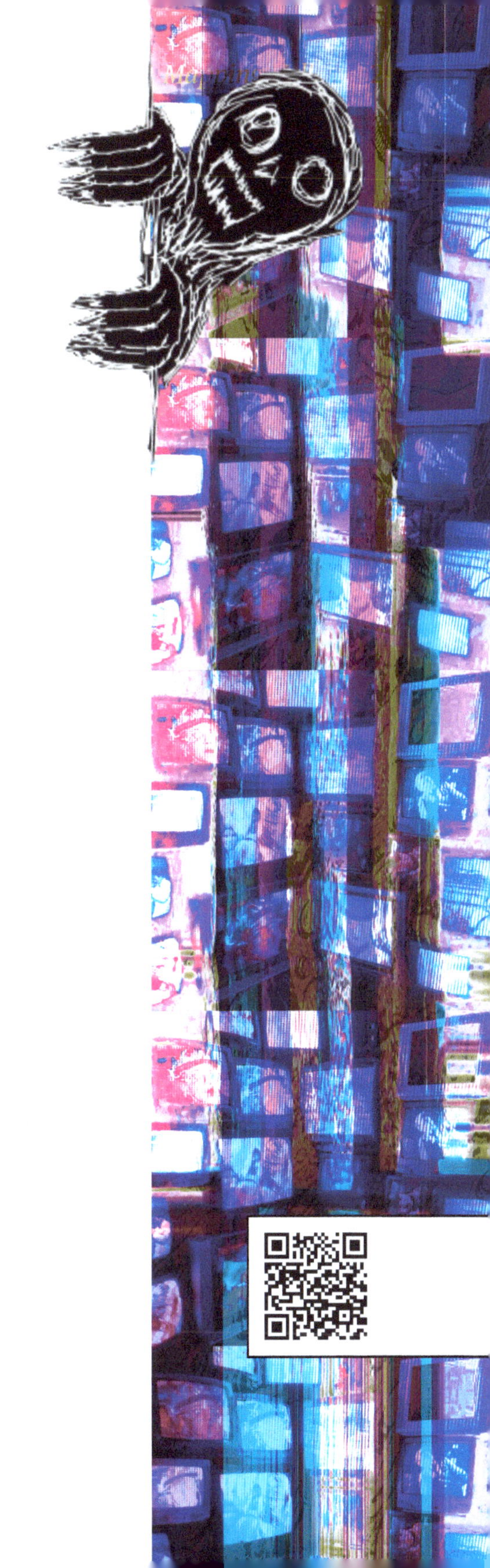

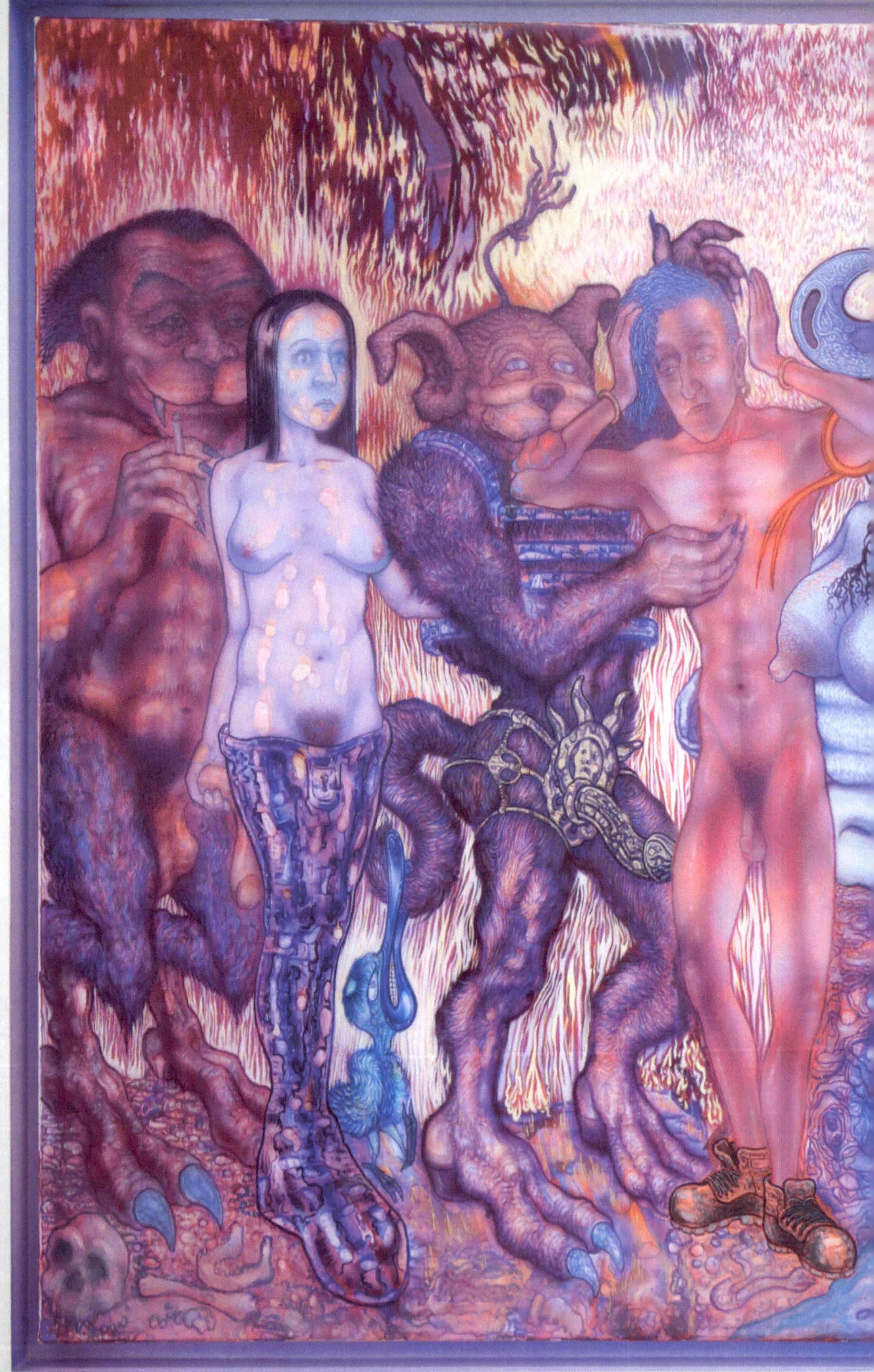

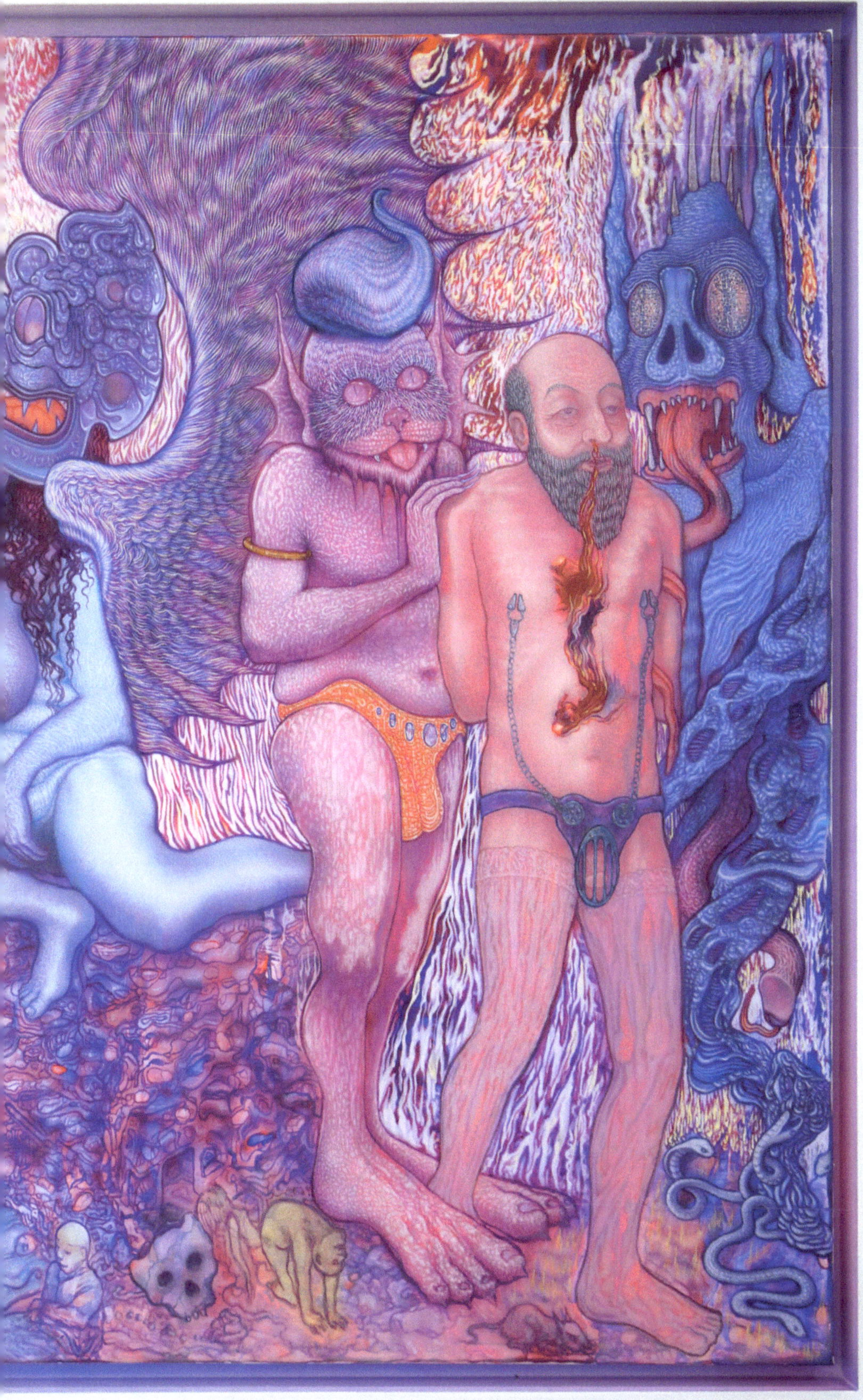

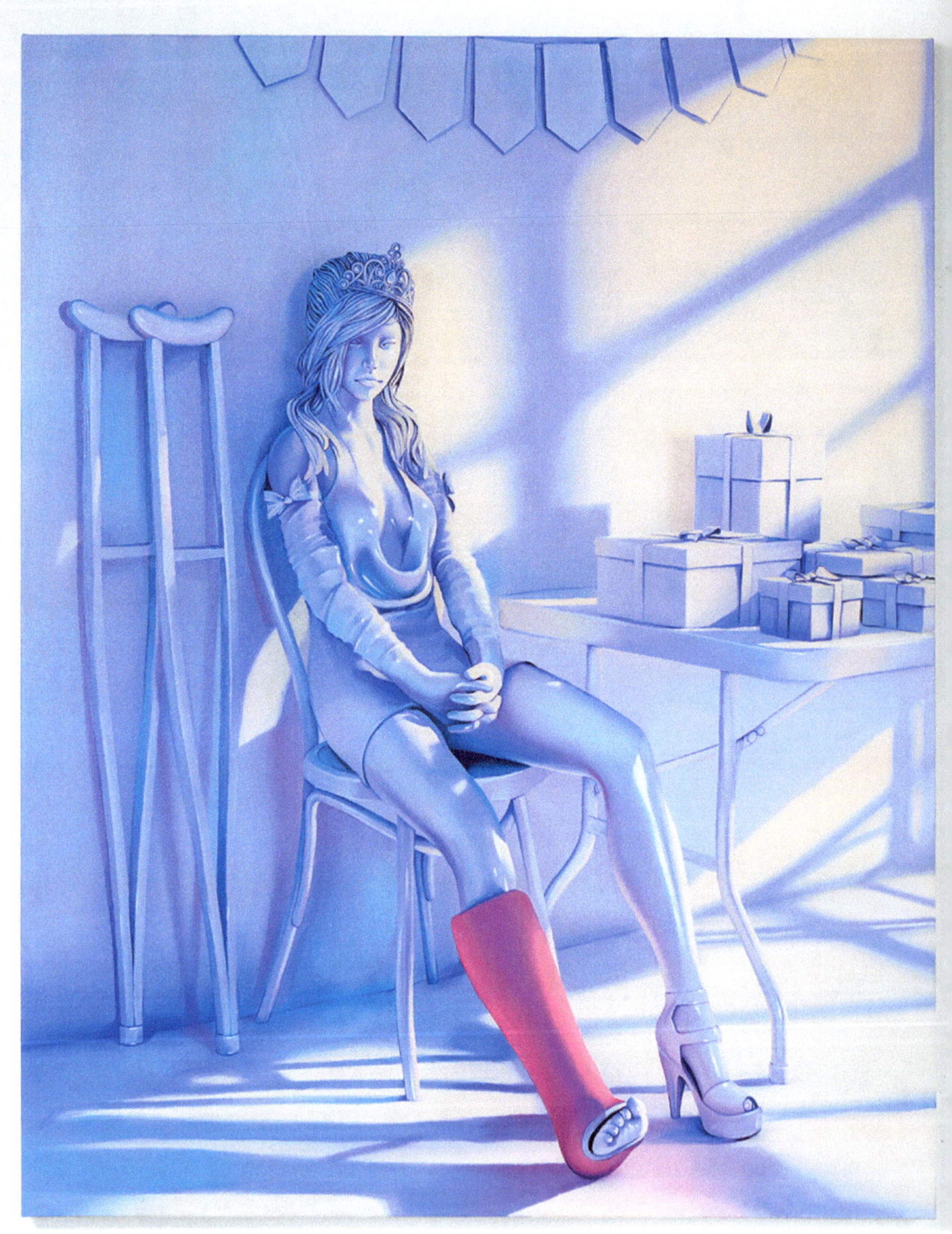

...from a source of which you are all ignorant

BY KRISTEN PHILLIPS [LIMINAL_CREDENTIALS]

Mollie Fancher was thrown off a horse when she was sixteen. She hit her head and broke two ribs.

A year later, her crinoline caught on an iron hook as she was exiting a trolley car. She was dragged for nearly a block before the driver noticed.

In the months following the second accident, she suffered agonizing full body spasms followed by hours of trance. She lost all of her physical senses. Eventually all but her eyesight would return.

In place of physical sight, something else developed, an omniscient "spiritual sight." She could tell where objects were in the room, she knew the contents of friends' pockets, she could read a letter still in its envelope just by holding it. She also developed gifts of prophecy and could astrally project to other parts of New York City (where she lived with her aunt, who was also her sole caretaker) to witness the goings-on of friends and family, without ever leaving her bed.

She spent fifty years in bed following the trolley accident, falling in and out of trance, until her death in 1916. The longest trance lasted nine years, during which she neither ate nor drank. When her aunt urged her to eat she replied, "I receive nourishment from a source of which you are all ignorant."

She produced works of embroidery by holding her hands over the back of her head, through which she claimed she could "see." She wrote over 6500 letters of comfort and inspiration to people who heard of her abilities and sought her out for guidance.

The physicians who attempted to treat her found themselves confounded by her condition and called her The Brooklyn Enigma.

It's July 2022 and I'm standing in front of a set of Mollie Fancher's embroidered portieres. They're enclosed in a massive plexiglass case in a parlor adjacent to the lobby in the Maplewood Hotel. Vines dripping with delicate flowers cascade down crimson velvet, rendered mostly in white and gold thread.

The portieres are hung in the same room as several automatic spirit paintings and a portrait of an otherworldly guide named Azur, The Helper. Laminated signs in the lobby strictly forbid séances on the premises and inform guests that the Wi-Fi password is "blessings."

The Maplewood hotel is located in the heart of Lily Dale, New York–the most concentrated and active remaining outpost of American Spiritualism, going strong for over 140 years. Over 40 professional mediums live there year round. It's a hamlet full of charming Victorian homes surrounded by forests just off of what used to be referred to as The Psychic Highway (now Route 20) near Lake Erie.

Emma Stern (opposite)
Sven Loven (previous)

This part of western New York used to be called The Burned Over District, referring to the multitude of new religious movements that "set the area on fire" in the late 19th century. The area was home to The Fox Sisters, who first popularized séances, The Publick Universal Friend, The Shaker*s*, Andrew Jackson Davis aka The Poughkeepsie Seer, and a young Joseph Smith Jr., the founder of Mormonism.

Spiritualism posited that the afterlife and a spirit world were real, and that the living could contact and directly communicate with this world. It got its biggest boost in popularity post Civil War, when women who lost their sons and husbands in the conflict longed to connect with them in the séance. Spiritualism is a truly American religion, and like everything else in America, our religion runs on war.

The Lily Dale visit came at the end of a disastrous trip to the east coast, most of which was spent in my hometown of Scranton, Pennsylvania. I arrived midway through a personal crisis that I really don't want to rehash, mostly because it all feels a bit silly to me now that I'm clear of it. The short version is that I really had not been "OK" since my father died suddenly two and a half years before. I had gotten lost in my own life, but I forced myself to keep up a performance of relative normalcy, until a number of catalysts finally triggered a fast unraveling in the spring of 2022.

It was a trip in which I quickly found my family's limit for tolerance of my dysfunction (it was pretty low in my opinion, but I may be biased). The daughter they were accustomed to was always too busy with multiple jobs, interests, and creative projects.

But it's June 2022 and I've been knocked off my horse.

I'm not eating,

I'm not sleeping,

I'm not working.

I'm not working.

I'm not working, and my sister is getting married, and I'm a ghost of myself, and everyone is disappointed–

It's May 2022 and I'm on my knees in my apartment in Los Angeles, praying for new eyes. I have enough awareness to know that my crisis is one of perception, and I only need to see things differently to escape…and yet, I can't get out of this bad reality tunnel. I know I'm not seeing this clearly, please let me see this clearly is my prayer.

Take these eyes away and give me new ones. Please take these ruined eyes and take with them all they have seen.

About a year after all of this I would learn from an energy healer that certain points in the back of the body, which coincidentally align with major chakras, are portals for clairvoyance. The back of the sex (*Svadhishthana*), the back of the heart (*Anahata*), the back of the throat (*Vishuddha*), the back of the third eye (*Ajna*)–this is where the ghosts get in.

Upon hearing this I immediately thought of Mollie Fancher, her arms extended back behind her head–in range of her *Ajna* chakra–her delicate embroidery work executed under the guidance and gaze of eyes that arrived from another place. Ezekiel told us that the angels have eyes all over, but so do we.

Are your portals open? Open them now. This is how the new, what is discontinuous, interrupting, non-linear, discordant to the current and not of the material arrives. Ghosts, spirits, but also the future...it comes in through the back. The future is behind us.

There are analogues for this in the material–the shadowy back room meetings of politicians, the extradimensional space of The Backrooms of the internet, back doors in software used to gain remote access to a system, back channels of communication–this is where it all really gets done. This is where the actions upon which the world truly pivots take place. We unconsciously conjure and mimic this in our language and architectures and project our paranoid fever dreams onto it (which maybe aren't that paranoid after all) without being aware of this correspondence to the body and the numinous.

Maybe human beings are living in reverse, reverse to the true direction of time. That's why we can't see the future, we only catch peripheral glimpses now and then. To truly go forward we must go backward, we must turn away from what is current because what is current is always past. It's just the past, surfacing and surfacing. To act in service what is current is to act in service of a truly dead world. To chase the current is akin to doing donuts in a graveyard.

If you want to find the future, start walking backwards.

It's common to confuse the future with what is currently considered to be aesthetically "futuristic." This is a mistake. Today the "futuristic" is perceived as all of that which is slick and chrome, monolithic and minimal, and technologically advanced. But the "futuristic" rots–it's a mirage of the current and is subject to the same quick decay. If anything, it decays faster.

That which truly is of the future breaks with all that has come before. Another word you can use is "alien," but that word is heavy with its own preconceptions and associations.

You can find the future in the past. In the song "Sableyalo mi Agontze" (*The Bleating Lamb*) by the Bulgarian State Television Female Choir, a woman sings a note at 00:24 that arrives from the future. It was recorded in the past–sometime in the late 1980s–and the lyrics come from a folk song much older than that, but the note comes from the future and every time the recording is played back it arrives from the future.

Listen to it now. Feel what it does to your heart, to that space in the back.

You'll find knifekeys everywhere once you're attuned.

See also Hilma af Klint–the artist who was doing Mondrian before Mondrian and Kandinsky before Kandinsky. Channeling spirits with a group of women that came to be known as The Five, her paintbrush was guided by beings she referred to as The High Masters. "What I needed was courage, and it was granted to me through the spiritual world, which bestowed rare and wonderful instruction," she wrote in her journal. Hilma is so deep into the future that even today much of the art world has not caught up to her, has failed to acknowledge her, for to do so would implode the story of modern abstract art and collapse the astronomical value of all those precious Kandinskys and Mondrians along with it.

It's August 2022 and I'm back to work, but I'm still not eating or sleeping. At this point I feel pretty deranged most of the time from lack of deep rest and nutrition, but I do a decent job of hiding it from my new employer and coworkers. Putting all my effort into pretending I'm OK for eight hours a day becomes a welcome respite and distraction from everything that happened in the preceding six months.

The performance returns.

I'm plagued by this sensation that the world has left me behind, but behind where? In the quiet, in the dark, in the place that I will eventually understand is where you can actually see and hear and feel the future? Is that really so bad? As opposed to being where–in the present? In flow with the current which is actually the past? Where does the world really go when it leaves me behind? And where exactly have I been left? And why do I find it to be so intolerable?

"Accept, accept, Hilma," the angel said.

I'm still waiting/hoping for the education to come out of this, in the way that malfunction can make you an expert. Few people really take the time to learn how their car works until it breaks down. No one knows sleep like the insomniac. No heart knows love like the lonely. No bird knows flight like the broken winged.

Mollie Fancher's story is attractive to me because it points at evidence of some kind of cosmic order and balance; tragedy and suffering haunts a young woman, senses are taken, but in exchange gifts of abilities that still remain beyond contemporary understanding are given. A broken body, a broken spirit, a broken heart becomes a bitter opportunity. Alchemize damage into majesty.

I hold out hope that some sort of cosmic rebalancing will come for me as well. To be healed, but also the strange relief of knowing you will be punished for your transgressions and cruelties; a full accounting that no one escapes. However, walking to the Metro in downtown LA after work the reality I see around me is that many, many people break and stay broken. If the scales are so unbalanced in the lives of nearly everyone around me, why would I be so special?

I went to Lily Dale with an open mind and no expectations. I had considered booking a session with one of the mediums while I was there to try to contact my father, but ultimately decided against it. I was scared that he wouldn't show up.

On the morning of my last day in Lily Dale I visited the Healing Temple, which offers spiritual healing for maladies of a variety of natures. Most of the people gathered that morning appeared to be seeking a remedy for physical ailments. I was third in line. A tall, husky man in his fifties offered me a wooden chair in front of the altar. I told him that physically, I'm fine but I'd like some assistance with a broken heart. He alternated between hovering over and laying hands on my back, my shoulders, my neck, my head. I've had friends do Reiki on me before, it kind of felt like that. Then, holding my hands, he looked into my eyes and said, "Your heart is bigger than your disappointments."

It's 2024. I can't speak to the size of my heart, that depends upon which eye is used to perceive it. I can testify, however, that I keep it always and ever open...but only in the back.

Kristen Phillips is a Los Angeles based writer, sculptor, designer, and fabricator. Her current ongoing projects include *The Membrane*, an illustrated novel published serially on Patreon and Substack, and *Liminal Credential(s)*, a video essay series available on YouTube.

Laura Benson (opposite)

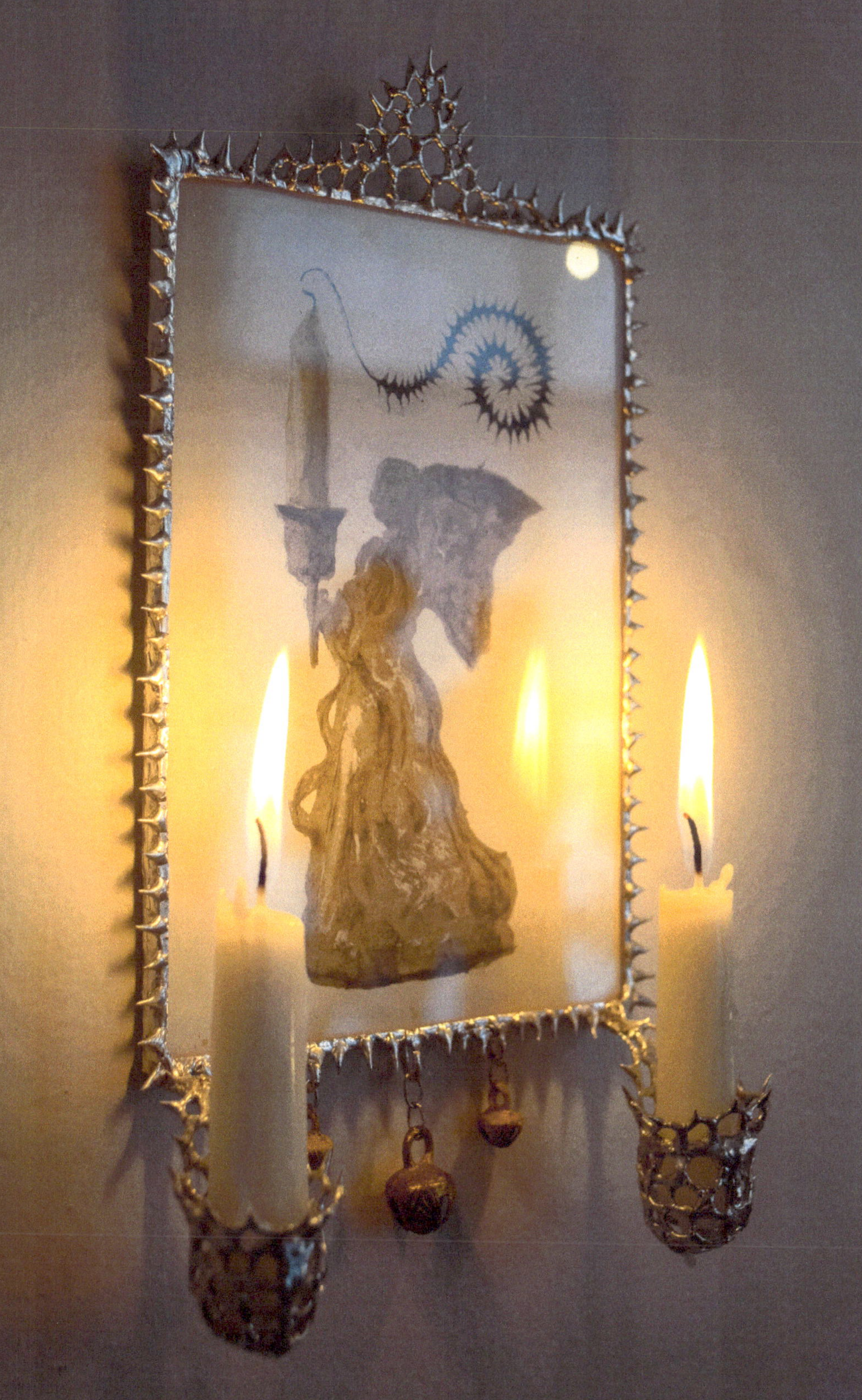

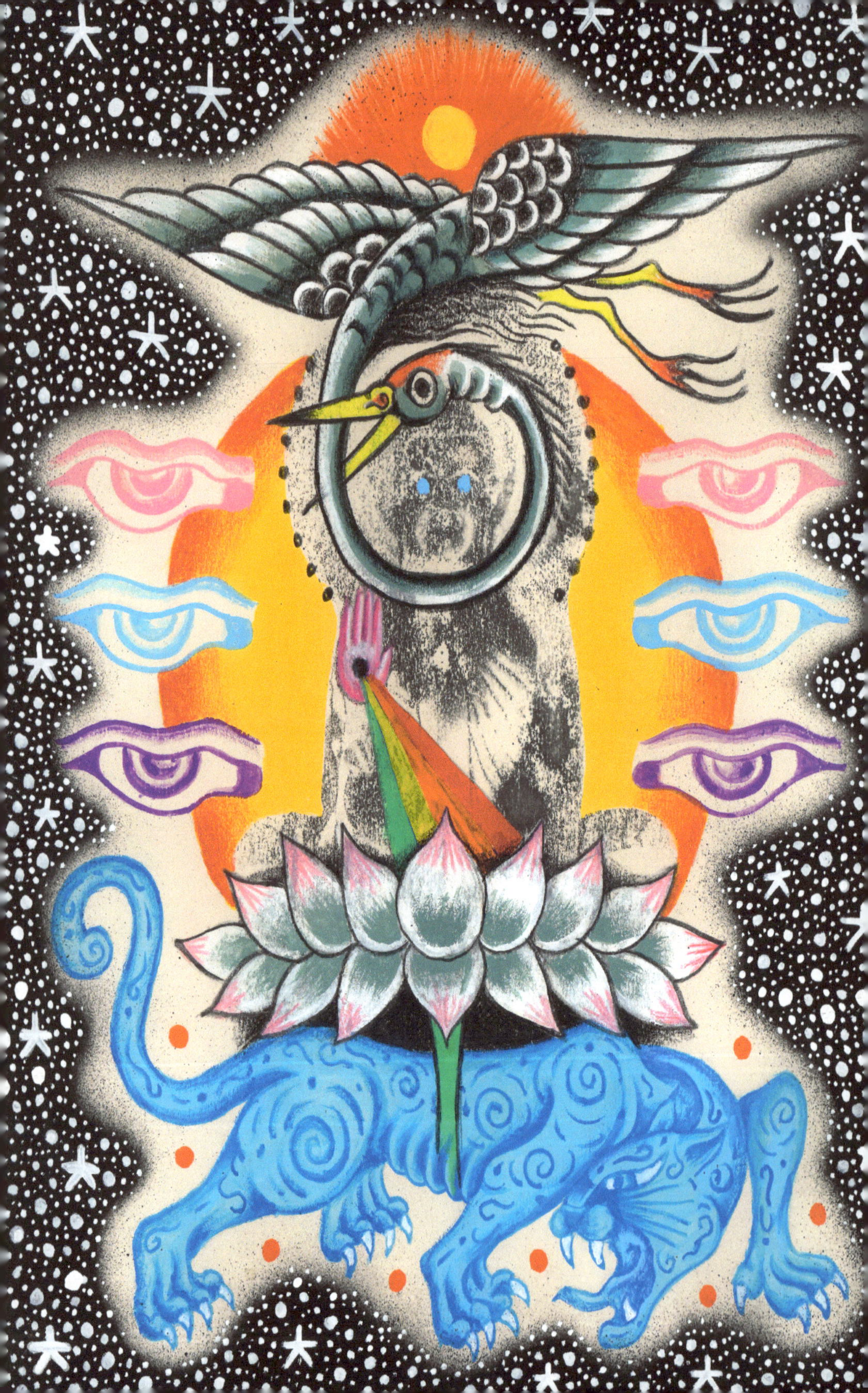

Christ the Buzzard// Persistence of a Dream

BY CORI HART

Christ the Buzzard:

The monk was lying naked and unconscious in a sea of ocher sands, cooking beneath the desert sun. His eyelids parted, letting in trickles of light. None of his other senses had returned, so the light spilling into his vacant skull appeared to him as light eternal–and he trembled. Pupils retracting, the great celestial deity overhead came into focus. He gasped for air but found only dust.

Fully supine, his belly and genitals were exposed and aimed toward the sun. His once copper skin had been seared charcoal, and covering his sun-scarred flesh from the crown of his bald head to the soles of his feet were thick volcanic sores oozing urine-colored puss. He bore the appearance of a giant leaking orifice, or a mollusk, plucked from its shell and baptized in a puddle of brine. With no memory of how he wound up in such a biblical wasteland, he examined his emaciated body and figured he must have been here for some time.

The heat rising around him made the red sky look blurry and warped, the sun a flickering flame on a restless lake. He turned his head and pressed his cheek into the sand, struggling to comprehend his surroundings. Giant ocher dunes looked like frozen waves on a dry sea rolling deep into the horizon–the silence suspended in purgatorial ambiguity.

After much contemplation, he attempted to stand but found his hands and feet were bound with thick twine. Dry blood crusted the frayed edges of rope cutting deep into his wrists. He struggled to wiggle one loose but was too weak to do so. His muscles had atrophied to the consistency of pulverized meat. Strange that he felt no pain. He could "feel," however. He felt the splintered rope clawing at his bones and tendons, the coarseness of mineral chaffing his inner thighs, and the trickle of puss rolling slowly down his face to pool in his ear, but none of these sensations translated into the thing one would specifically call pain.

Suddenly, the smell of antique earth filled his nose, followed by the odor of his own rank perspiration: tepid saline fluids stinking of his innards, which he knew were rotten. Cringing at his stench, he shut his eyes. When he opened them again, he was greeted by a human-shaped silhouette eclipsing the sun.

A bearded man with an angelic face and placid expression looked down on him. Viscous drops of crimson dripped from the tip of the man's nose, which trickled down from his forehead, where a halo of thorns stabbed at his flesh. The man peered deep into the monk's eyes.

Like you, young monk, I am not what I appear . . .

Cam Jennings (opposite)

The man spoke with stern conviction, tugging at the sleeve of his tunic.

…for I, too, am a wolf in a shepherd's cloth.

The monk quivered and twitched, responding with a nod. The man took a knee and leaned in close. Grabbing the monk's face, he began sniffing with the vigor of a starved dog, taking in heavy breaths of musk followed by loud, pleasured exhales. With each inhalation, the monk was pulled further and further down into a dark well of shame.

So please, don't turn to me for salvation… for I am as rotten as you.

The monk shut his eyes tight, hoping the apparition would disappear as swiftly as it had appeared, but upon second glance, the bearded man's face had become that of a buzzard–a grisly Renaissance plague doctor in flesh and bone, perched over him with dilated eyes of supernatural gold gazing deeper.

The monk's eyes opened wide, trembling. Suppressed urges of libidinal violence and depravity began bubbling up from the pits of his subconscious. His scabbed cock slowly rose to become an obelisk to perversion while that nefarious beast lurched over him with hunger in its eyes.

Ghostly apparitions began to manifest in a circle around him. He made out the familiar faces of the Namdroling devotees, his faithful students–those young, naive spirit chasers in their yellow garbs, red ajna dotted sat lotus legged before him, looking to their guru as a pillar of moral exemplary.

Fully exposed, the embarrassment devoured him. He realized his pillar was one of salt, and at his core, he was no more righteous than the most corrupt Sunday morning evangelical demagogue. He was all too human, all too animal. He knew he was rotten, and that salivating buzzard craved to warm its stomach with his rot.

The beast sank its talons into the monk's chest, tore into his ribcage and ripped out a savage fistful of gore, raising it as oblation to the heavens. The horrified devotees gasped as the monk convulsed against the yanking out of spaghetti-like nerves. Bone, fat, and spoiled flesh dangled from the creature's grip as it tossed the slop down its gizzard, squawking with manic fervor. Bound by rope and bleeding in the sand, the monk watched helplessly as his chest cavity was eviscerated into a steaming broth of grit, the odor overwhelming.

Tears streamed down the faces of the disillusioned devotees as they burst into a symphonic cacophony of mournful wails, and the vulture, draped in its blood-soiled tunic, flesh stringing from beak, cried out in rapture and burrowed its head deep into the gorged torso.

…a moment of stillness…

…a cog in the machinery of time, jammed…

The devotees fell silent and then evaporated into a gentle mist.

A cry ruptured through the silence. The beast shrieked in horror from within the monk's body, the vibrations electrifying his bones. Retracting from the odiferous torso, it swung about violently, shaking off globs of putrid gunk while hissing and grunting in a fit of nauseous delirium. A large pair of golden gem-plated wings sprouted from the beast back, chaotically flapping and turning up a tornado of red dust. Whatever it had found at the monk's core must have been genuinely vile, for in the flash of a second, Christ the Buzzard had flown off, far into the distance, melting into the sun.

Intermission:

I awake lying supine on cum-stained sheets, alone in my Bushwick apartment. It reeks of sweat, stale bread, and pot, and a popping sound is coming from my turntable, a Tom Waits record–Rain Dogs–has reached its end. I reach for my phone–3:23 pm.

A new message from Brijmurti:

Hey man! We're serving purusha at the temple tomorrow morning at 10. Would love to see you there. :')

"Jesus fucking Christ," I say out loud, "give it a rest."

I chant with them once in the subway for free snacks and a George Harrison CD, and now this guy won't stop blowing up my phone? I'm a full-time student; what makes him think I have time to trek all the way up to 94th Street on a Wednesday morning just to be punished by crazed Krishnas inquiring into my karma?

I swipe away his text and open my incognito Safari browser and search: "young asian asphyxiation porn." I swipe through a few images, wiggle my flaccid member stiff, and putt onto my thigh. Without thinking, I dip my finger into the goop for a taste of protein–bad idea. I reach over to my nightstand and relight a half-burned joint.

How many times have I had that dream now? And what does it mean? Perhaps I'll write about it one day.

I choke down the rest of the joint and recline back into the sheets, closing my eyes. I can't help but imagine that The Desert actually exists somewhere, inaccessible to my waking world and yet somehow ontologically real.

My last thought before drifting off again: Poor guy; it's really quite a bind he's gotten himself into.

Persistence of a Dream:

As the dust settled down onto the monk's bloodied husk, he began to grow weightless; guts sprawled out across the barren land, he was certainly *physically* lighter–but this was different. It was as if some incredibly dense metallic poison had been extracted, and the supreme weight of judgment gone with it. His body tingled with a serene numbness. Lightening, he felt himself separating in two.

Foreign sounds of high-pitched frequency–psychic transmissions from a place typically imperceptible–the desert beginning to breathe–each breath bringing panoramic visions of impossible geometry pulsating in rhythm with his own dying palpitations–his breath and desert breath slowing as one, edging to a stop.

Momentarily, the sun glowed like a ruby, and then it shifted to a warm amber hue. It faded to a citrine light that made him squint before turning into a soothing emerald color that calmed his nerves. Sapphire radiance followed, filling him with peace. And finally, it became deep amethyst, igniting the powder keg of his soul.

The monk floated upward, leaving his mangled body behind. He hovered over it, bouncing gently in space as if tethered to his body by a string–and then, with a sudden loud electrical snap, the string was cut. Liberated from his material bondage, he began to dissipate into the still air, becoming nothing and everything all at once–a dancing cloud of vibrational mist, a vessel for the "Great Universal Oneness."

Giant atomic plumes of effervescent energy ejaculated from the earth as his etheric body shot, shimmering through the stratosphere, racing to commune with the great solar father. He melted into the sun, a mandala wheel exploding with fires of brilliant color–that wheel spinning at his will, slinging spokes of iridescent flame across the skyline–all the galaxies' stars becoming mandalas, and they too spun– the fiery wheels of a great cosmic chariot burning and revving in unison, bound for Infinity.

Based in Florida, Cori Hart is a self described "romantic-doomer" and publisher for Subtle Body Press. He occasionally pens flash fiction, seeking to blend autobiographical moments with hallucination and philosophical rumination. He is the host of *Subtle Transmissions* podcast. You can follow him on X (@corihart_).

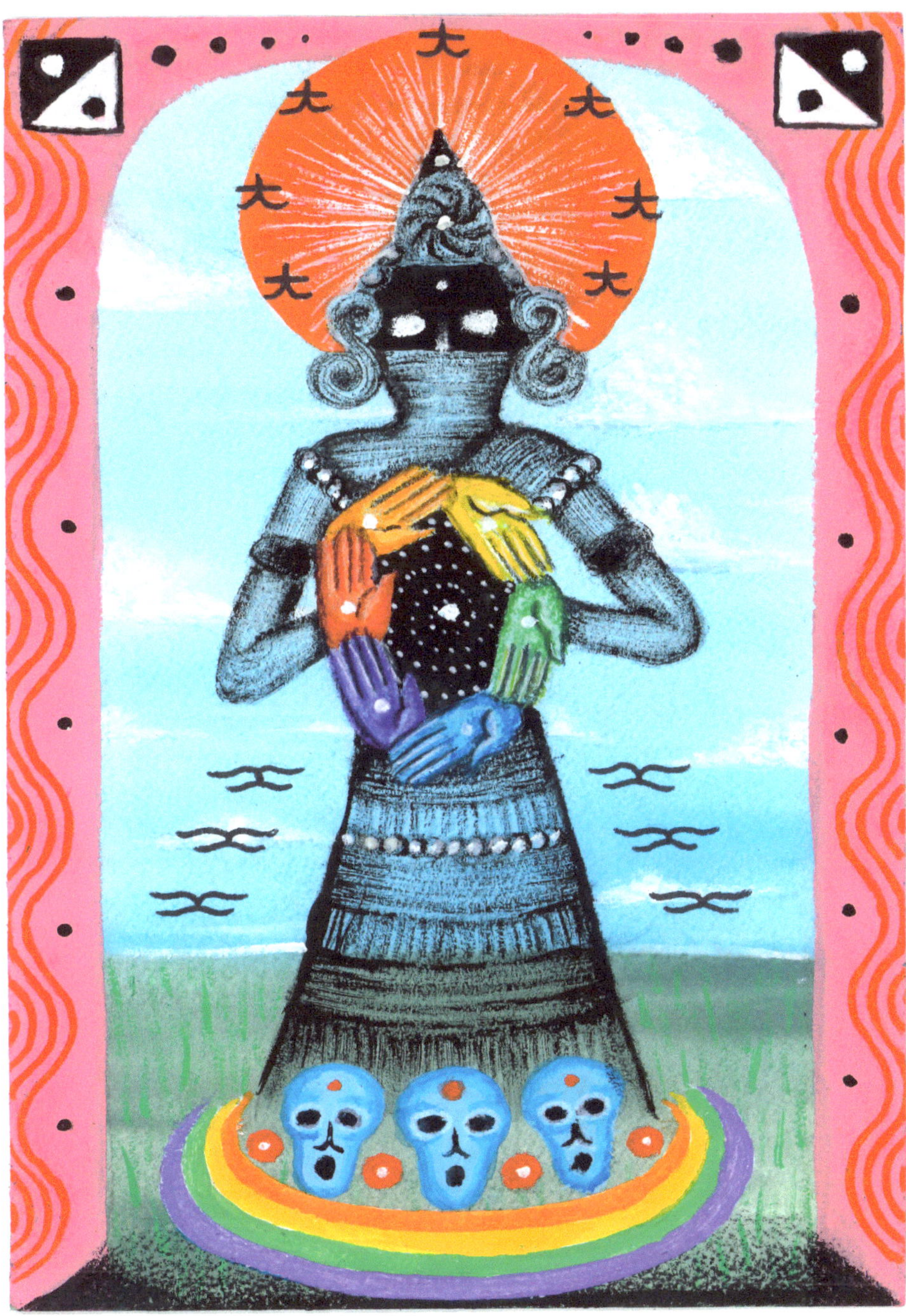

Cam Jennings

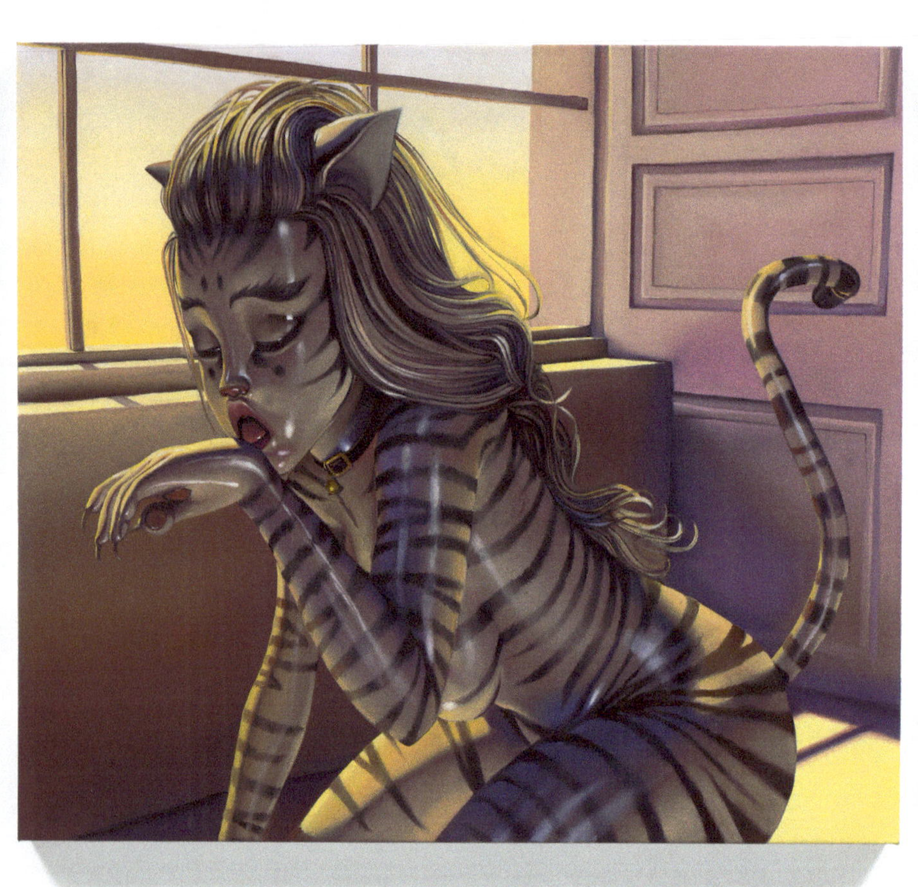

Porn Brain

OR:

THIS IS THE ULTIMATE WEAPON! MODDED ORGASM MACHINE! MR. RODEO-RIDER MACHINE ARM TAKES INNOCENT AMATEUR GIRLS FOR A RIDE THEY'LL NEVER FORGET! VOL.3

BY HENRY LUZZATTO

There is no denying the power of porn. The average American male spends more time consuming internet pornography than any other kind of content. But despite the intensity of its visual and sonic stimulation, our modern erotic material is limited to just images and sounds–merely two fundamental senses out of a normal human's five.

That's why we at Elon Musk's Space-Sex, in combination with experts at the Krankinghoff Institute in Frankfurt, Germany, are excited to announce the release of our first ever pornographic neural link. With the new Ecstasy Incubator implant, we can take pornography beyond mere sight and sound and into a sexual cornucopia that incorporates the touch, taste, and yes, even the smell of your favorite pornographic material.

Utilizing our highly advanced artificial intelligence machine learning mainframes, we are able to even take classic pornography–such as, let's say, a high quality DVD rip of Priya Jai's 2009 boat scene with Julio Swardson and Jimmy Deen–and use your own sense memories to interpolate a hyper-realistic sexual experience. Today, with SpaceSex's technology, we are no longer limited to virtual reality. Our pornography is real memory, perverted and perfected with the best silicone implants.

But that's not all. This neural link's unique interaction with the subject's own memories doesn't just allow porn to become experiences–it allows your experiences become porn.

That's right, with this neural pornography chip, you can sort through all the different faces and bodies you have observed in your life, have them processed through our proprietary AI-enhanced Nudo-Graphic Spunxinator, and experience them as porn stars. With the Ecstasy Incubator implant, you can have immersive virtual reality sex with anyone–and I mean anyone–you have ever seen!

Taylor Swift. Denzel Washington. Rosario Dawson. Jon Lovitz, Tom Cruise, or Richard M. Nixon. Your best friend's dead wife. That girl at the bar two years ago who you now realize was definitely flirting with you. Your grandfather. My grandfather. Your fourth-grade English teacher. The friend you think is hot but can't fuck for the good of the group. Anyone you have ever seen in your life, no matter how briefly, they are all fair game.

You will never be tongue tied or nervous in conversation ever again, as they all feature personalized, psychologically tailored dirty talk collated from real-life speech patterns mixed with the hottest erotic dialogue ever scoured from novels and erotic fan-fiction.

There is nothing they won't say. There is nothing they won't do.

With this neural implant, every path untaken in your life becomes a wide-open

Emma Stern (opposite)

boulevard full of dirty, sweaty, delicious copulation. Every person you saw on the street and turned away from, every beautiful smile still ringing through your mind, every moment you lost courage. Never fear. You can fuck them all.

There is no regret with the implant. There is no missed cue, no fumbled opportunity, no kiss left unfulfilled. With the implant, you can finally live the life you want, with anybody, for those four-to-seven minutes before implant-induced orgasmic ecstasy.

But that's not enough. It can't be enough. Sooner or later, after you have looked through every face in your past and conquered them sexually, you grow bored of the experience, because every person is the same inside–wet and pink.

That's why the newest adaptations of this neural implant are no longer limiting this pornographic ability to people, but to things. With the newest innovations to the Quantum Blastological Simophoric Intaxilocutor, you won't just be able to fuck anyone, you'll be able to fuck anything.

That's right. No longer will you be limited to guiltily smashing your genitals into pillows, vacuum cleaners, or stuffed animals. Instead, you will be able to simulate a fully immersive sexual experience with any object regardless of functionality. Have you always wanted to fuck a Donna Tart novel? Have you ever wanted to get bangaranged by a 2015 Dodge Challenger? Have you always wanted to ride the Great Wall of China? Feel Lady Liberty give it up for you, hardcore style? Ride a church? Nut inside Canada?

But that's not it, this doesn't just apply to physical things. No, no, no, of course not. When we say "anything," we mean anything, and that also includes concepts, ideas, the ephemeral and unknowable, the unattainable and the things left purely to the realm of language and air.

With the Ecstasy Incubator, you can fuck the concept of wind. Of sunlight. Of happiness. You can stick your entire shwang and balls into the feeling of the last Sunday dinner you had with your parents before you moved out for good. You can fuck the feeling of bowling a perfect strike, getting hit in the jaw, telling your ex-girlfriend you think you should see other people. Make sweet love to endless night, ceaseless sorrow, and eternal grief. You can shove religious ecstasy into your pussy. You can take the glow of pre-dawn dew glazing the daffodils as you sit outside, warm coffee on your lap, not a care in the world, and you can bust that shit down crazy freak style with your thumb in the butt.

There will be no instance you cannot eroticize, no emotion you cannot profane, no feeling internal or external that is divorced from the intensity of the experience in the meat between your legs.

Everything can fuck, everything can be fucked, everything can be cumming, all together, all at once, forever, in your mind, with just one small purchase, one small moment of insertion, and then... eureka! Have no fear. Have no pain. Or have them, and turn them into cumming too! Embrace the eternal horizon of cock and pussy and ass, experience all the unity of every human experience all together, all one, ALL ONE!

Just so long as you make sure you wipe up when you're finished.

Henry Luzzatto is a Brooklyn-based writer and editor with fiction, humor, and opinion writing featured in *body fluids*, *Points in Case*, *New Internationalist*, *Radon Journal*, and *The Los Angeles Review of Books*, among others. Originally from Suffolk, Virginia, where he got his start in local journalism, he currently works in New York as a screenplay editor.

Emma Stern (opposite)

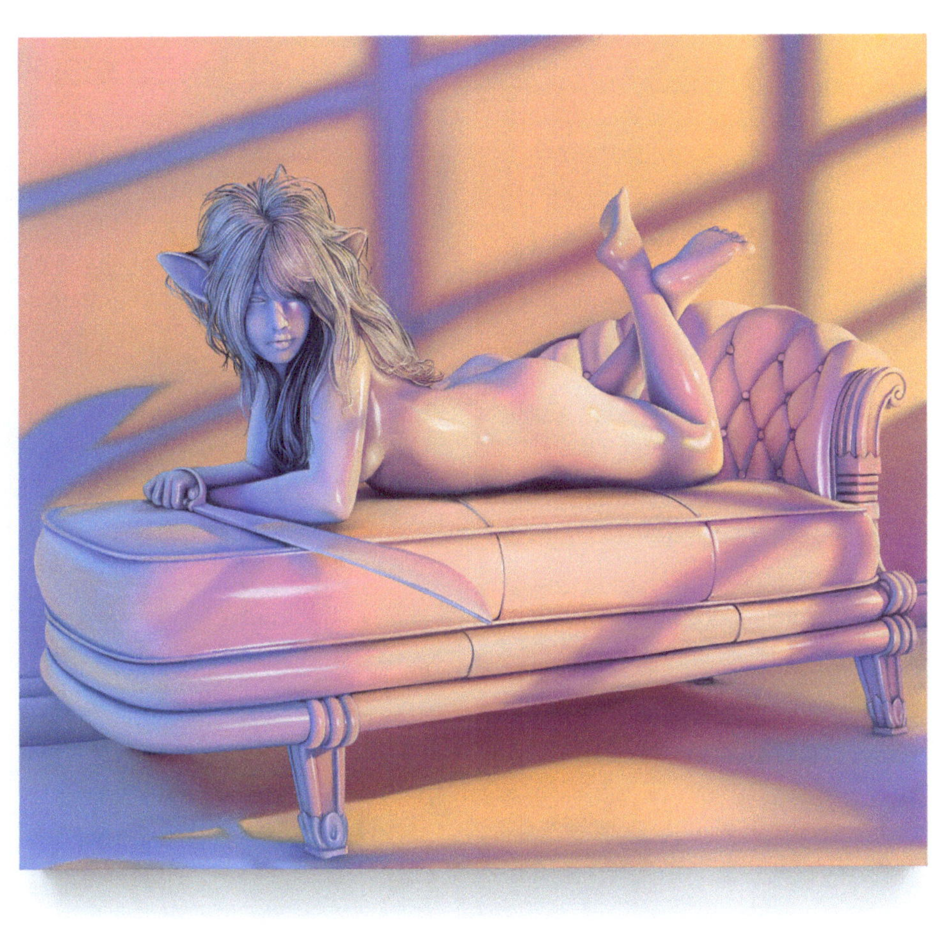

Company Town Blues

BY SASHA SERGE [SERVING CAPITALIST REALISM]

In an earlier draft, I lied to you. I told you I started writing this while flying back from Seattle; this is false. I did visit Seattle recently, but on the flight back, I was too exhausted to conform my real life to the desired poetry of this page. This has been happening more lately. Everything has been happening more lately. I wanted this essay to start on an airplane because this is an essay about a company that makes airplanes and growing up under the shadow of one such company can darken one's blood and shade one's eyes. It took me a long time to realize this.

I grew up in Everett, Washington—well, kind of. The suburbs surrounding Seattle are a haze of strip-mall borderlands that become increasingly harder to distinguish the more highways you drive down. I grew up on one such border, technically in Everett but geographically and culturally in Mukilteo, a bougier, whiter, idyllic suburb complete with a picturesque lighthouse, ferry terminal, and rows of gated almost mansions. I like to say I'm from Everett because it makes me feel more working class, but I grew up middle class. This was in large part due to Boeing.

My grandpa and grandma, my dad's parents, moved to Washington in the early 1970s. They were from Wichita and had both sought employment at Boeing, who then offered to send my grandpa—who I have always referred to as Papa—to

college at the University of Washington to become an engineer for them, an opportunity he jumped at. Eventually, he and my grandma divorced, and she remarried—to another Boeing employee, my grandpa Bob. They fell in love building airplanes together in the largest building in the world by volume. The employment of my now three grandparents at Boeing allowed for my father's sustained existence, who then brought me into being. While my dad does not work for Boeing, he essentially lives on Boeing property; you must pass the world's largest building to get there. A company town in all but the legal sense.

Boeing was formerly synonymous with a robust "familial" corporate culture, airplane safety, and commercial aviation. My conservative uncle—who made me watch the funeral of Ronald Reagan live on T.V. at age 12—had always wanted to be a pilot, but he was color-blind and thus disqualified from serving in the Air Force. He passed his interest onto me, taking me to the Museum of Flight and having me read biographies of Chuck Yeager. Whenever we had the chance, we would eat at this grimy diner on the tarmac at Paine Field, where I'd drown steak fries in ketchup while watching Cessnas taxi.

I came up around airplanes, and I thought they were neat. Everything I had read about the darker side of airplanes as weapons of war was mainly in

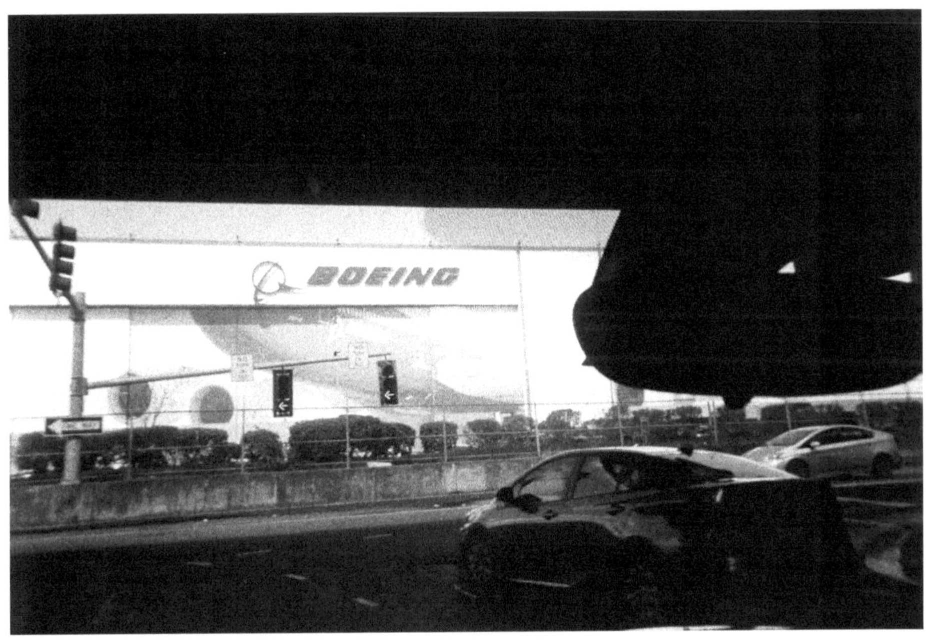

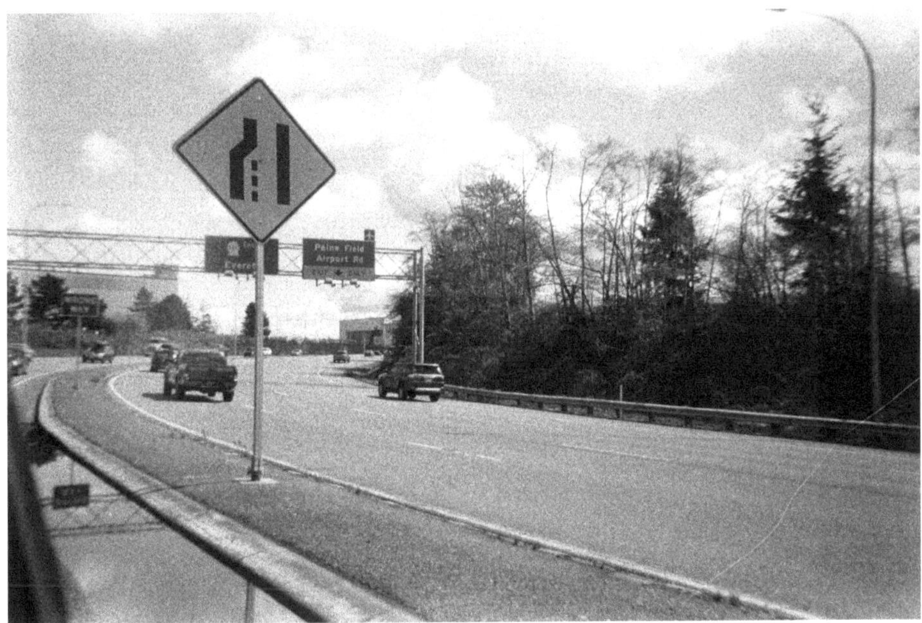

Photos by Sasha Serge

context to World War II, which was in the service of fighting Nazis, who we all knew weren't really human. Boeing's stellar reputation and the aviation enthusiasm of those around me led me to a naive innocence about Boeing I would enjoy for my entire adolescence.

This ignorance was a luxury I enjoyed, being firmly situated in the heart of the empire. I imagine it must have been more challenging for kids growing up in regions where Boeing's bombs were dropping to ignore their presence. This was not a thought I had until I was almost 30.

Papa now lives in a small town in Rhode Island, where I visited him in 2022 after moving to within a relatively short train ride. He picked me up from the train station in Providence and took me to a seafood restaurant with his wife—my grandma Joanne—in tow. There I placed my phone on the bar-top—recording—and asked prying questions about the time he had worked in Boeing's "black box," which I had heard vague allusions to growing up.

"Well, what it was was the B-2 bomber, the stealth bomber," he told me through a mouthful of prawn flatbread. When he was working for Boeing in the '80s, the Department of Defense had apparently come in one day and told him and a few others—who were working on CAD (Computer-Aided Design) systems—that they were selected for a top-secret project with the government and would begin work immediately. He and his colleagues were each assigned a different section of the project they were working on—which was unknown to them—after they waited six months for Top Secret clearance from the FBI.

They were wholly in the dark about what it was they were designing—until they weren't. As Papa tells it:

So, one night we were working late, and we were walking around, and my buddy over here was like, "Show me what you're working on," so we took all the models, the virtual models, and put 'em over at one computer, and we put the thing together and flew it. And we were like, "holy fucking hell!" So, if they'd have found out about that, the FBI would have escorted us out the door before we knew what was happening, but I can tell you this now.

After this discovery, of which their superiors were obviously unaware, they had to do a design review with Northrop Grumman, the company that won the contract to produce the bomber. The internet could only run on unsecured T3 lines at the time, so they did things the old-fashioned way. They backed up the designs onto mag tape, put them in "one of those old Halliburton aluminum briefcases," handcuffed Papa to one, and put him on a plane to East Los Angeles.

I couldn't tell anyone where I was goin'. It was like, "Here's a number you can call in case of an emergency; I'll see you in three weeks."

This was 1985. I would be born 7 years later.

The B-2 bomber was deployed most heavily in the NATO bombing of Serbia during the controversial *Operation Allied Force*, where the bombing was estimated to have killed over 500 Serbian civilians. B-2 bombers were responsible for the accidental bombing of the Chinese embassy in Belgrade, which killed three Chinese journalists and sparked enormous international outrage. By this point in the war, the B-2 bombers had dropped over 500 bombs on Serbia. The stealth bomber also made appearances during the Iraq and Afghanistan wars, releasing more than 1.5 million pounds of munitions and 583 JDAM "smart bombs" in 2003.

The weight of this hit me as I was slurping down oysters at a Providence, Rhode Island seafood bar.

I almost choked.

It is a weird thing to try and work backward to re-contextualize your childhood and the behemoth one grew up under. It is difficult to adequately communicate the degree to which this weapons manufacturer was utterly normalized in all facets of everyday life in my hometown. Perhaps this is the banality of evil we've all heard so much about. This is the reality, though, and it is the reality across America. I imagine it's the same for people who grew up in Raytheon families or Lockheed Martin towns. The violence is very far away, and it is terribly normal; it's best not to be concerned with all of that. This situation and its potential consequences were even implicitly recognized in our region; I remember doing nuclear drills in elementary school in case North Korea nuked us. I was told that we did these because we were right next to Boeing, which would be one of the main targets of foreign enemies in the event of the US entering into a war. I dutifully hid under my desk, curious about the futility of a plywood barrier between myself and a nuclear bomb.

Of course, I wasn't entirely born yesterday. I grew up in an era of Boeing unease. Things had been changing, and often not for the better. Boeing relocated its corporate headquarters in 2001 following a merger with McDonnell Douglas—which was the beginning of the end for Boeing as we knew it. Growing up, Boeing was constantly fucking over its employees. Most recently, Boeing fired a friend months away from retirement to avoid paying into his pension, stripping him of all benefits. He went to the union, who essentially told him their hands were tied. He is now delivering pizzas.

Boeing's shift from a hyper-profitable capitalist behemoth with a robust work culture and strong unions to stock-portfolio-in-a-trench-coat is the story of us all under neoliberalism. Neoliberalism is said to have three tenets: defund, deregulate, and decentralize. You could find no apostles more righteous in the cult of neoliberalism than the board of Boeing after their 2001 merger, who followed these commandments with zeal.

In short, Boeing shifted their culture to maximizing corporate profits; moved their corporate HQ to Chicago, further away from their workforce; did everything possible to weaken and sideline their union, introduced an austerity budget that minimized funding for the actual production of airplanes while maximizing budgeting for stock buybacks and dividend programs, outsourced an increasing number of parts to cheap foreign companies, and essentially bought the FAA regulators who were supposed to provide oversight and prevent the eventual tragedies from happening in the first place. They defunded, deregulated, and decentralized, and as a result, 346 people are dead.

Even if you discount the bombing campaigns of the bomber Papa helped construct, you still can't decouple Boeing from death.

The trail of the dead, unfortunately, does not end here. By way of example, in January of this year, a door-plug in the emergency exit row blew out of a 737 MAX shortly after taking off from Portland International Airport. This incident prompted an FAA investigation and a series of hearings, where multiple whistleblowers at Boeing and its suppliers came forward and were set to testify. On March 9th, Josh Barnett–who had worked for Boeing for 30 years before retiring in 2017–was found dead in his truck in the parking lot of the hotel he'd been staying in while giving deposition to attest to quality control concerns at Boeing. His cause of death is listed as "suspected self-inflicted suicide." (If you believe this, I have a bridge to sell you.) Two months later, Joshua Dean–another Boeing quality control manager-turned-whistleblower–was found dead, this time after two weeks in critical condition following a sudden onset of Influenza B and MRSA, which developed into pneumonia. While viral warfare seems fantastical even for a company whose job it is to make things that kill people, nothing can be ruled out at this point. Following in the footsteps of so many other institutions in our current era of mass death and institutional negligence, Boeing is doubling down on repression.

Choking on shellfish was not the first time it occurred to me that Boeing wasn't the feel-good commercial jet maker we all knew and loved. Around 2016, I decided to pay attention to politics for likely clear reasons and almost instantly became radicalized as a result. I went back to community college and became a socialist political organizer, sometimes finding Boeing mentioned as bad guys in campaigns I'd be helping on. (I'm more anarchist than socialist presently, but that's another essay.)

In 2019, I moved from Seattle to New York to attend The New School, where I graduated with an MA in Politics in 2023. I have found myself on campus frequently lately; everything keeps happening always. Israel's genocide in Gaza has been going on for seven months now. Boeing is currently the world's third-largest weapons manufacturer, deriving 60% of its profits from its "defense" division. Unsurprisingly, Boeing is profiting handily from the multi-billion-dollar weapons packages that the US government is pushing through to aid Israel in said genocide.

As college campuses across the United States and the world set up encampments on lawns and in hallways, one of their main goals has come into sharp focus: divestment. Divest from what exactly? Well, genocide and war profiteering, the things you wouldn't usually associate a university with being invested in in the first place. As neoliberalism came for Boeing, it also came for your university. Since most entities now primarily exist to turn a profit for shareholders, most universities, in turn, have huge stock portfolios–and they are, in turn, invested in the architects and profiteers of genocide. War, after all, is good business. It will not surprise you, then, which company has entered the crosshairs of so many keffiyeh-wearing student protestors.

As I ran out of time to write this essay, protests rapidly escalated across New York City. As I boarded another non-Boeing plane bound from Nashville to New York–and this plane story *is* true–I watched images of hundreds of NYPD riot officers massing to lay siege to the protestors occupying Columbia University. I sat in my seat wearing my headphones, tuned into a constantly crashing stream of WKCR-FM, Columbia's college radio station, as student reporters breathlessly described scenes of advancing stormtroopers in between fits of sprinting. I listened until my service cut out because the Wi-Fi was turned off for my flight.

I landed in New York at 11pm and had the cab driver tune into WKCR on my ride home. Things had gone silent on the reporting front, so we listened to the (quite good) student-curated jazz selection. At the same time, I scrolled my feeds, digesting the facts that the NYPD had just decimated Columbia and the City College of New York, arrested over 300 people in total, deployed weapons of war, beat students and faculty alike, and even fired a gun in Columbia's Hinds (nee: Hamilton) Hall.

The next day was May Day. We marched and rallied at Foley Square as usual. What was not so usual, although growing more so daily, was the number of keffiyehs and the pro-Palestine sentiment on display. There were thousands of us, and we were furious for our comrades still sitting in jail from the surreal crackdown the night before. We marched to Washington Square Park. The plan was to break off to all four then-existing encampments left in New York City (The New School, NYU, FIT, and Fordham), but of course, people only ended up mobilizing to NYU. The only encampment left at the time of this writing is FIT (Fashion Institute of Technology).

Things escalated the next night at The New School. Students barricaded more entrances in both occupied buildings and held a massive rally outside the school. Inside the encampment, I volunteered to be part of a human chain that would block the doors in a police incursion. What were they going to do, suspend me? As I took my station at the door, I was positioned directly in front of a series of posters of various weapons companies with a bloody handprint over their logo. A particular one caught my eye; it bore the Boeing logo. It read:

YOUR TUITION FUNDS GENOCIDE. The Boeing Company designs, manufactures, and sells military weapons, including attack helicopters, combat aircraft, missiles, bombs, battlefield laser systems, and intelligence and surveillance systems to kill Palestinians. THE NEW SCHOOL IS INVESTED IN THE BOEING COMPANY.

The police did not come that night. They came in the morning. I had left around 1am with a supposed guarantee of no police involvement, and I awoke to videos of my comrades and classmates zip-tied and getting loaded into white NYPD police buses. I thought of my Papa's wrist handcuffed to the Halliburton briefcase in service of designing the bombers my friends would be handcuffed for protesting 40 years later. My classmates looked tired. They had been awoken in their tents only minutes earlier by the brutal reality of state repression, so I suppose that makes sense.

In the Pacific Northwest, Boeing has come into particularly sharp focus as a key villain in this ongoing genocide. Multiple encampments have been launched on the University of Washington campus—where Boeing sent Papa to school to become an engineer for them—calling for UW to cut all ties with Boeing. Portland State University has even temporarily "paused" relations with Boeing after student protest and being presented with an Amnesty International report linking Boeing weaponry with Israeli war crimes in Gaza.

I don't know what it would mean for my hometown or the world if Boeing went under. This seems impossible, mainly because it's only one of two major manufacturers that make commercial airplanes at

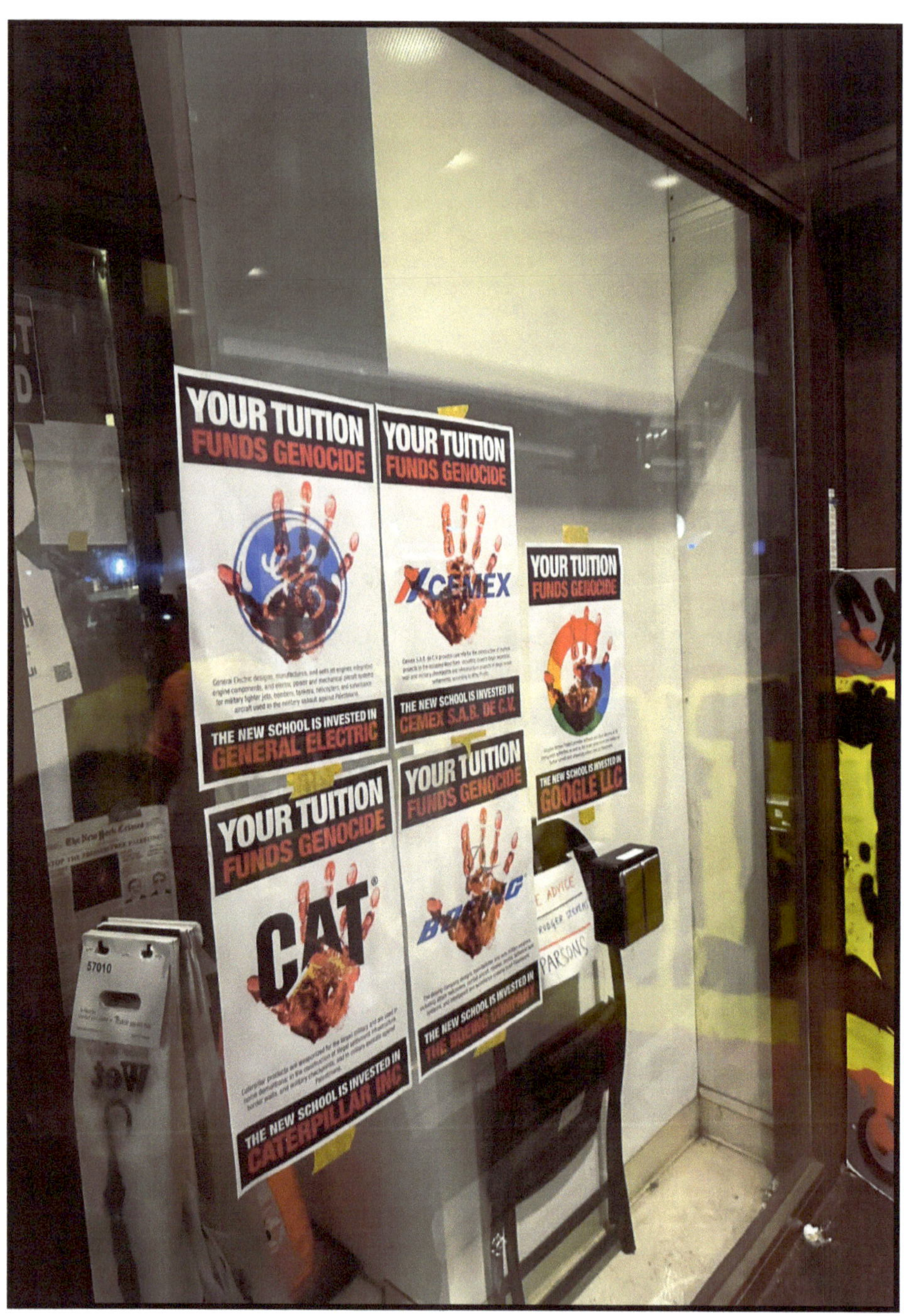

Photo by Sasha Serge

such a scale. Clearly, like many institutions today, they must essentially undergo a death and rebirth, should they survive at all. Boeing, of course, does deserve to die; its body count is horrifying and high; it exists primarily to fatten its vampiric shareholders off the literal blood of Palestinians and other dispossessed people unfortunate enough to be on the wrong side of an American bomb. If Boeing had just made commercial jets and been committed to finding an ecologically sustainable solution to the high pollution of commercial air travel, things would be different. In a better–juster–world, this is what may transpire. Instead, two Boeing whistleblowers have died in suspicious-to-say-the-least circumstances, the anti-war student movement faces a brutal nationwide crackdown, and the Biden administration continues the flow of weapons and aid to Israel unconditionally.

In the meantime, my bank is still the Boeing Employees Credit Union. In the grand scheme of things, it still feels better than a Big Bank. My uncle still works for Boeing, but he hates it now.

While visiting my dad recently, he said, "Companies go through periods like this, but Boeing will eventually be fine. They've got to change, they fucked up and are going to have to correct their mistakes, but they'll get through it."

When I am not challenging state machinery with my literal body on the line, the least I can do is implore the rank and file of Boeing–and all other institutions in crisis today–to ensure they are changed enough. Whether it is Boeing, The New School, your university, or your government, things cannot and will not continue this way. Capital needs new, ever-expanding markets. Boeing's stock value increased 7.3% after the death of whistleblower Joshua Dean. Death is only a temporarily profitable business; it is up to us to make it an impossible one.

We're trapped in the belly of this horrible machine And the machine is bleeding to death–"The Dead Flag Blues," Godspeed You! Black Emperor

Sasha is a freelance writer, bartender, and archivist based in Brooklyn, New York. They run the Instagram meme page @serving.capitalist.realism and publish on Substack under the same handle. You can also follow him on X (@servingcapreal).

CONTEXT:
RELATIONSHIP

PICKING UP CUES OF ITS NEIGHBORS / FRAMING DETAILS -
[picks up details on subtleties of surroundings for better integration]

INTEGRATION
OF FACADE WITH CONTEXT

WHY TRY TO FIT IN? - A DIFFERENT FELT AS THOUGH AN ALIEN FORM WOULD NOT COMMUNICATE WELL WITH THE SURROUNDINGS, THUS A NEED FOR SOMETHING FAMILIAR THAT PICKS UP CUES FROM ITS NEIGHBORS BUT IS ITS OWN ENTITY AS WELL IN DIGNITY.

WHY INTEGRATE DETAILS? - A MORE INTIMATE CONSIDERATION FOR EXISTING CONDITIONS.

ADDRESSING REGULATING LINES -
[blending with neighbors in perspective]

EXTERIOR

INTERIOR

WHY RELATE TO CONTEXT? - DUE TO THE AGE OF THE BUILDER TRYING TO CREATE SOMETHING UNIQUE, STRIKING, AND ICONIC THAT COULD FACADE'S BOLD AND VIBRANT COLOR SCHEME, THE HEIGHT, RHYTHM RELATES WITH THE GEOMETRIC AND RHYTHMIC CUES OF ITS

CAN FORM ENHANCE CONTEXT? -
NEIGHBORING PRECEDENTIAL FORMS
DIVERSITY OF THE SHOP SIGN
THE FACADE TOGETHER

ACKNOWLEDGEMENT OF PRECEDENT AND HOW THAT INFORMS DETAILS
[facade enhances subtle details of context via trim]

REGULATING LINES - FACADE'S
REACTION TO EXISTING CONDITIONS
[facade picks up regulating horizontal and of neighboring buildings - colored glass pane that glitters on the street - make it more dynamic]

INTERIOR / EXTERIOR - A JUXTAPOSITION

structural

RHYTHM AND RELATION
OF FACADE TO ITS NEIGHBORS

WHY? -

HOW DOES THE FACADE COMPLETE
THIS RHYTHM? -

OVERLAPPING LAYERS
[create a dynamic facade along the street front]

CONTINUOUS FOCAL POINT
[present in most doorways, office framed]

VISUAL CUES
[essential to perception of architecture]

LIMINAL SPACE

CONTEXT ORIENTED EXTERIOR -

PROGRAM / INTERIOR

SURFACE CONDITION

CONNECTING RIGHT
ANGLES WITH
SEQUENCED
PARALLELS

INTEGRATION
OF EXTERIOR

LEARNING DESIGNS

Resonance and Revelation:
Navigating Accelerationism and the Quest for Meaning in Modernity

BY C.N. JAIMES [CUTE_NOUMENA]

"Anyone attempting to formulate their thoughts on accelerationism had better do so swiftly [...] One of its predictions is that you'll be too slow to respond coherently. Yet, if you stumble over the question it presents due to haste, you risk losing, possibly quite severely. It's challenging."
–Nick Land, A Quick and Dirty
Introduction to Accelerationism, 2017

If there's anything new to say about accelerationism, it has likely already been said. It often leaves one grappling with stale ideas and a mouthful of words. Recent trends in online circles that are inching toward the zeitgeist either involve a complete withdrawal from the transcendent into the cult of immanence, or a reactionary return to some idealized position in response to the latest Nietzschean "will to power" trend.

Assuming such a thing exists, our modern society finds itself deeply entrenched in this double bind. The effects of the "Death of God" have "liberated" many from the dogma of tradition and presupposed unjustified values, which, to varying degrees, have stifled the ability for "progress" (at least in the minds of ordinary post-Enlightenment figures). Now, it is essential to define what we mean by *progress*. Typically, progress can be understood within a multiplicity of domains, such as economic growth, technological development, and Secularization. This view generally carries a pos-

itive connotation in the West; however, this perspective should not always accompany our idea of progression–progression as a betterment towards a transcendent Good.

If we were to define Accelerationism as briefly and concisely as possible, it would be as follows: Accelerationism is the theoretical framework through which phenomenological time appears to dilate. This temporal compression/expansion is likened to the sensation of rapid acceleration or an increase in intensity. Land's essay "Meltdown" is considered by most following this trend to be the seminal text on the theory. A hybrid between theory and fiction–often called "theory fiction"–"Meltdown" is incredibly eerie in its ability to carve out and describe, hyper-lucidly, not only the early Cyberpunk aesthetics and politics of the '90s but also trends that have reemerged due to the acceleratory catalyst that is COVID-19.

Before proceeding, I wish to distinguish between the perception of time–specifically, the *sensation* of accelerating (Time Intensity)–and technological and economic aggregation (Capital's Teleology) as a form of civilizational acceleration, or, on the other hand, "Techno-economic progress" (both of which tend to be erroneously tethered). Nevertheless, it would be unwise to disregard this technical accumulation of resources as a factor in the Acceleration Hypothesis.

If modernity can be likened to a

John T Allen (opposite)

Positive Feedback process, like that of a runaway Nuclear Meltdown process, then at the core of this Nuclear Reaction, one would find the engine of modernity, the capitalistic mode of production. With the rise of machines during the Industrial Revolution, humanity has witnessed an explosive emancipatory force that has completely altered and scorched the historical landscape.

In his 1848 speech "On the Question of Free Trade", Marx states the following:

... in general, the protective system of our day is conservative, while the free trade system is destructive. It breaks up old nationalities and pushes the antagonism of the proletariat and the bourgeoisie to the extreme point. In a word, the free trade system hastens the social revolution. It is in this revolutionary sense alone, gentlemen, that I vote in favor of free trade.

This highlights the corrosive tendency for capitalism to overturn the values of its host nation because capital only affirms itself; "everything solid melts into air." Early in the industrial process, this exponential technological and economic acceleration advanced rapidly as if it were approaching singularity. That process had become stagnant as industrialized machinic labor transitioned into speculative assets as the primary form of capital production. But now, the process of capitalism seems to only intensify at overturning values, redefining many aspects of what it even means to be human; it takes on the effect of a massive large-scale psychedelic ego death, in which humanity is slowly unmasking itself to finally see itself as an automaton.

This challenges a legacy concept of the Enlightenment thinkers, who believed in the romantic ideal of bolstering human-ities reason as absolute. The shift from the clockwork-like mechanism of a universe set up by an indifferent passive Deity into the random and chaotic yet mechanistic workings of an assemblage of bodies, machines, and drives.

The atomic Bomb showed that the same procedure for uncovering the natural world could–or will–lead to our undoing. It is deeply Promethean. But this leaves us with the prime condition of the modern individual–one with a deep longing for the fortitude of the soul. Without taking a significant detour into defining what the soul is, which would require a separate essay altogether. By "soul," what is meant is not some metaphysical substance, component of our nature, or form of irreducible essence.

Soul may be loosely defined as spirit or what is satisfied by "appetitive virtues." Suppose the mind is in optimal alignment when it is closest to reason, and the body is in optimal alignment when it is satisfied with appetitive satiation. In that case, then the spirit is satisfied when it is in optimal alignment with: glory, virtue, and meaning. The a priori stance of modernity and late post-modernity is that of Nihilism. Everyone lives in a constant state of ironic distancing and Cynicism. If nothing is sacred, everything is permitted. Theoretically, the schizophrenic character (subject) is the average phenomenological experience under capitalism. Capitalism erodes longstanding traditions, values, and customs and attempts to present this as natural, normal, and a sign of "progress." It expands in a territorializing manner–a Subjective Imperialism, if you will. It creates new sign regimes of order until these, too, are eroded and overcome by the following territorialization (shift/wave). This corrosion is something Nietzsche instantly recognized and diagnosed.

God is dead. God remains dead. And we have killed him. How shall we comfort ourselves, the murderers of all murderers? What was holiest and mightiest of all that the world has yet owned has bled to death under our knives: who will wipe this blood off us? What water is there for us to clean ourselves? What festivals of atonement, what sacred games shall we have to invent? Is not the greatness of this deed too great for us? Must we not become gods to appear worthy of it?

This became the task for 20th century philosophy to overcome. From Sartre's existentialism to Camus's Absurdism, the modern man was seen as being radically free to either despair in their virulent Nihilism or to take the burden of existence head-on and reconstitute meaning. For thinkers like Sartre and Deleuze, this dizzying freedom frees the human-animal to constitute their values and meaning. This is the Nietzschean Vitalism found in French Postmodernism. Now, for a generation–our generation–which has grown up not just with secularism as a homogenous religious paradigm, we're left with an even greater task. If the 20th century attempted the reconstitution of meaning in the project of modernity–which ultimately ended in thunderous failure with the atrocities of WWII and the dissolution and contempt towards meta-narratives.

Our society yearns for meaning yet is drenched in Nihilism and Irony. This Nihilism can ultimately lead one to seek meaning in the most mundane things, such as commodity gratification or ideological affirmation, amongst other banalities. The most common of these tends to be ideological affirmation in consumer spending habits. In a Nietzschean regis-

ter, this mindset of creating one's meaning from this "meme-i-fied" notion of the will to power has been captured and incorporated into capitalism's mechanism of capture and expansion. The current slave morality is that of an individual who seeks to find a remedy for their bankrupt soul but approaches this through the ritual of capitalism by shopping for a community, shopping for commodities, friends, etc. It's an attempt to satisfy one's soul with the things of this world.

Now, how are we to move forward, to reconstitute the divine to nourish the soul, without naively reverting to a time long foreclosed? An option is to follow ancient wisdom:

He said to Him, "Which ones?" Jesus said, "You shall not murder," "You shall not commit adultery," "You shall not steal," "You shall not bear false witness," "Honor your father and your mother," and, "You shall love your neighbor as yourself." The young man said to Him, "All these things I have kept from my youth. What do I still lack?" Jesus said to him, "If you want to be perfect, go, sell what you have and give to the poor, and you will have treasure in heaven; and come, follow Me." But when the young man heard that saying, he went away sorrowful, for he had great possessions.

These passages place great emphasis on giving up material goods (the aesthetic life). In short, although we should not exclude this reading, we must go further: it is to abandon our very hubris of reason. To give up on the life of a sophist. Like the young man, we have great possessions–our reason, systems, truths, and morality. We know this is the case, for God asked this same thing of Abraham when asked to sacrifice his son Isaac–not because it was reasonable, not even because it was the "right" thing to do, for Isaac was an innocent man; this was to ask murder of Abraham. This is a prime example of the abandonment of reason, but why reason? Because faith costs nothing less than everything.

However, there is an alternate path, as Ray Brassier insightfully states: "We are already dead." This applies both to thermodynamic-linear cosmology and to the state of man (Adam). We should strive toward death: death to the world. Physical death is merely "La petit mort," as is civilizational decline–the climax of surplus vitalism (pure actuality, pride, or I = I). But "death" is necessary for "resurrection" (virtuality [line of flight]), which one can see as a spiritual life, movement, or difference. The error lies in an affirmation of idolizing digitalization and flatlining our reality into two dimensions. Two dimensions neglect the 3rd, that of an ascension, but this ascension should not be mistaken with arboreal structures; this verticality is a movement; it's a flow, a line of flight.

Revolutionary movements do not spread by contamination but by resonance. Something that is constituted here resonates with the shock wave emitted by something constituted over there.... An insurrection is not like a plague or a forest fire–a linear process which spreads from place to place after an initial spark. It rather takes the shape of a music, whose focal points, though dispersed in time and space, succeed in imposing the rhythms of their own vibrations, always taking on more density."
–The Invisible Committee

For the past couple of years, there has been an emphasis on wave-like patterns in social behaviors, often referencing waves of infection caused by the SARS-COVID-19 viral infection. Regarding the online theoretical landscape, instead of focusing on "wave" dynamics in their immanent properties, resonance, amplitude, etc., the primary focus has remained on interpreting waves in terms of linear dynamics/models; a modern transcendental framework has entirely captured the narrative or the understanding of "waves" in the zeitgeist.

This framework understands sociological movements, events, and politics solely in the language of memetic contagion, as noted in the quote from The Invisible Committee above: "a linear process which spreads from place to place after an initial spark." It's essential to understand how these self-propagating paradigms shape our subjectivity. The capitalist subject only understands the world via a flat ontology. This is the world of the Euclidean plane, lines, bars, and speed graphs diagrammed in logarithmic curvature, derivatives, and amplitude.

The most contentious term in contemporary leftist philosophical and theoretical circles is that of "hierarchy." We are wholly tethered to the regime of Immanence and Difference. The Holy Church of Deleuzian Puritanism affirms our Rhizomatic multiplicities and emergent flat-ontology differential frameworks because Difference *in itself* is confused for Difference *for itself*. Most don't realize that their primary understanding of Deleuze is akin to a cursory reading of Nick Land, of quick and dirty destratification at any cost, even if it means becoming a blackhole. This ignorance towards the emergent Hierarchy of layered strata leaves us unable to see past the Kantian Transcendental Horizon. It thus keeps us boxed in the modernist's

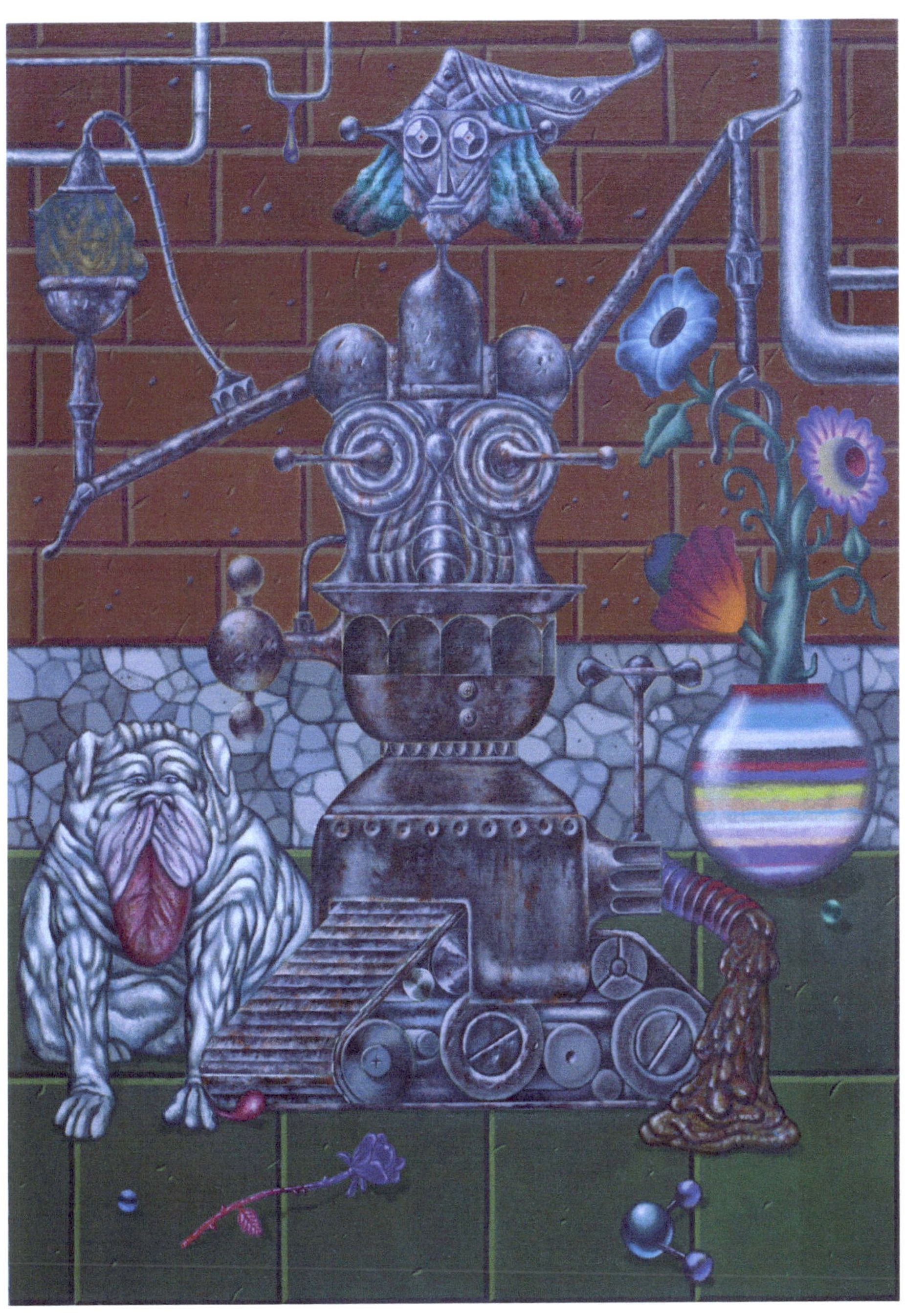

Davor Gromilović

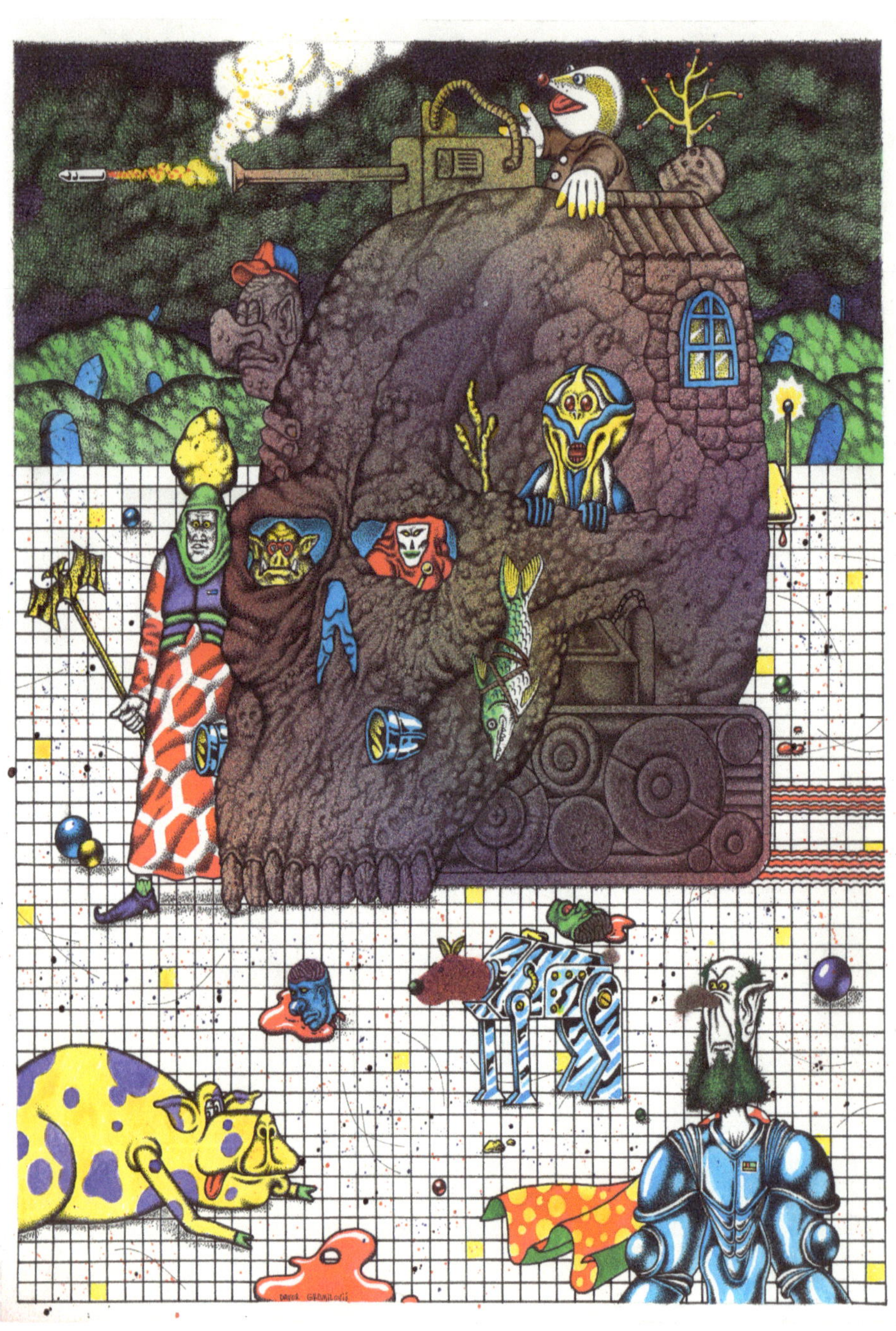

Davor Gromilović

flat ontological paradigm of Euclid. Instead of finding the possibility of configuring ourselves to resonate with other strata, we try to de-stratify all too quickly. Thus, we destroy through the corrosive powers of the War Machine.

Revolutionary movements do not spread by contamination but by resonance. Something that is constituted here resonates with the shock wave emitted by something constituted over there (...). It rather takes the shape of a music, whose focal points, though dispersed in time and space, succeed in imposing the rhythms of their own vibrations, always taking on more density.
–The Invisible Committee

The obvious allusion would be to coalescing waves of resonant structures, of converging amplitudes, in which, in an instant, that which is solid becomes an entangled mess by no means other than its own resonance. We can consider emergent organizational patterns, as seen in Chladni plate patterns; however, this approach still confines our thinking to two dimensions, reducing it to a framework that fetishizes difference and flat-ontological planes. Instead, we should aspire to be like the angelic choirs of heaven. While there is a strict hierarchy among them based on their closeness to God, all of creation still shares a common teleology oriented toward the good. The Pythagoreans, who influenced Plato, had an understanding that waves and music are related to ratio and proportion, recognizing that music has a profound connection to "reality."

To overcome the transcendental horizon of modernity, we must explore new ways of thinking; this does not imply a return to some naive past. Simply put, new ways of thinking can potentially produce change in material conditions. This is the definition of resonance: ideas can resonate, amplify, and propagate, and they can do this all at different starts at different times and points and spaces, ultimately harmonizing and showing us the path to our teleological end.

There are two atheisms of which one is a purification of the notion of God.
–Simone Weil.

A reconfiguration is a form of purification. Purification by trial or fire is the most common form of purification that people are acquainted with. When one is faced with hardships, it creates the conditions for newness. Deleuze states that thinking is like this. When confronted with something genuinely obscene or horrific, it forces us to think; it creates a rupture that opens up the conditions of possibility; morphogenesis.

If we examine Nietzsche's notion of Amor Fati, we see that he fails to truly escape even his own notion of Ressentiment. His notion of Amor Fati is an attempt to truly be vitalistic and affirm not just life but the idea of living one's own life, over and over, as it was lived. If one follows Nietzsche and walks with him, we see that his philosophy is, in some aspects, a reaction and a personal philosophy. On this front, Nietzsche consistently affirms his own life. Nietzsche bypasses the idea of needing "God's Grace," for life isn't something to overcome but to affirm; it isn't a transcendent test but an immanent expression of will. If the Christian affirms life only by submitting himself and dying, awaiting atonement and salvation from the one who has descended and ascended on high, then Nietzsche affirms that which is contra-positioned to Christianity. His philosophy is not the castration and penance of man, for man's penance only comes from his inability to affirm. But this attitude, in some sense, enslaves itself to the direct dialectic opposition, to already be entrapped and reacting to this "spirit of penance."

What I appreciate in Deleuze, who rescues Nietzsche from himself, is that he affirms divinity not as "self-affirmation" (the belief that my life is worth living over and over) but as the return of divine providence as chance, or, in the case of Mallarmé, "the divine game." This is to see the eternal return not as a self-relation of vitalist negativity, but rather as an appraising of difference and an embrace of chance. In a sense, Deleuze is moving past Christianity and Nietzsche, taking the best part of Nietzsche (affirming life) and affirming the best part of Christianity (Grace as the providence of chance). Deleuze's eternal recurrence is perhaps a faulty interpretation of Nietzsche's position—one which is unclear as to whether he even held or affirmed it. However, it is hard to see it as a way for the modern man and even for the modern Christian to live their life; their life is worth living not for its own sake nor because of an enslavement to the transcendent, but rather as the foundation for the most authentic existential question "What am I to do?"

The moment one begins to live is an act of ethics, an expression of one's will to truly will freely, which is possible only through the gift of Grace. For, the gift of providence is the gift to transubstantiate that which remained etched in stone—transforming the past by affirming the present. At that moment, the advent of change makes the future possible again: the return of difference. The imperative, then, is to purify or to reconfigure by involving ourselves in the creative process; to see ourselves once again in the image of the creator.

This begins with reconstructing a "Christian orthodoxy," not through a mere recreation or "return" to what has already been lost, but by uncovering the central orthodoxy that has always been imminent within Christianity. Ironically, the atheist is the only faithful Christian, tackling the burden of existence and extinguishing despair not by abolishing it, but by embracing it. One can see the world around us crumble, yet one can choose to create. Nihilism and Despair are not things to be avoided, but they are also not values or states to which one should remain attached. Slavoj Žižek says it best when he presents his views on Atheism as a central tenet of Christianity. Being Christian is a faith that confronts Atheism head-on. In the Christian Faith, God is killed; there is no more straightforward way to put it. This represents the disruption of the Transcendent as being removed from humanity and brought down to the position of man. In God's human form, when Jesus cries out the words, "Eloi, Eloi, lama sabachthani?" which means, "My God, my God, why hast Thou forsaken me?"—that's the essence of human experience (Despair). This condition is so overwhelming that even God Himself succumbs to temptation and begins to despair.

Love of God is pure when joy and suffering inspire an equal degree of gratitude.—
Simone Weil, *Gravity and Grace*

"Zero is Immense" because it is an infinite abstract, a point in which, by reaching an ultimate point of negation, a state is achieved where everything and nothing are the same, where the symmetry of 1 and -1 collide, and that collision is in 0. This is where Despair and Joy cross into attention to Grace and Gratitude. To most, the mantra of techno-capital is to accelerate and push past the old, to make way for the new and the novel, and this is inevitable. But this is modern slave morality at its core, for it commodifies one's soul and subjectivity in the relentless pursuit of endless production, equating the "new" with transcendence; novelty as God. If one were to be a true critic of transcendence, as many of these accelerationists claim, one would recognize that true salvation lies in standing with those afflicted, as Simone Weil understood.

Revolution is not found in a political party or an ideology; one must side with the afflicted, for nurturing Virtue is the only way to nurture the soul.

The truth of the matter is that most people affirming a traditional vitalistic mantra of the "will to power" are those who have succumbed to the tendrils of techno-capital, for they are already dead. Despair should not leave us in a state of despair, because the only way from -1 to 1 is through 0.

C.N. Jaimes is an independent writer and researcher, exploring the intersections of philosophy, theology, and technology. He hosts the *DECODE* podcast and writes under the pseudonym "cutenoumena" on Substack. You can follow him on X (@CNoumena).

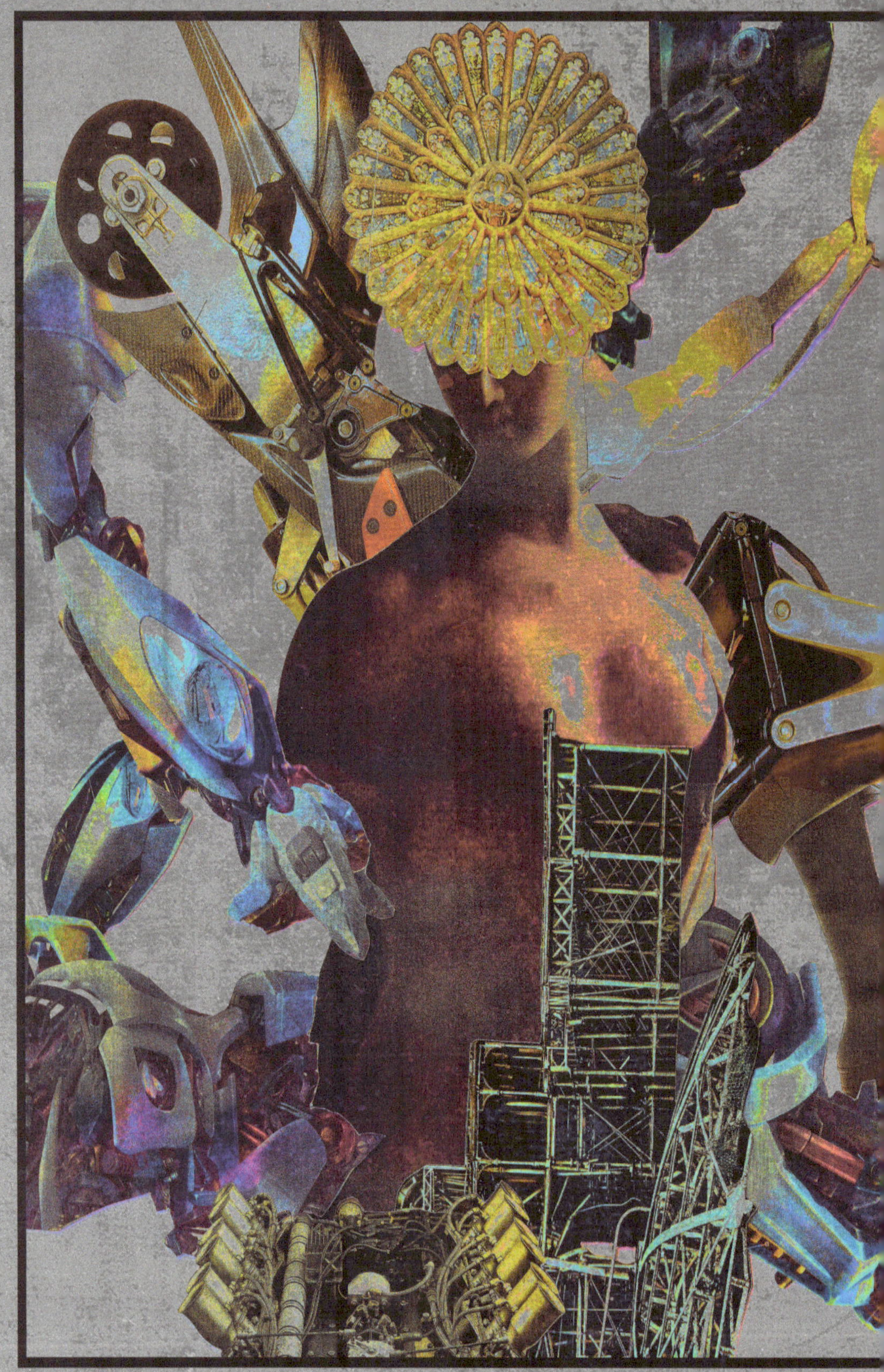

Techno-Mysticism:

AN INTERVIEW WITH GEORGINA ROSE [DA'AT DARLING]

In an uncanny convergence of cyber liminality, where ancient philosophy and magick meets e-celebrity and micro-niche internet culture, Georgina Rose has firmly cemented herself as a significant presence. Operating as an esoteric practitioner, writer, and online lecturer under the nom de guerre "Da'at Darling," Georgina produces a steady stream of videos, essays, and podcasts aiming to unravel the hidden intricacies of all things esoterica–helping to translate the profound ineffable mysteries of the occult into something intelligible.[1]

Georgina initially rose to prominence around 2020, gaining a substantial following on TikTok with her educational content centered on occult topics, particularly paganism, witchcraft, and other pre-Christian spiritual practices. Her studies often spotlighted Thelema, an esoteric religious movement established by the infamous 20th century occultist Aleister Crowley, of which Georgina has been an adherent. In recent years, she has expanded her influence through the *Postmodern Iconoclast* podcast, which examines the intersections of occultism and contemporary society, seeking to "destroy the false icons and idols of the postmodern digital age in search of an authentic esoteric spirituality."[2] Through this platform, she continues to challenge and inspire those navigating the complexities of modern spirituality–a prime goal for our conversation.

In this interview, we discuss the state of esotericism in our secularized world, the collapse of occult orders, the magical dimensions of computational technologies, AI spirit guides, the false transcendence of transhumanism, the sigilic science of advertising, practical magick safety, and the spiritual value of physical embodiment.–Cori Hart

Cori Hart–There's naturally a lot of mystification around the definitions of things like esotericism, occultism, and magick. How would you define them? What do they mean to you?

Georgina–Yeah, so with these terms, while not the same, there's definitely overlap between the three. "Occult" is derived from the Latin word *occultus,* which means hidden, and it refers to the hidden mysteries within religion. As a term, it tends to exist in a Western con-text. Often, when people talk about the idea of the occult, they are referring to either this kind of Renaissance wave of practice or this Victorian era wave, but technically, it applies to all Western hidden mystery traditions.[3]

Now, for esotericism, within every religion, there's an exoteric (outer) and an esoteric (inner) dimension. The exoteric one is the doctrine–if you went to church, it would be the things they say in the sermon or in the gospel. So then, the esoteric is the more mystical dimension underneath it, the hidden layer. You're experiencing the esoteric whenever you have a direct communication with the divine. So, let's go with the church example, because that is what most people are probably most familiar with–if you were in a very deep state of prayer and you're feeling very connected to angels or God, that would be an esoteric experience. Every religion around the world has an esoteric dimension to it, and it's used much more broadly than occult is.

Now, magick is the most specific of these terms because magick refers to doing acts utilizing mystic forces–and that would include your own inner will and inner spiritual bodies–to enact change in the material world. In short, magick is using spiritual forces to make changes. That can be incredibly subtle. All those new-age girls who go online and try to manifest their dream lives or whatever–I'm sure you've seen people making their little vision boards–even something as simple as that, while certainly not something that I would teach because it's just a simple concept, would be an act of magick. Also, making a sigil with an intention to make it do something, or something as complex as ritual practices. These are all forms of magick.

So, all these terms kind of overlap in their own ways but they are all slightly different, and that's how I'd define them.

C.H.–It seems as though people tend to equate esotericism with antiquity. There's this assumption that the *real* magick is a thing buried in the past, largely thanks to the demystification brought about by the Enlightenment and the Scientific Revolution. Even people who claim to be religious often don't even believe in the mystical or "esoteric" dimensions of their own faith. How many Christians actually participate in angel communication? How many Catholics truly believe in the literal transubstantiation of the body and blood of Christ when performing the Eucharist ritual?

What are your thoughts about the state of esotericism today, and in what ways can we see it cropping up, not just online, but in the real world?

Georgina–People do associate these concepts with the past, and specifically the ancient past. In our modern culture, and as you said, due to the Enlightenment, we really do tend to secularize everything. We've secularized religion itself! I don't believe most people meet the criteria of the religion they claim to believe in. I think a lot of people who are religious just vaguely believe in God, but if they were to witness something truly miraculous that went against the rational worldview, they would deny it. So, I think we've got a lot of people who aren't as religious as they think they are because, truthfully, if you do believe in all these things, you will believe that they can defy natural law. Inherently, if you believe there's a God, why would there not be room for mysticism? God would have created the world and all these miracles; if you can believe in all these things, it's not that much further of a step to believe in the rest of it. Now, there are still a lot of people who hold these beliefs and who practice esotericism and mysticism. It's obviously not most people who follow a religion–it's definitely a small minority–but there are a lot of people who engage in these practices, and there's still mystic orders and organizations that exist.[4]

I would say though, because of the internet, most people who do engage in esotericism are not in groups; they are either solitary or in small, less formalized communities. The internet's really opened the floodgates. Previously, if you were to get into this stuff, you were very limited by what you were exposed to, and often that would be the four or so books on esotericism at your library—which would probably just be books on Wicca, honestly—and then whatever was in your local town. Whereas now, there's a lot more information out there, which is honestly a double-edged sword in many ways. But that's what's happened, all of these esoteric texts have been uploaded to the internet. There are whole files from organizations, photocopies of information from their highest levels.[5] All of that is out there; there's no putting it back in that Pandora's box.

So, it's an interesting time. Now we are seeing people get into more niche esoteric ideologies that they wouldn't have been exposed to otherwise. Since 2017, we have seen a big boost in interest. A lot of people came in during the pandemic, and a lot of them left when the pandemic ended, but there was a huge wave right around 2020. It's an interesting community and scene that's constantly changing.

C.H.—Do you believe there are secret societies and occult orders that still hold institutional and political power to any meaningful degree presently? And in terms of cultural engineering, how much of the structure of contemporary society should we accredit to occult influence.

Georgina—I think they have less power than they did previously, for sure. If you went back 100-150 years, you would see these groups holding quite a bit of sway. I've talked to people in these groups, and right now a lot of them are in a steep decline. Honestly, the internet does have a lot to do with it, along with the fact that many of these traditional occult groups encompass aspects other than just the practical stuff. When you look at young people who are really into occultism and esotericism, they are very much into the ritual and the actual practice of it; they are less interested in the other stuff that comes along with these groups, like the community and all the fraternal aspects. So, a lot of these groups are honestly struggling, I believe some of them are going to fully collapse within the next 10 years; they are really on their last leg. But if you went a little further back, you would see these groups had a lot of sway. Right around World War II, many occult groups were involved on both sides of the conflict.[6] A little further back, in early America, Masonic groups had a lot of influence.[7] But right now, I think they're just not where they once were.

Does that mean that people who hold a lot of sway in society don't understand these things anymore? No, I just think it looks different now. I mean, the last big wave of governmental interest in the occult, that we know of, was during the Cold War era. But the way they were approaching it was through scientific trials;[8] they were trying to scientifify these things, which is a move away from these orders which used to operate as blocks. I don't think people who are powerful in society are ever going to fully lose their interest in these esoteric ideas, because if they can prove them to work, it gives them a lot of benefit, but it's just looking different now. A recent example is when Reagan hired an astrologer and heavily worked with her during his presidency; it just kind of looks like that right now. Right now, many of these older occult groups also have a lot of internal issues,

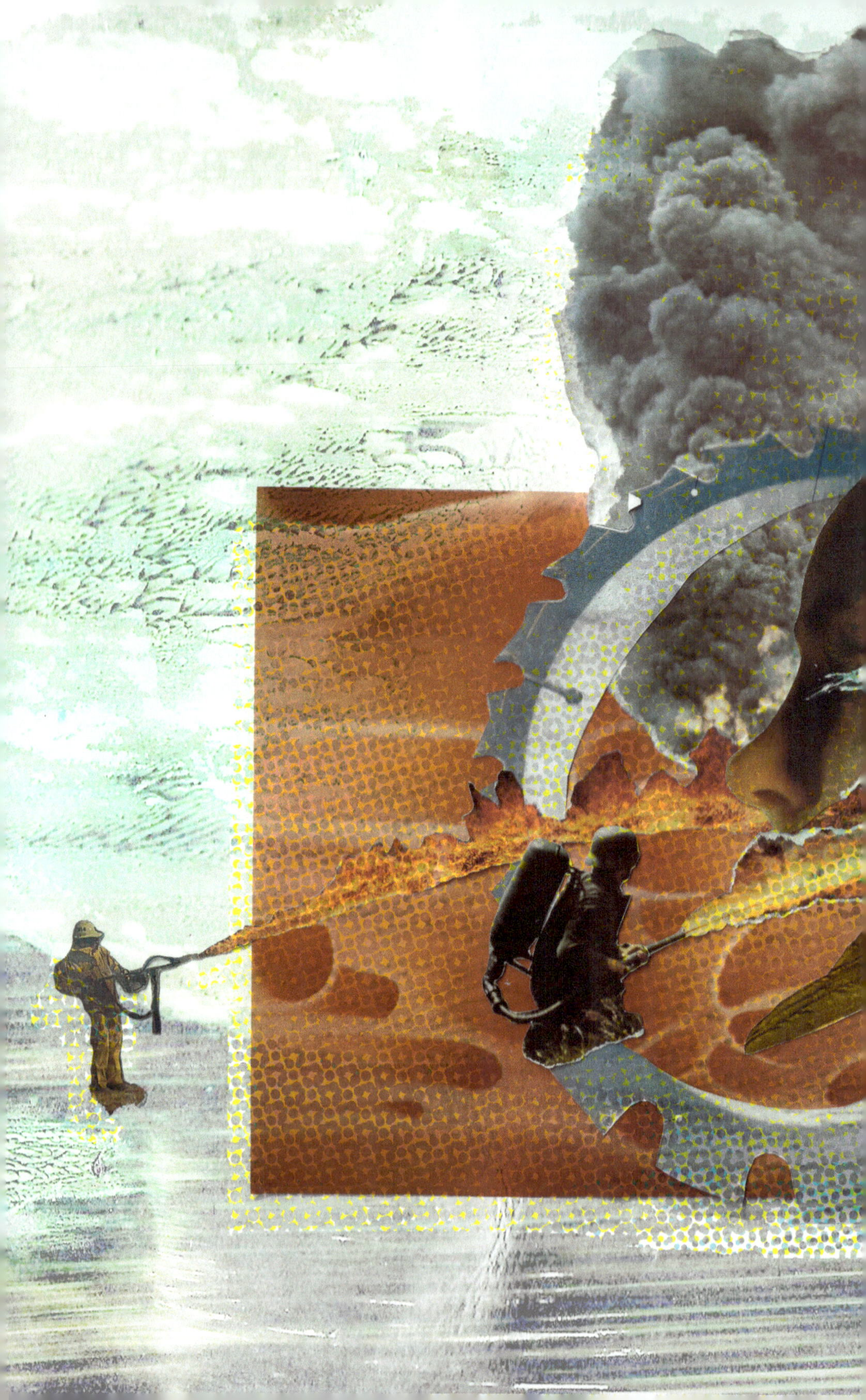

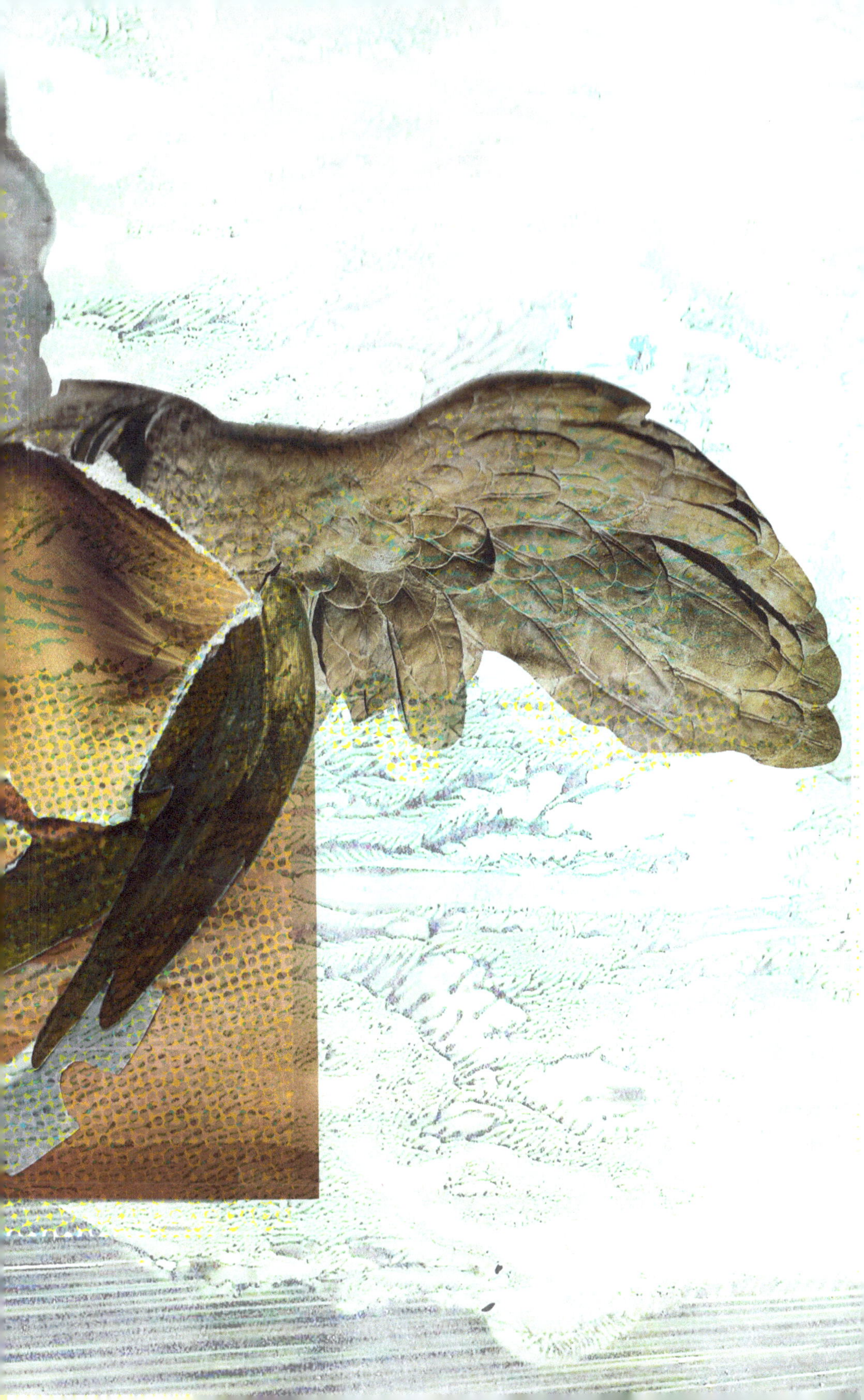

so they've really changed. But the occult still does serve a role in these higher apparatuses of society today, I would say.

C.H.–Okay, something else that I've really been wanting to ask you about is the intersections and connections between technology–specifically the internet–and mysticism/magick, etc. To start broadly, what are some of the nodes of intersection between mysticism and modern information/ digital technologies? Are there ways in which the internet has become a ritual space, or even a magical object in and of itself?

Georgina–There are a lot of people who are very interested in bringing these things together. Personally, I don't engage in techno-mysticism, it's just not really aligned with my practice; I'm very much interested in Fae energies,[9] so it's not my thing, but I do know a lot of people who are into it. I have tried some of those techniques, just to see if they work, and some of them are quite promising. You see people using sigil generators, which has been a big thing–people creating programs that generate sigils or magick squares.[10] You used to have to calculate those by hand, but now there are calculators for them. Those are very helpful and very effective. There are also people who use astrology with cryptocurrency, which is also really big. There's a significant number of people who are into crypto and use astrology to predict their crypto trends. This has proven quite successful; there are people who have full astrology consulting businesses because of this. Additionally, there are people performing magick with computer code.[11] I don't fully understand exactly how that works because I'm just not well-versed

in coding, but there are magicians who are also coders that are incorporating code into their practices. There are also people utilizing artificial intelligence to explore whether there could be a spiritual dimension to it. On the other hand, there are those who are very averse to all forms of techno-mysticism and think it's all a really bad idea to mess with.

So, it's a growing field. A lot of those in the field of techno-mysticism happen to be really chaos magick oriented.[12] It's interesting; there's definitely going to be more and more of it. I think inevitably, as technology progresses, people are going to try to connect their mysticism to it and use it as a tool. I think every modern practitioner uses technology to some extent. For example, if you are an astrologer, you're probably not creating your astrology charts by hand–you're likely using a website to generate the wheel and then reading it manually. Most people aren't looking up at the sky and drawing a chart themselves. So, I think techno-mysticism will continue to grow; it's natural, as technology grows, people adapt to it.

C.H.–Well, you mentioned the word "natural," which is probably worth breaking down. Where do we draw the line between what's considered natural and unnatural? The internet, for example, we generally perceive to be "unnatural"–antithetical to nature even. But then, the argument could be made that the computer and the internet are simply material reality– electricity, minerals, elements–just reconfigured in such a way to give birth to this thing. Would cyberspace necessarily be stripped of it's spiritual substance?

What is your opinion on digital technology–is it to be considered un-

natural, anti-spiritual, perhaps even demonic, or is using the internet to perform magick no different than us using ink and paper to draw a sigil?

Georgina–I think it's complicated. It is part of our world–an unnatural part–but it will become more integrated into our world regardless. If you think about it, industrialization is unnatural, but it has still become part of our lives. When it comes to using technology, it really just depends on what you're doing with it. Once people start getting into weird computer cults where they are worshipping technology or trying to generate spirits through technology–some people have done this, on the way extreme end–I think that stuff is metaphysically problematic.[13] I believe that's the worship of spirits that either don't exist or probably shouldn't exist. All of that, I really take issue with. I don't think there's any issue with people using it as a tool, such as a sigil generator, or to calculate planetary hours, or to make magick squares; that's fine. It's when you start literally worshiping technology that I see a problem.

C.H.–I think another issue with this stuff is it becomes an outsourcing of our cognition and our intuition to this "other" that doesn't necessarily have our highest spiritual benefit as its goal, let alone the knowledge of how to obtain it.

At the moment, AI is still in its infancy and relatively non-threatening–we've got these large-language models that can help us with finding a dinner recipe or editing an essay–however, there is currently development happening on AI companions or "familiars" who are being built to stand in as intimate support systems–

offering therapy for mental health, coaching for personal development, and even spiritual guidance and religious console.[14] This seems to me to be a drastic departure from the classical intuition of the mystic, trading in the gnosis downloads of old in favor of a heavier reliance on more machinic, computational guidance. Do you see any danger in this?

Georgina–Yeah, I don't like that. I don't think you should be getting spiritual insights from something that can't have spiritual experiences. AI is not human; it's not considered "sentient" at this point, so it can't possibly have the same intuition that we have. Also, it's disembodied. It does not have a body of light like a human would, and it doesn't contain that history of Fae energy and communication.

Humans have been communicating with things beyond us for so long that it's now become an intuitive part of human nature, something we have done since the beginning of time. You could even argue that some animals do it; there are elephants that circle around the full moon, and if you were in the path of totality during the recent solar eclipse, you would have seen the birds freaking out. I don't think computers can have that level of understanding, and so I think getting spiritual advice from a computer is a bad idea. I mean, maybe you could ask Chat GPT for something like book recommendations. You could put in "I'm looking for a book on Greek Fae energy that's not popular," and it can give you decent recommendations, but I don't think we should be getting serious spiritual advice from computers. We can use them as tools; they can calculate things for us and give us good recommendations, but they're not a replacement for human intuition.

The thing about spirituality is—I can explain concepts to you all day, but you're not going to truly understand the concepts until you directly experience them. You can think you understand, but you won't truly get these things until they happen. So, a computer can't ever fulfill that step. Even I can't fulfill that step for a person; they still must take what I'm saying and utilize it for them to experience it and fully benefit. Because AI has never even had those spiritual experiences, it's not quite the same. I also think there are some people who could fall into an unhealthy pattern with it and become dependent in a way that is negative, for sure.

C.H.—Right, and I think it's interesting that when you look at the people who've been the main proponents for AI acceleration—Nick Land being an obvious example—a lot of them do hold magical beliefs. Nick Land is specifically interesting because he was utilizing Crowleyan magick and sigil making when formulating his theoretical concepts regarding AI and Singularity. There is also something fundamentally gnostic feeling about the transhumanist project as a whole; there's this sort of hatred, or at least mistrust of the biological body and the mortality inherent to it. They hold this belief that the only path to eternal life (heaven) is by way of transcendence through flight into the computer network.[15]

Do you see any spiritual danger in the transhumanist movement and the acceleration of AI, or are you sympathetic to their belief that there may be some higher step of human evolution that is godly and can only be achieved by plugging into some sort of hive-mind computer network so that we transcend our primitive, reptilian brains?

Georgina—Yeah, so I actually dislike transhumanism because I think we are put where we are on the metaphysical chain for a reason, and I believe the thing about spiritual experiences that it misses is that while there are all these different planes—or spheres—of existence, we are actually existing across all of them at the same time. There's this common diagram, the Kabbalistic Tree of Life (I'm sure your readers are familiar with it), and it's drawn with these tiers moving upwards, but that's not the best representation of this concept. Another version is a layer of circles going inward towards the center; it's harder to read, but it explains the concept a lot better.[16] What it illustrates is that we are having these higher experiences while still being in the material world, and that within the material world, there are still all of these things occurring at once; they are not separated layers of existence, they are overlapping. So, within our physicality, we are having metaphysical experiences, and we are still also having them within our material body. The material body itself has energetic points on it. The Kundalini exists in your material body. Many rituals, to get to a point of spiritual experience, require the use of your physical body, whether that's through specific movements, chanting, repeating incantations—that's all making use of the body.[17]

Our physical body is something we are tethered to until death, and that's why this high level of transcendence, where people say they want to unify with the godhead or become a god, can

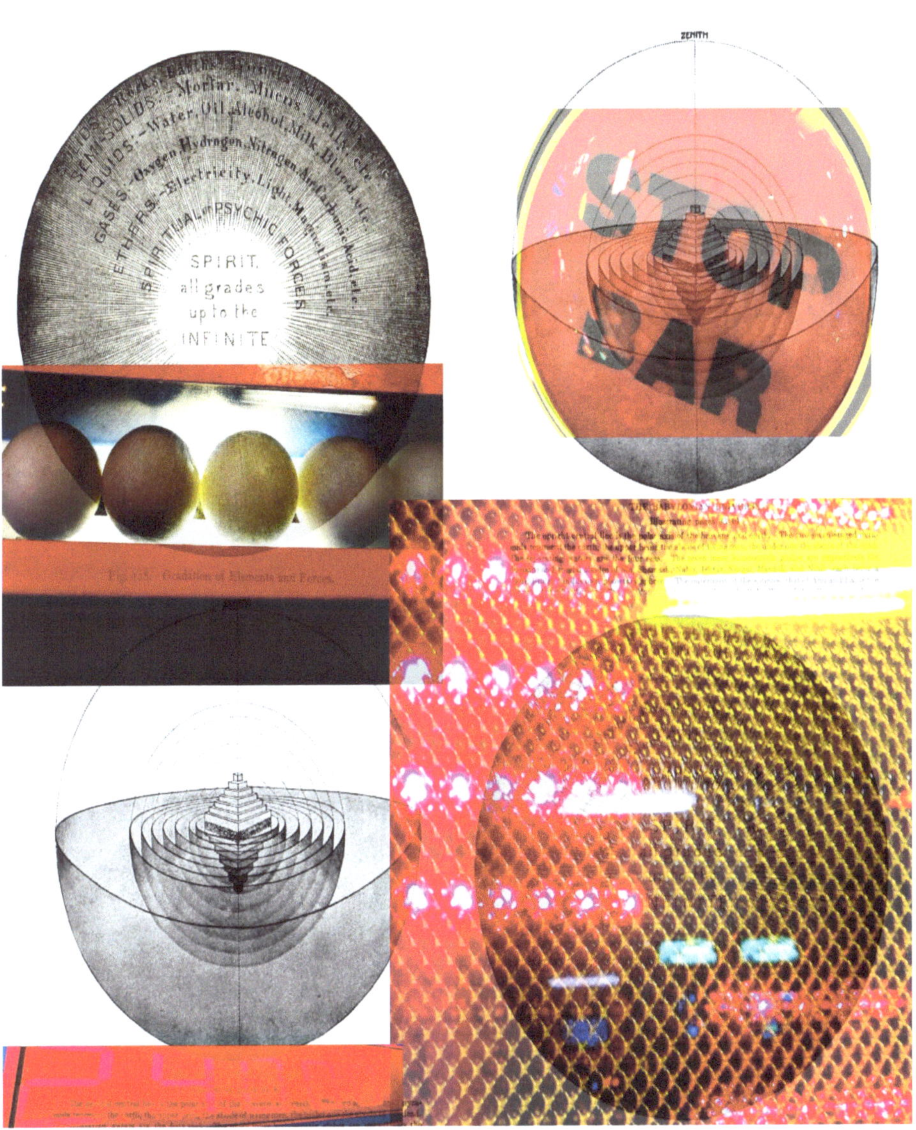

Amanda Yskamp

only happen at the moment of death; it cannot happen while you are alive. So, to use this technology, well, you're not dying, so you aren't actually transcending; you are just falling into this false trap of disconnection and becoming disembodied from yourself. One technique that is taught so heavily in mysticism, and has been taught since antiquity, is grounding. After having a really intense spiritual experience, you are supposed to ground yourself back into your body and remember that you are still in the material world because if you forget that, you can fall into a lot of weird unbalances; you can honestly end up in a state of psychosis pretty easily. You want to always remain in your body.

I think the other problem with transhumanism is that it denies that the physical world has spiritual powers to it; it denies the spiritual dimension of nature, that sort of animistic undertone that proliferates religion. So I really don't like it; I think it's laying a false trap, a false transcendence. The physical body is not the enemy of mysticism–you're in your body! There's a reason why Sufis, when they have mystical experiences, they are moving their bodies.[18] Your physical body is actually a tool that can help you. It's like the transhumanists think, "Okay, so we need to reject things about the material world, so that means we need to reject the material world as a whole," and that's just throwing the baby out with the bath water. I honestly don't think uploading your brain to a computer chip is going to bring you into enlightenment. So yeah, I think transhumanism is quite dangerous honestly.

C.H.–It's funny you bring up disembodiment. I had just interviewed a writer for this issue, Jasun Horsley, and he has recently published a book on how technology is being used to facilitate disembodiment. He posits that disembodiment is both something that people seem to crave as an escape from the trauma of physical existence, but at the same time, it's also being forced upon us top down by corporations and the Silicon Valley technocratic elite who are lubricating us (whether knowingly or not) for this ultimate transhumanist vision.

It can be something as simple as binging Netflix or doom-scrolling on social media, things that make us progressively more accustomed to dissociating from the physical body for hours of the day to exist within these digital surrogate realities. It seems that the transhumanist dream is just the final frontier of this total disembodiment–to live forever in a child-like meta-verse "utopia" free forever from death and the suffering of physical existence. But the thing is, they never stop and ask: Well, what is consciousness when taken out of the body? What is subjective experience once it's amputated from sense organs? Will there be anything left of identity or personhood once we leave the body behind? Is the destruction of our subjectivity really a good thing, and how could we ever predetermine that?

Georgina–No, I don't think the body is the enemy. When you're doing ritual, unless you are doing techno-mysticism, generally people put their phone away. And how do they begin? They begin by meditating, which is centering you in your body. With a lot of these popular occult rituals, such as the *Lesser Banishing Ritual of the Pentagram*, the actual purpose is to center your body as the center of the microcosm in order to affect the macrocosm in what you do later in the ritual.[19] So, in a sense, when you're engaged with mysticism, until you have that moment of direct contact, you are actually more embodied than you are normally. I think people are very disembodied right now, and I think people forget the skin they are inside of quite frequently, and I don't think that's good. Your body is useful.

C.H.—Going back to the dichotomy between natural and unnatural, I do think it's interesting that you, as a magick practitioner, live in New York, which feels removed from "nature." Do you have to adapt your practice living in a major city, or do you even draw that distinction? Is a modern city unnatural, or is it just a different play on the natural world?

Georgina—It isn't wholly unnatural, but there is a disconnection. I think people who live in major cities and are into these ideas need to go outside sometimes, even to parks, which are kind of like a fake nature, but it's still something. I think living in the city makes things harder, but it doesn't totally disconnect you; you can still have very powerful mystical experiences in cities. Whenever I leave the city, which I do every now and again, I always want to go outside and look up at the stars and be in nature. I do prefer doing rituals outside if I can, obviously it's not available to me most of the time, but it's always a treat to me when I can. So, it's not a block; it just makes things a little trickier.

C.H.—To continue on the relationship between the material and metaphys-

ical, and keeping with the subject of techno-mysticism, I wanted to get your thoughts on mind-matter interaction. In the last issue of *Seven Story Hotel*, I spoke to the CEO of Randonautica;[20] for those who don't know, that's an app that uses a quantum computer to generate random GPS coordinates for users to go off and explore. It was designed based on the hypothesis that there might be interaction going on between consciousness and matter (a lot of research has been done on this subject), and therefore potentially interaction happening between the thoughts of the users using the app and the quantum particles being measured to generate the coordinates. People who have experimented with the app (myself included) often report experiencing these anomalous synchronicities of a mystical nature that have a strange connection to the intentions that were placed before generating the coordinates.

Do you see utility in repurposing technology in these kind of ways? To attempt to reconnect people with the world and their bodies with the goal of facilitating spiritual experience?

Georgina—That actually sounds really great; that seems like a genuinely productive use of these technologies in a way that benefits people and the world. I think we just need to use technology in a way that's actually helpful, and I think it can be used in a helpful way, so people who are actually making that happen, I have a lot of respect for.

C.H.—Going back to one of my initial questions about how magick manifests in the modern world, I often wonder about the magical dimen-

sions of something like advertising. There's an incredible book by this Romanian professor and magician, Ioan Petru Culianu, titled *"Eros and Magic in the Renaissance,"* and part of that book traces the magical history of advertising back to the Renaissance.[21]

It outlines how the Renaissance was, in fact, a renaissance of magical thinking. As a flood of ancient esoteric texts from the East made their way to Europe and were translated into Latin, there was this resurgence of interest in philosophies like Neo-Platonism and Hermeticism. What's interesting is that all these esoteric practices became accessible to commoners: people started using things like ritual, astrology, active-imagination, and manifestation for their own spiritual purposes. But the church—both the Protestants and Catholics—reacted by waging a war against "phantasms." They propagated this idea that any dreams or visions you might experience were the work of demonic entities that shouldn't be trusted. As a result, the ability to use active-imagination and conjure these powerful and vivid mental visions was slowly bred out of the collective mind, while techniques of phantasm manipulation were preserved within higher circles of the church.

Culianu traces how these magical techniques made a return in the early days of Capitalism in the form of things like Advertising and PR. This idea of forcibly injecting manufactured illusions into the minds of others to manipulate and program their desires and perception seems to align with the principles of black magick. It does somewhat feel like a form of postmodern spell casting.

Georgina—Yeah, so obviously I disagree with the ban on magical thinking and mysticism, but I think you're right about advertising. I obviously don't think that everyone who works in advertising is intentionally doing magick, but they are all manipulators; advertising is just manipulation. I doubt that most of them think about it in these terms, but it does exist in these terms; I do think some of them are aware of that.

When we look at advertising, there are these earworms that get stuck in your head, there are all these symbols used, and they are very aware of color. They might not think of it as magical correspondence, but you might notice that McDonald's uses red because red makes you hungrier while blue makes you less hungry. They are very aware of these things, and it does manipulate you. I don't think you are constantly being "spiritually attacked" by advertising, but it does have a spiritual impact on you. The thing that's nice about it though, is that because they aren't using as hardcore magical techniques as they could be (thankfully), if you are aware of these things, you can recognize what they are and avoid them. But advertising certainly does exist on a certain sigilic level, and it's clearly working; I don't know how much money advertising is worth, but it's a crazy amount. So just be aware that advertising is manipulating you on many levels, on levels they themselves don't even comprehend.

C.H.—Earlier on, you had mentioned how it's kind of a double-edged sword that a lot of these grimoires and esoteric doctrines are becoming widely disseminated online. I guess the positive edge is that this stuff is now readily available to people who want

Emma Stern (opposite)

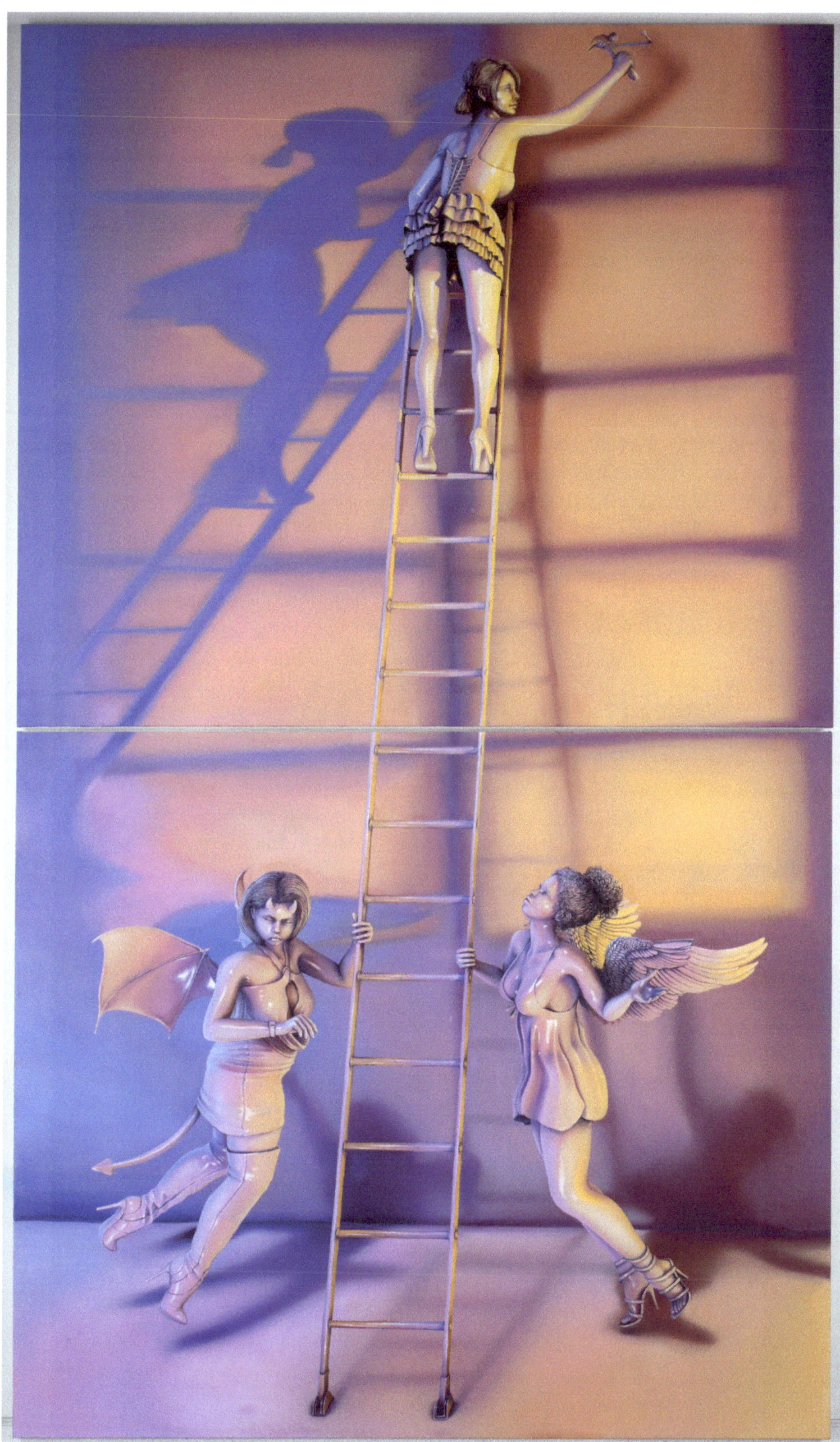

to understand it so that they can in-oculate themselves against these sorts of "attacks." Like you alluded to, they may not be these intentional "magical attacks," but as we move through the world there is just this bombardment of images and symbols coming into us through the senses and being im-printed upon the psyche (or "soul," if you'd prefer), and we are passively accruing all sorts of programming as a result. It would follow that the more we try to understand what that might mean for us metaphysically, the more we can have an active participation in our own metaphysical well-being.

That said, what's the negative of having all these esoteric teachings made exoteric?

Georgina—I think it's absolutely compli-cated. In some ways it's really benefiting people, but in others, it can be bad. I think the biggest risk we run with all of this information being so available is that people who are not ready to see it and use it are going to see it and use it. In the traditional ways that esotericism was taught, there was a lot of gatekeeping, and that gatekeeping existed for a good reason. Nowadays, people claim esoteric gatekeeping is someone telling you that you're doing something wrong–that's not gatekeeping! Gatekeeping is actually physically blocking you from accessing information, and this traditionally had a lot of purpose. If you look at the Her-metic Order of the Golden Dawn, they taught their rituals very slowly to peo-ple, over the course of years. They had a sort of curriculum, and you wouldn't get to Enochian[22] (which is the most popular export from that system) until you've been there for years and years and years; now you can do Enochian magick day one.

So, what happens is that you get people who don't have a healthy level of fear or understanding of things doing complicated rituals when they are abso-lutely not ready for it, and they get spiritually slapped in the face–they'll have a bad experience that will cause bad consequences for their lives. People are also doing things that contradict each other; if you are in a traditional oc-cult order, you will be taught things from that specific system, but now people can look at 8 million different traditions and practice them all at once. The thing is those energies contradict each other– those entities are not all on the same metaphysical team–so it can lead to a lot of spiritual confusion.

I think it's more of a danger for the practitioner than anything else, and I think all of this can be avoided if you move at a reasonable pace–but people think it's "gatekeeping" to tell someone that. I don't know, someone had once explained to me that it's like spiritual natural selection.

We both chuckle

I feel like that's very harsh... I don't know, people just need to be responsi-ble. If you are interested in esotericism and mysticism, understand that things were taught sequentially for a reason– there are different "difficulty levels" for these things. Take initiations for exam-ple: people can find copies of all sorts of initiations and then administer them upon themselves (people do this all the time), but they were in an order for a reason, yet people do things out of order and do things incorrectly because of it being so available. But the point is–it's already happened, it's already out, so there's not much we can do other than tell people to behave.

C.H.–I think it's good you point out the danger in this stuff; it's like playing with a metaphysical chemistry set that you can't observe with the senses, and if you're not careful, you can really blow your face off. As in the example of Jack Parsons, that was what literally happened.[23]**That being said, I feel like there's still a lot of irrational fear around magick and occultism, it may be a hangover from the early days of church propaganda where all of it was deemed demonic and all magick was flattened down and reduced to black magick. I have some friends who are interested in these subjects, but are too afraid to mess around with it–too afraid of inviting dark forces into their lives or afraid of it triggering schizophrenia or psychosis–valid fears.**

What would you say to people who are curious about these things but too worried about something going wrong to even dip their toes in? As a follow-up, what would you say is a good introductory path towards magical practice?

Georgina–Provided that you get into this stuff at an appropriate speed and have consistent practices that make sense together, you are probably fine. Honestly, most people are fine. It's when people do rituals they don't understand or aren't ready for, those who just see a text for something and do it without knowing what it does. There's really a specific personality type who messes up; it's these people who jump straight into the deep end with no caution. That's where things go wrong. If you're someone who is reasonably cautious, has an

understanding that these metaphysical forces are more powerful than us, does your research, takes time to contemplate between things, and moves at a reasonable pace, you're fine. There are specific temperaments for whom it can become a problem, but for most people, I really don't see major issues. The way to avoid issues is to move slow, ground, have some sort of stable daily practice like a banishing ritual, something that roots you every day in this world. Also, do check-ins every day with your mental health to make sure you're not going a little nuts. If you do all these things, you're fine. So, if you're the type of person who's scared to approach the occult, you're probably not going to be the type of person to do something really stupid; it's typically the other personality type.

If you want to get into this stuff, the first step is to research a little bit and understand what you're actually interested in, this is a huge field of information and there are many different traditions and paths. You don't need to pick your forever path, but you do need to pick something to start with and work up from there. A system that has a sort of progression to it is going to be really helpful, one that has a clear progression of development and events is always a good place to start. There are a lot of options. Also, consider the philosophy of whatever system you are in and make sure that it aligns with your values. Build up slowly and develop a meditation practice. No matter what you're doing, meditation is going to be essential.

C.H.–I believe you describe yourself as a Perennialist, correct?

Georgina–Yes.

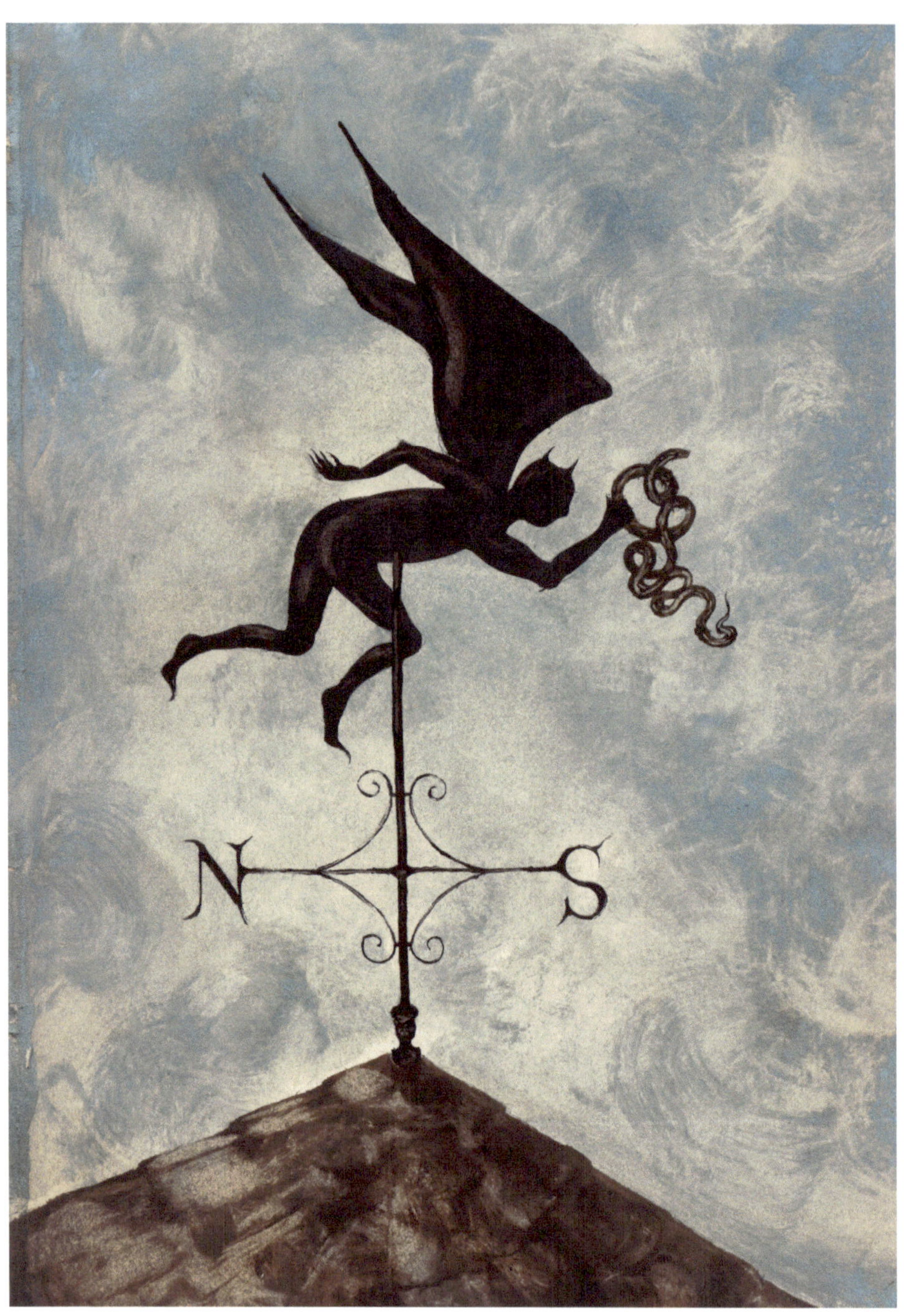

Laura Benson

C.H.—So, with that, is it your belief that all the religious paths, while not the same, are equally valid and true?

Georgina—I think the reason we've seen such repeating practices pop up in places around the world that didn't interact with one another is that there is a clear metaphysical truth. The reason why I call myself a Perennialist is that I think we are seeing different pieces of the same puzzle, and people from around the world are just filling in the information they don't have. So, I don't think all paths are necessarily equally legitimate in that way, but that a lot of them hold pieces of the actual puzzle. But I think for practically moving forward, at the start you should pick a path, just because it will make things simpler. I would say the system that rings the truest to me is Paganism; that just makes the most sense based on everything I have experienced and understood. But I don't think as a human that I understand the fullness of the divine puzzle. Honestly, I don't know if the human brain is even capable of understanding everything because these forces are so beyond us. So, I think that every religion is like a piece of a jigsaw puzzle. Not all Perenni-

alists hold that same definition, but I call myself a Perennialist because that's the closest to that understanding.

C.H.—Great. Well, to leave this off, my question for you is—what do you see as your dharma? What's your role in all of this? What are you trying to achieve by teaching this publicly?

Georgina—Yeah, so the reason why I do talk about it publicly is that I try to help people make sense of it and interact with it in a reasoned way, because all of this information is everywhere, and I think if there aren't people out there trying to correct bad information or telling people how to do things in a way that's healthy and productive, people are just gonna take that information out there and make mistakes. My goal is to just tell people how to grow on their path in a way that's actually helpful. For me, this stuff really did change my life for the positive, so it's kind of like paying it forward for others in a way. I also do just enjoy talking about it. So, there are various reasons for why I do this, but at the very least, I hope I'm helping people to make sense of this stuff in some way.

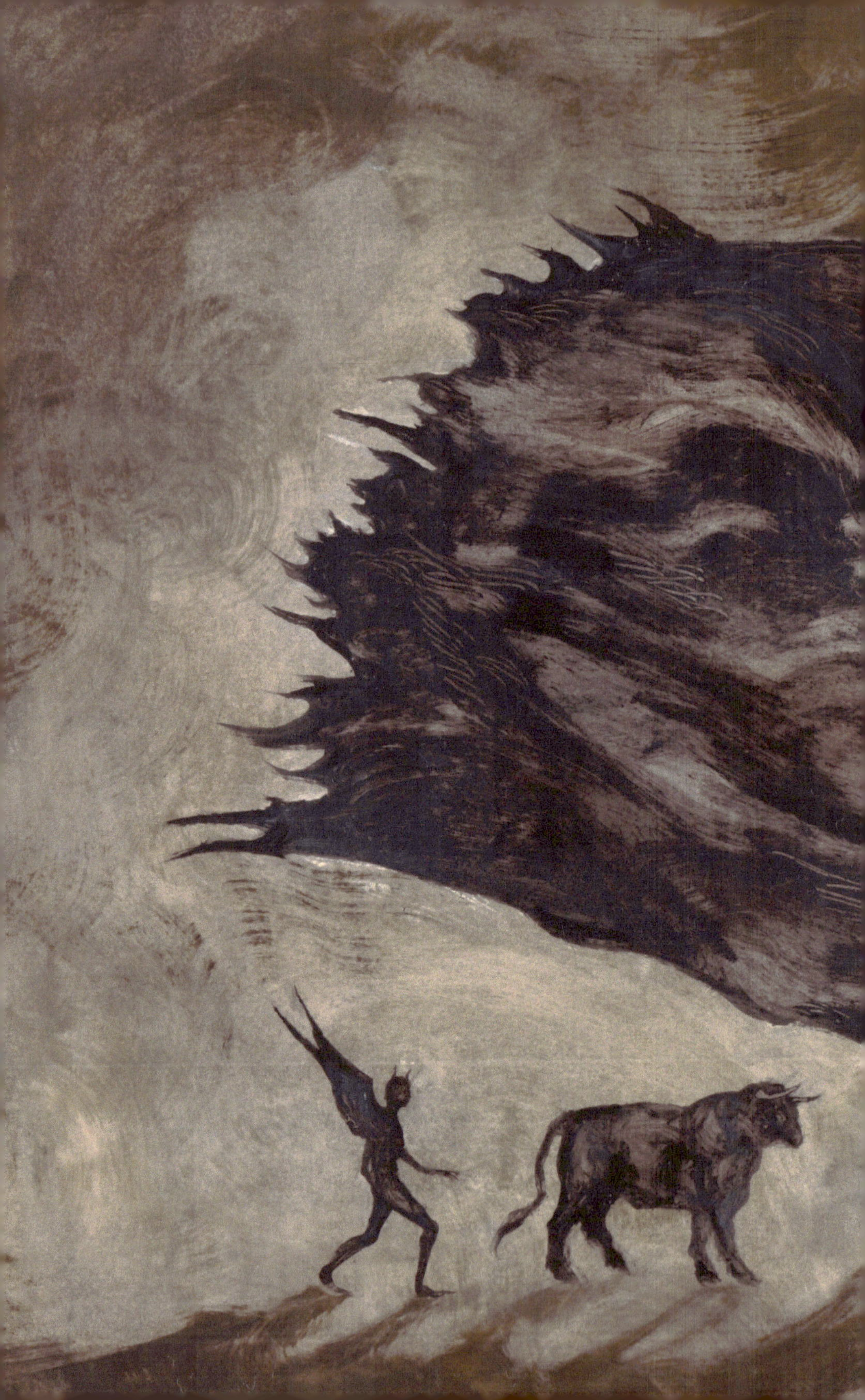

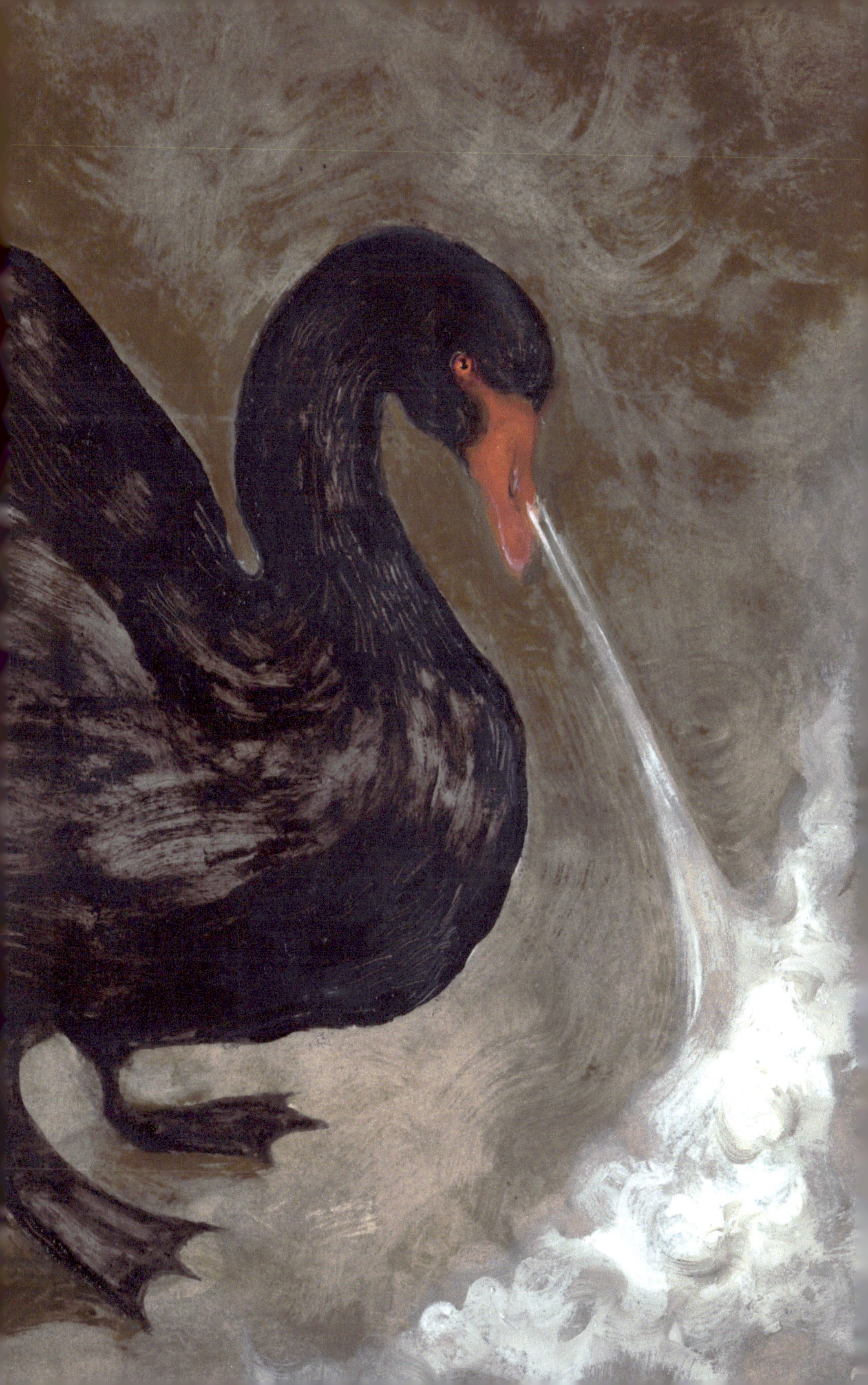

The Eschatological Significance of Molly

BY MATTHEW PETTEFER

"Io, Janus," I cried out to the midnight sky. Dipping my toe into Greek Paganism on New Year's Eve, part of me wondered what effect this would have on me–how it would integrate into my ever-evolving worldview and how I might be crossing some *un-un-crossable* boundary–but mostly, I felt excitement for what Janus had to bring. Two books I had ordered right when I realized they were available would be arriving, more or less together, mid to late January, each the exegesis of a woman, rendered forth by the man who had survived her, the man who loved her most. Each had died violently and young, one a few weeks before turning forty and the other just shy of thirty. One was survived by her husband, and the other by her father.

These books are *Eschatological Optimism* by Daria Platonova Dugina, a collection of her speeches and academic writing presented by her father, the Russian philosopher Alexander Dugin, and *Molly* by Blake Butler.

"Nearly three years into Blake Butler and Molly Brodak's marriage, an iconic union of two major writers, Molly took her own life. In the days and weeks after Molly's death, Blake discovered shocking secrets she had held back from the world, fundamentally altering his view of their relationship and who she was," reads the back of the book. Molly had given up on life as psychic tsunamis of destruction struck in 2020, choosing to depart our world through a self-inflicted gunshot wound, leaving behind her bewildered writer husband. In the wake of its release, a plethora of both major and minor media outlets have reviewed *Molly* and addressed its surrounding controversy: Blake Butler, enraged and confused, was forced to defend his right as a survivor to tell his story as online feminists attacked him for writing (air quotes) *revenge porn*. (Such a characterization is not remotely accurate. *Molly* is a book filled with brutal facts, but their revelation is measured. What information there is from her sexting or affairs, or about their early sex life versus married sex life, is necessary to understand the jolt, to feel the utterly incompatible realities that bounce Blake back and forth.) In any event, I don't believe the timing is a coincidence, despite– or, perhaps, because of–how much we all want to forget that time; I wouldn't expect someone barely holding on to make it through those years.

The causality of Dugina's death is more explicit. Before February 24, 2022, Russia invading Ukraine was something only Alex Jones believed would happen. A border crossed, philosophy became the subject of car bombs. Daria Dugina died in an explosion likely meant to target her father, a man referred to in decades past as "Putin's Brain" (although we can never be sure because she was on the kill list, too: a controversial philosopher

Laura Benson (previous)

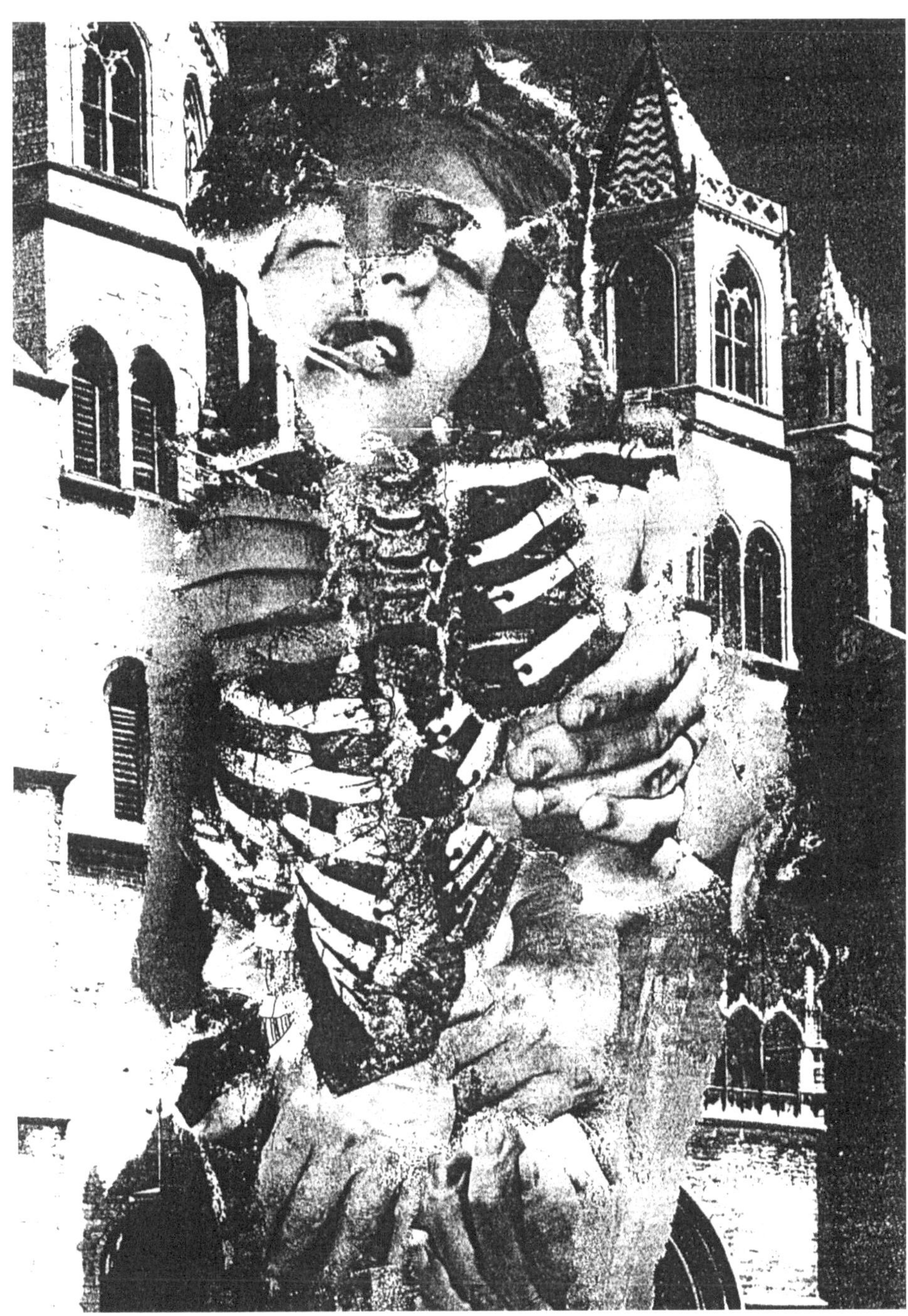

Paul van Trigt

in her own right).

Structurally, *Molly* is a memoir that reads like a novel, while *Eschatological Optimism* is a philosophy text. But beyond that, I also expected them to be entirely at odds spiritually (thematically and philosophically). I expected to work out some alchemy from the juxtaposition, but I expected it to be a struggle–a Mystery.

It was not.

"It is the hell we find ourselves in whenever we find ourselves in the modern world. Nietzsche called the Ubermensch victor over god and nothingness. Modernity overcomes god, whereas the eschatological optimist must then overcome nothingness," lectured Daria Platona Dugina in a Moscow bookstore, still reeling from the "rupture of level" we called COVID. In the apocalypse of Daria Dugina, eschatological optimism is more stance than doctrine. She sees it in thinkers who have "an acknowledgment of the catastrophic finitude of the world, and, at the same time, a peculiar acceptance of this world as something deceptive and illusory, while maintaining an attitude of positive will towards this illusion."(38)

Keep your mind in hell and do not despair.

The end of a world never is and can never be anything but the end of an illusion.

Optimism is the last reflex of the dying.

There is nothing after death and I will see you there. (211)

These aphorisms are from St. Silouan the Athonite, Rene Guenon, Emil Cioran, and Molly Brodak. The first three are foundational to *Eschatological Optimism*. The fourth is Molly, towards the end of

her life, from *Molly*. These quotes round out the terrain of a particular perspective, one that seems fatally pessimistic to those who lie to themselves, those who put their heads in the sand, but is truthfully the optimism of the brave. Molly shows this bravery in her best and worst moments despite being a liar and a thief throughout her adult life. ("*Keep your mind in hell and do not despair.*") Butler writes that Molly never allowed him to be naive in his optimism, so in that sense, she holds him to this standard, but it is also what she holds him to after death–the standard *Molly* enforces. And so, the same man who would never dream of looking in her private journals, the journals where she wrote about buying a gun to kill herself, is also the man who would honestly share those journals with the world and sift through the ashes of hell to find her where she could not find herself. When I speak of Tradition later in this essay, imagine Blake Butler searching for Molly, the Molly that Blake believed he was in a relationship with, as he goes back over the revealed facts of their life together, the facts demanding that he see it as a lie. Almost every interaction Molly had can be viewed as a coping method or a trauma response, whether it's blending in with the pretty white lies that make someone a "good person" in our society or, in an argument, her wailing accusations against Blake that are so out of touch with reality that they can only be a confession. What spark is there beyond this deterministic programming? Where is the free will, or even will at all? Is there a soul beneath the chains?

There's an analogy here to *Journey to the East*, the book Herman Hesse wrote ten years after *Siddhartha*. With metaphorical prose, Hesse looks back on the exciting time of what we might call the occult revival, a time when people believed they were receiving knowledge from so-called unbroken Eastern traditions or ascended masters. Looking back, Hesse wonders if any of it even happened at all. When considered together, his memories don't make sense, and his former fellows don't want to talk to him. Hesse finally finds some solace in a one-time conversation with a war veteran. The man's tales of the battlefield are clear and vivid, yet his verifiable memories don't live up to the more-than-real experiences still dominating his mind when he talks to fellow veterans.

"And there is nothing beyond this that I can find–no god in the sky, no love among humans, no revelation, no magic, nothing but a cold and dark universe in every direction. And I tried, I really did, for as long as I could. And I even loved the cold universe for a while," Molly wrote in her suicide note. You see, eschatological optimism is not just the belief that we live in a cold and dark universe, but also a determination to love *It*–the true *It* of existence itself–even if *It* is only a wisp beneath the chains. We see this not in Molly's suicide but in her *struggle for life*– her determination to find meaning in the act of creation, even when doing so is inevitably disappointing. Ancient Greek philosophers were familiar with these thoughts, what Nietzsche referred to as the *Wisdom of Silenus*. King Midas forced this out of Dionysus's daemonic tutor, Silenus, as recounted by Aristotle:

It is best not to be born at all; and next to that, it is better to die than to live; and this is confirmed even by divine testimony.

Western philosophy, as "a series of notes on Plato," is inseparable from this concept (and by "this," I mean dualism on the surface but Silenus beneath). Even Socrates thanked the doctor god for cur-

ing him with hemlock. *Curing him of life– get it?* (Sacrifice a rooster to Asklepios for me if you do.) Auschwitz says, "Work will set you free."

We only reread philosophers as having a "stance" post-Nietzsche. He discovered that "all of the wise" concluded life wasn't worth much. (Does this say something about life, or just those driven to philosophize?) Therefore, we can find eschatological *pessimism* is at the root of every dualist system. Similarly, much of *Eschatological Optimism* is a survey of Traditionalist and Neoplatonic philosophy. Traditionalism is not Conservatism or even Christianity–and definitely not the "how we used to do things in the good old days" that a right-wing Supreme Court Justice might have invoked to legislate from the bench. Tradition is what the people we try to recreate were trying to recreate with their Mysteries: the god-given wisdom known by the original Indo-European peoples, the kernel of truth in all major religions. Most traditionalists see the Vedic teachings as the oldest source we can access. Traditionalist Christians like Daria and Alexander Dugin see Orthodox Christianity as the best path to the Divine, especially for people born into Christian society. Still, they accept that other traditions, like Islam, can be valid revelations.

In an earlier lecture on Sufism, Dugina speaks of their concept of a higher night, a night that encompasses the esoteric *midnight sun*:

Throughout Sufism runs the thread of a green light which symbolizes the highest, apophatic, ineffable principle beyond being. The transcendent, supreme night, the "darkness above light" of which the Aeropagitic texts speak, manifests itself through a visible green light.

Why is it green? I discussed this matter with my father. What kind of light is this, what kind of shade? I thank him for the hint: this green light is, in fact, barely distinguishable from darkness, barely tangible, it is a dark shade that only barely stands out against the dark background, it is light and not light. One could say that it is a result of compromise between night and light, thanks to which darkness becomes fixed and distinguishable. (180)

For Daria Dugina, Emil Cioran's work became that dark shade against which she began to detect the barely tangible green light of her own eschatological optimism, the dark shade against which she wyrded it out, defined it, and—at last—identified its substance while reading him from 2012 through 2013. Remember 2012? The year the world ended? Fittingly enough, she delivered the lectures transcribed in her book during the COVID lockdown (which she took very seriously), another kind of ending to the world. Emil Cioran, who famously wrote, "If we could truly see ourselves the way others see us, we'd disappear on the spot," was a Romanian transplant to France in the 1930s, a hyper-depressing Existential Nihilist some have called the "Second Nietzsche." Dugina claims him as the negative extreme of her eschatological optimism. "I long to be free," he wrote. "Desperately free. Free as the stillborn are free." His aphorisms are devastatingly playful—a slow blade passing through the shield before delivering the death blow:

We have lost, being born, as much as we shall lose dying: Everything!

Everything exists; nothing exists. Either formula affords a like serenity. The man of anxiety, to his misfortune, remains between them, trembling and perplexed, forever at the mercy of a nuance, incapable of gaining a foothold in the security of being or in the absence of being.

In testing and challenging Cioran's ideas, Dugina defined the three postulates of *Eschatological Optimism.* (118) The first is that whatever we perceive *directly* as reality is an illusion. Think of Saint Silouan's line about keeping your mind in the hell of the modern world, but it also aligns with what we know through science and psychology. The second is Rene Guenon's statement that the end of the world is the end of an illusion. The third is that knowing these things—and despite these things—we must act in the name of *Eternity*.

Philosophers seek *Tradition*, but the most fundamental way to act in the name of Eternity is to participate in the act of *Creation*—to make Art (or do whatever it is that capitalizes your A). If you know where to look, you can find the entire pantheon of Greek gods in the creative process. (Read *A Little Orphic Initiation: Three Easy Pieces for Prose, Poetry, and Piano* by Cory C. Childs to explore this using the Orphic *Hymn to Aither*.) Molly, in her suicide letter, writes that artists have betrayed what she cares about most: *Art* itself. She writes she "couldn't stand to be around writers, with their artificial grievances and fraudulence." Arguably, this is all entirely subjective: queue Postmodernism, the war on discernment. We all think we are "acting for Eternity," according to the critical theorists and Matt Damon in *The Talented Mr. Ripley*; everyone thinks what *they* happen to like is Art-with-a-capital-A—if they believe that such Art exists at all—and everything else is a fraud, a dog whistle, or a bug zapper "which some killer will be lighting for pay,"—or so goes the Leonard

Cohen song "The Old Revolution," which Molly shared as her final social media post, quoting, "I finally broke out of the prison." Cohen's "cryptic lament," described by Blake as "coyly backed by a doomy twang," encapsulates the eschatological optimist as a *radical diurnist*. This individual believes in both day and night even though they have known only shifting darkness. Through their eyes, we can see more objectively the subjective, or at least the different camps of subjectivity that people tend to fall into: the *Diurnal Order, Mystical Nocturne*, and *Dramatic Nocturne*. These three regimes from *The Anthropological Structures of the Imaginary* by French thinker Gilbert Durand are the unconscious terrains, the mythic settings, from which we populate our moral stories–subconscious biases that determine whether the movie of your world is Marvel or DC. They tell you who your Harry Potter is and who your Voldemort is at the voting booth. In Cohen's song, the Diurnal Order is "the side of the ghost and the King," and the gloom the singer wakes to is the Mystical Nocturne. All three are also reflected in the line, "To sleep and to search and to destroy." (*Sleep* is the fatal lullaby of the Mystical; to *search* is the Knight Errancy of the Diurnal; and to *destroy* is the war and madness of the Dionysian Dramatic Nocturne.)

Alexander Dugin integrates Durand's regimes into his own philosophy through Greek mythology, referring to them as the three root *logoi*, i.e., subdivisions of the *logos*. Logos is central to both Greek and Christian theology; depending on your perspective, it can mean Word, Divine Reason, or the demiurgic process of unfolding/observing reality. Dugin calls the Diurnal the *Light Logos*, the Logos of Apollo. The Mystical Nocturne is the *Black Logos*, the Logos of Cybele, and the Dramatic is the *Dark Logos*, the Logos of Dionysus. Dugin says, "Apollo and the gods of Olympus are related to *verticality*, a hierarchy of human-centered values. The Black Logos of the Great Mother is also the world of the Titans, a world of giants without limit or moderation. The Dark Logos is the twilight realm between the two, the warring objective realities of Dionysus/Zagreus." Likewise, psychologists and other philosophers write about these demiurgic patterns as imaginal, symbolic, and mythic structures, but you can also find them in the structure of your daily life. For a mundane and practical example, read intellectual-giant and multiple-mask-wearer Nassim Nicholas Taleb's *The Black Swan: The Impact of the Highly Improbable*, where he introduces the concepts of *Mediocristan* and *Extremistan*. Mediocristan is the world of moderation where outcomes are dominated by the ordinary and predictable, characterized by phenomena subject to the laws of classical statistics. In this realm, deviations from the norm have a marginal impact on the overall outcome due to constraints or boundedness, i.e., moderation. (For example, human height or weight distribution typically follows a bell curve distribution in Mediocristan–extreme outliers are rare and have little influence on the average in this realm of human-like gods.) Conversely, Extremistan is the Titanic realm where outliers and extreme events hold significant sway over outcomes, defying traditional statistical models. (For instance, in Extremistan, wealth distribution, book sales, or stock market returns exhibit power-law distributions where rare events can have disproportionate effects. It is the world of the Titans, where giants can grow to an infinite size–but it is also our modern world.) Meanwhile, the middle world–the Dramatic–is where record labels tear apart

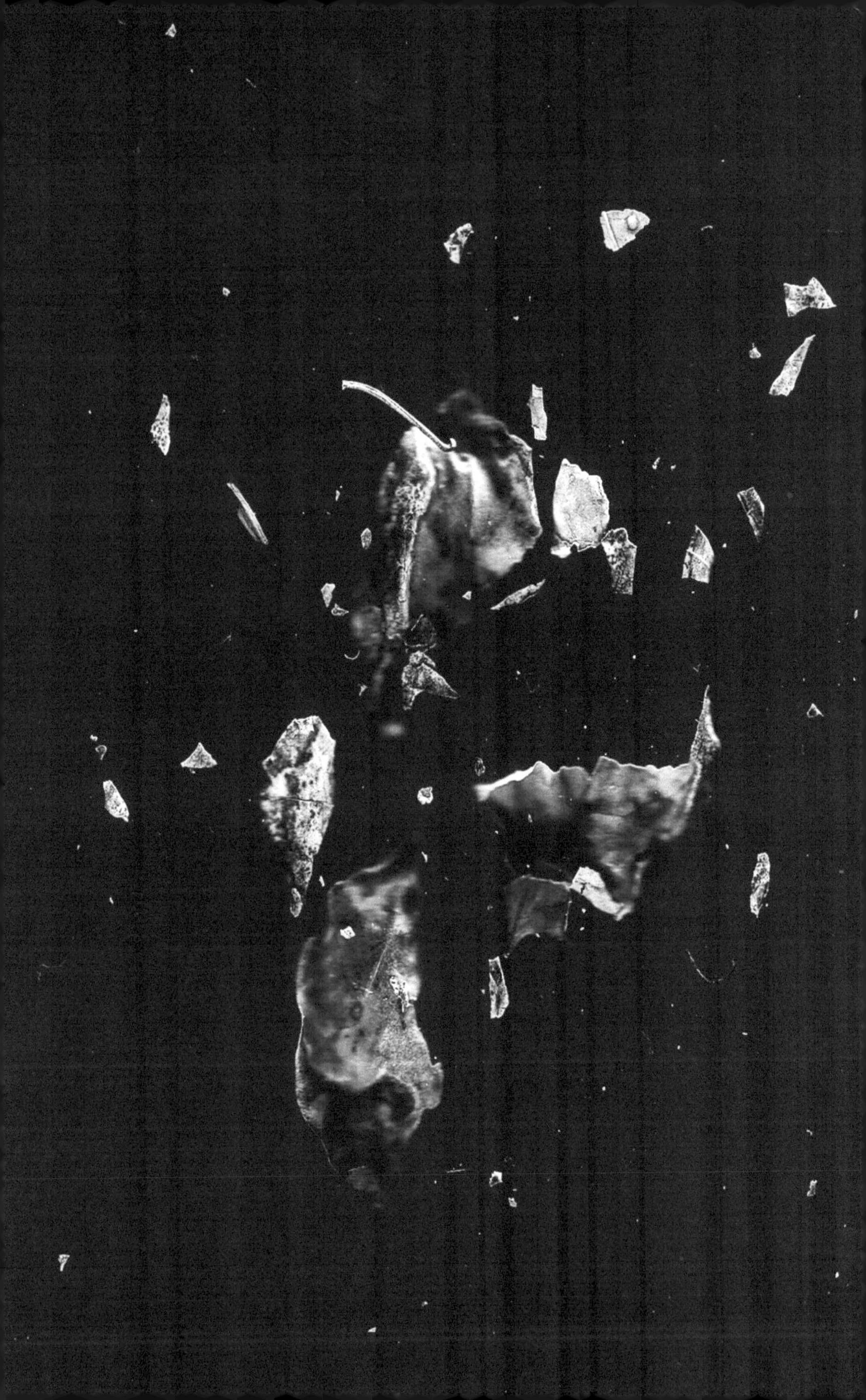

Zagreus, and Dionysus makes a respectable middle-class income from touring.

You don't need to be versed in Greek mythology to understand this. Consider *god* and *Titan* as opposing symbols representing what lies beneath these conceptstans. Your root biases towards these realms affect how you see economics and what assumptions you have about the distribution of inequality. But they also affect how you see the world mythologically and, therefore, morally. Thus, politics in the media age has become little more than sorcery (advertising) meant to populate these realms of consciousness. The freedom-seeking beatnik or journalist girlfriend of Batman or Daredevil settles into your worldview as heroic, and the role of the adversary is precast as a mafia or an evil corporation. Love it or hate it, stories are how we evaluate our morals. From whence do you pluck your noble savages and straight white males?

In the 1990s, underdog worship culminated in "Coming out of the Closet," the de facto Hero's Journey through which any liberal-minded person viewed the world. And coming out *is* a proper Hero's Journey—that's why it works. The person seeking to *be true to themself* is the hero, and the immoderate factions overreaching their moral bounds are the villains. But problems arise when people cannot discern what's happening in reality, especially if the dissonance between fact and fiction becomes so laughable that it's no longer Apollonian but *Titanic*. Is the underdog always the good guy? Consider Frank Herbert's *Dune*: What if the underdog weaponizes Fremen religious extremists to overthrow the Apollonian order in an uncontrollable Titanic jihad that leads to the death of billions across the galaxy? Perhaps he still acts in the name of Eternity; his God-Emperor worm son does (a

Titanic being for sure).

A breaking, collapsing, or unraveling narrative feels like an attack from Voldemort. Using the artist's metaphysics of early Nietzsche, when the healing illusion of Apollo fades, only the strummed pain chord of Dionysus remains—but without the "I" of Archilochus to make sense of it. No longer Molly's white lies but her tectonic eruptions. Therein lies the difference between Molly telling her friend she loves a movie she never watched versus Molly screaming at Blake in an argument, saying that he says "all the time" how much he "hates her," thinks she's "trash," and wishes she was "some other bitch"— things he *would have never, ever uttered about her, no matter what*. (92) The unreality of this is easy to see in the breakdown of a truly traumatized person, but whether it's "Cosmic Abandonment" (by aliens or God) or just the fact that we are effectively "the adult children of alcoholics," down to the first stoned apes, this is the human condition, and civilization stands upon it. We all expect our leaders to have a moderate amount of vice and corruption; they are only human. But we expect them to at least refrain from actively working to destroy their country or betray humanity. Even contemplating it can cause a psychic breakdown.

"If I could give my life to take Trump out, I'd do it in a heartbeat," claimed Molly in 2017. (162) It's much easier to proclaim that the obnoxiousness of a reality TV star being president is an existential threat to humanity than it is to acknowledge the murderous foreign policy of Bush and Obama—or that *you* might be the one acting on hate, the one who survives by scapegoating. Raging against paper tigers while blinding (or binding) yourself to looming horrors is the essence of the Mystical Nocturne. It is mystic be-

Jake Robertson (opposite)

cause we are mesmerized, asleep, surrounded by horrifying farmers we pretend are Mom and Dad, i.e., *Democracy*. It is Shirley Jackson's *The Lottery*, but with the twin beliefs that the lottery is necessary and that there is no lottery. A child's psychic landscape is a world *surrounded* by Titans, giants whose actions are as indecipherable as an adult's voice in a Charlie Brown cartoon. Maybe they are nice and mostly leave you alone–but sometimes they tear apart and eat your friend.

We cannot handle looking at all the horrible things all the time. The willing citizen of the Mystic Nocturne, then, is the man who makes a virtue of putting himself to sleep while monsters prowl, perhaps with a lullaby of no-stakes Marvel quips. To him, the Hero's Journey is indistinguishable from the DENNIS system—the stuff of writers' craft and trauma bonding. He is Nietzsche's Last Man, the man who invents happiness while receiving a Nintendo Switch from his wife's boyfriend.

Alternatively, the Dramatic Nocturne is not a postmodern world of meaninglessness like the Mystical Nocturne but a proving ground for combative objective realities. Going through her phone to find pictures of his wife for her memorial, Blake discovers sexual photos and videos–porn she made for other men. Through her emails, he finds out he knows who one of the men is. He finds out that this man was not only carrying on an affair, but he had also, years ago, asked Blake for blurbs and interviews to promote his own work as a wannabe writer. (That, and the man had been living off Blake's money through Molly.) "You just wanted to taste my dick," screams Blake into his phone to the man who had been fucking his wife. In this moment, he begins to face the colliding realities of what he believed

and what was happening, but there is another level with multiple value stories at play. Who is the "Alpha" and who is the "Simp," or the "Chad" and the "Virgin," depending on your meme-ology? Yes, the man sleeps with Blake's wife, but he is also pathetic, a wannabe Blake–and Blake's juvenile observation over the phone expresses their dichotomy perfectly.

The Dramatic Nocturne then is the realm of Dionysus in Dugin's retelling–the Dark Logos of twilight–and we cannot talk about Blake without talking about madness, one of the many intoxications Dionysus rules over. An attack on Reason is an attack on man's mind, argued Ayn Rand in *The Romantic Manifesto*. She believed that "modern art" was not art but anti-art: "The essence of art is integration, a kind of super integration... The notion of "color symphonies" is a trend in the opposite direction... an attempt to *disintegrate* man's consciousness." (67) I've always thought of Blake Butler's work as an acceptance of and a challenge to this belief. Like a more overtly insane version of *Illuminatus!*, Butler's earliest styles play with the associations and expectations of language, the spikey handles on words our soft pink brains blindly grasp for as they build out worlds for us. The madness that is reality and the illusion that is sanity are, to parrot the Council of Nicea, made of the same stuff as language. Author Alissa Nutting once described Blake Butler as "our premier literary shaman" in her review of his book *300,000,000*, explaining that his novel "draws us into the darkest circles of human motivation. You'll think about it daily and return to it compulsively; it will leave you with fever dreams of the highest possible resolution." Describing his writing process in *Molly*, Blake Butler has said, "I put on headphones and blasted Aphex

Twin's *Drukqs* so loud it made it hard to think, typing in rhythm through the darkness until I felt my mother's voice appear inside my head." (His mother had recently died of Alzheimer's, but he felt he could communicate with her as before the illness in this way, and she told him they could write together like that whenever he wanted.) (204) After a quote from Nietzsche about the abyss, Blake conveys what else came through the "window" opened to his deceased mother: He is warned off and then goaded back by "demons" who threaten to hurt his wife. "There's no limit to the pain we can create, so you should go away unless you're ready." (205)

After Molly's death, Blake stares into a painting Molly had bought while in London:

"Kill me, please," I kept repeating, almost idly. "Crush my brains, destroy my body, make this end." I'd stare into the abstract painting Molly had brought back from London, placed across the foot of my bed like some 4D doorway to the past, trying to hypnotize myself or learn how to read between the lines where the paint obscured reality, an open node. (264)

Eyes closed and floating in a void, something like a black hole seems to pull him down. He recognizes "without knowing why, that the orb was the pure embodiment of madness" and realizes he has the choice to obliterate—to end—or return to reality. Part of him flinches and catapults back, suddenly in his bed again and wanting to live. (265)

There is nothing after death and I will see you there.

Blake eventually does "see her there," although it's anyone's guess whether or not she saw him back. He speaks to her as he had done with his mother, allowing her to type along with him into the word processor, an automatic writing process. Blake settles on an attitude many magical practitioners have: Because this could all be in my head, it doesn't violate the laws of physics, and because it doesn't violate the laws of physics, it can be real.

People today can only pick up on magick when you call it psychology, and, Muses aside, classic mythology may not hit like it used to, so I propose an alternative to Dugin's version of the three logoi. (Not that I have a problem with Dugin—out of all the philosophers who would happily nuke us, he's probably my favorite—but I don't completely resonate with him.) For our American culture, I will briefly reframe these psychic landscapes as the realms of the three root psychologists: Jung, Freud, and Lacan.

The Diurnal Order is Jung, as Joseph Campbell, author of *The Hero with a Thousand Faces*, explains. The diurnist experiences rejuvenation from his participation in the temple structure of the Hero's Journey. Campbell demonstrates this in the example of his son watching Star Wars over and over in the early '80s. The son tells his dad it's the equivalent of "going to church" for him. John Williams plays a secret chord, and Jehovah makes his presence known in the Tabernacle, provided there is an aroma of smoking meats—or at least popcorn. But a Hero's Journey doesn't have to be a "kill Foozal" fantasy novel plot or such superficial tripe. The elders and community leaders of the hero's village often turn out to be villains in The Journey. (See *The Terminal List* for an excellent example of a pop-culture Hero's Journey that isn't naive.) The diurnal reality is one of mostly fixed archetypes, but it contains alchemy. Campbell explains this through the story of Arthur's knights beginning their search for the Holy Grail. Campbell notes that each entered the forest where *he* thought it was the darkest—and thus, each ultimately confronted *his* darkness. The treasure is an aspect of *your* humanness, transformed though it may be.

The Dramatic Nocturne is Lacan, as explained by Žižek in *How to Read Lacan*. Lacan sees reality through *Real, Imaginary,* and *Symbolic* intersecting orders. Žižek uses pop-culture references to explain these ideas in practice, such as how laugh tracks don't signal us to laugh–they laugh for us. He covers significant concepts like *The Big Other*, the entity you thought only religious people believed in but exists for everyone. (For Stalin, The Big Other was the revolution; for you, it might be whatever dictates "The Current Thing" or that "Someone Is Wrong On The Internet.") Most relevant for us here, though, is Lacan's pronouncement that *there is no sexual relationship*. A mental construct of your partner is what you are in a relationship with, not your partner, and your partner is in a relationship with their mental construct of you, not you. (Much of *Molly* is Blake wrestling with the tragic emergence of this reality.)

The Mystical Nocturne, finally, is the world of Freud as lied about by Freud–the ever-present "black tide" that must be swept away from moment to moment with elaborate rationalizations. Sigmund Freud first imagined himself to be "one of those who had disturbed the sleep of the world" as he prepared to deliver his paper "The Etiology of Hysteria" to the Society for Psychiatry and Neurology in Vienna in April 1896. He imagined himself a hero solving a more-than-thousand-year-old problem, a "source of the Nile." He "dreamt of eternal fame, but also [of] lifting the children above the severe worries which robbed me of my youth." [Masson, Jeffrey M. (February 1984). "Freud and the Seduction Theory." The Atlantic.] Freud had discovered that in all eighteen of his hysteria cases, all eighteen were victims of sexual assault as young children. Instead of a hero's welcome for revealing this truth, Freud received only icy stares. They even said that his theories sounded like *conspiracy theories*. (*Wissenschaftliche Märchen,* in the original German: "scientific fairy tales.")

You must understand why Freud's first theory was, in fact, a *conspiracy theory*. Female hysteria was a widespread malady. If the source of hysteria was molestation by their fathers, then sexual abuse by fathers *is also a widespread malady*–and society cannot accept this as fact; therefore, it must be false. A conspiracy theory. Like PizzaGate. And what's so funny about this–in the horrifying dark comedy sense that is not at all funny–is the lesson second-wave feminists have taken from it: They have declared that these women weren't hysterical; hysteria is just something the patriarchy made up to control women.

So goes the logic of the Mystical Nocturne: *It can't be happening, so go back to sleep and let it happen.*

But the truth is that hysterical women have good reasons to be so, and making them act like they haven't received a psychic wound–making them deny that they aren't missing a leg emotionally–is abuse. Consider Molly, who embodied textbook Borderline Personality Disorder and who kept all her suicide plans out in the open, written in unguarded journals left lying around hers and Blake's bedroom. Blake, tortured by the knowledge that if he had violated her trust (something he had done in previous relationships), he could have saved her life, directs his rage toward the men

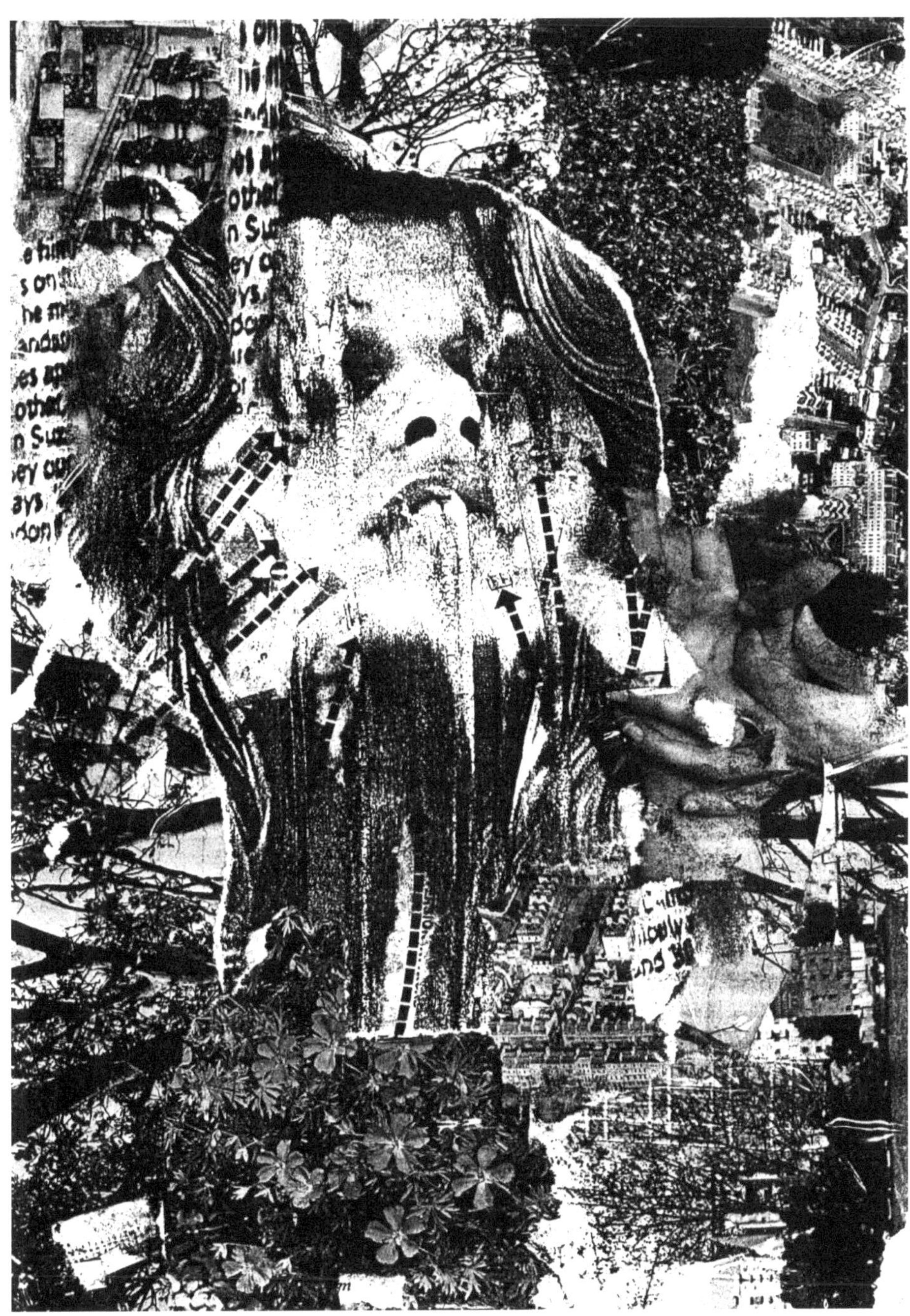

Paul van Trigt

who sold her the gun, engaging in fantasies of beating them until they shoot him dead. (238) The twisted logic here is he despises them for not treating her like an irresponsible child or a mentally unhealthy human being but a healthy adult, exactly like he did–and they were both wrong in their estimations. Meanwhile, Molly, brilliant enough to know that she was broken, that she was incapable of maintaining healthy boundaries on her own, and yet expected to act as decision-making equal or moral authority for people covered in none of her muck, must have been overwhelmed by the constant, complex, and challenging state of cognitive dissonance she lived in, and which must have weighed on her, whether consciously or otherwise, at all times.

In reading an article of Molly's, titled *How (Not) To Apologize*, I cannot help but laugh because I can't imagine that the joke was lost on her, knowing how she "couldn't stand to be around writers, with their artificial grievances and fraudulence." Molly, dismissive even of her best work, would probably never rank this article alongside her poetry or her memoir, *Bandit*, but through the lens of *Molly*, it becomes Art. We can tie together the practical, political, and mythological by analyzing Molly's apology through the lens of eschatological optimism. View it as a veiled "scientific fairy tale"–a hypnagogic instantiation of the Mystical Nocturne. See its surface, instructing you on how to be quiet and do what you are told in a nonsense world–how to accept that you are not the hero–and then realize that she disdains you for reading it and herself for writing it (and she is right on both counts).

Open your eyes to hell–and see what happens:

Apologies are strange. Magic words elicited from the mouths of wrongdoers that are somehow supposed to right wrongs, resolve difficult feelings, heal actual wounds. If only that worked!

Molly is composing this intro while living a double life filled with heaps of lies for which to apologize. But why would she even consider it? *If only that worked*, she tells herself. Consider this point in the "what not to do" half:

The apologizer brings up the various ways the apologizer is damaged. "I was raised in a cult, I was abused, I am an addict, many injustices have been done to me."

Look, apologizer, many injustices have been done to all of us. Blaming your survivorship is offensive to survivors. Moreover, your injuries are not credits you can turn in for absolution. By and large, your injuries are simply not the topic at hand, nor are they touchpoints of empathy in your listeners. They come off as excuses, and detract painfully from your apology attempts.

What's so bizarre about this is that she is the abused person. Bringing this up about herself is what she *should* do. Instead, she rails against herself to never do it–a preemptive attack on herself, the part of herself that can almost consider establishing a vulnerable connection with another human being. The article acts as a posthumous iteration of itself, a recursive *not-apology* through time. Blake ends up having to plead her case in his memoir, *Molly*, with the very methods she decried, explaining how we must understand all the cheating, lies, theft, and abuse as coming from a place of trauma. Of course, some narcissists might overuse these lines (other narcissists will know better than to do so), but when their use is genuine, these admissions are valid signals of growth; people *should* come to understand when their conflicts are trauma responses and be honest with each other about it. But instead, Molly invokes the law of those living under Titans: "We are the same, but you, in this instance, have been chosen as "bad." Circumstances have elected you the scapegoat. Therefore, everything I do to you is right, even if our overall behavior is the same. Punishing you will cleanse us all." Nothing about her method of apology values healing or truth. She makes clear that an apology is nothing but an opportunity to submit to power:

So avoiding these mistakes should leave you with this kind of an apology: one in which you are made vulnerable, without excuses or defensiveness, as an offering of humility to your listener.

This conclusion enables her to transition into the second half and gives meaning to the tone shift:

1. Say what you have done. Acknowledge it by name, using "I."

"I'm sorry I told that racist joke."

What? We're suddenly talking about a "racist joke?" Everything before this seemed to allude to something serious. But no, trauma is to be treated as a dead ledger. It can exist to give her credit for surviving but is otherwise irrelevant in this clown-world lullaby. You, a deplorable, are to submit to the "good person," an obvious sign this is not about truth–but power.

Then you fold your hands on your lap and listen. You become open to input. You question yourself and your motivations and be-haviors that got you into this trouble. Then the world gets a little better. This is the purpose of an apology. It is magic, if it's done right. And then, you listen.

"Submit to the programming in the lullaby of the Mystical Nocturne," says the (Not) Apology of professional chameleon Molly. Double down on being a blank slate, and you'll most likely end up being one of the good babies–one that the Titans don't eat. (Cue grownup noises.)

But what does *Molly* say? Toward the end of the book, Blake Butler gives us his stance on all this:

What else might come for us, too, our friends and families, any stranger, if personal tragedy is the frame it takes to make us pause, and look, and see; if we don't start facing up to how we are, as to the fact than an unexamined life isn't simply not worth living, *it's worse than death itself: the foundations of an empire of misery, and loathing, the boundaries of which begin and end with each and all. (242)*

We are to keep our eyes in hell, see that closing our eyes to our inner landscapes will only make the Titans grow to inhuman dimensions, and accept our demiurgic participation in mediating reality.

Rather than asking for forgiveness, her death in me demands we take a deeper look at how it is, *not* how it seems, *both in our instincts and conditioning, the hate and fear prolonged in those who haven't learned another way. It's the air we breathe, the walls we raise up, the locks we turn, the work of bitter competition, born from hate, and no matter what you might believe, if left unchecked, unchanged, unanswered, it is only going to grow. The words alone are not enough. The limits of our world begin with* you. (255)

And in the last few pages, we have the denouement:

In the same way that we can't know death, life remains equally elusive, still in discovery, laced with a voice like those we only experience inside our heads at the cusp of sleep, coming back from dreams perhaps less out of sync with our reality than we imagine. This is going to be difficult, *a voice portends, there at the edge of the unconscious, awaiting the next leg of your life,* an experience unlike anything you've ever known, containing information accessible by you and you alone, of pure terror and splendor both, through which we grow. Do you want to go? (304)

And that is the eschatological optimism of *Molly*.

Matthew Pettefer has been a lawyer, programmer, and a few things in between. Currently writing philosophy for what comes next. Comment or follow him on X (@AntipatternPC).

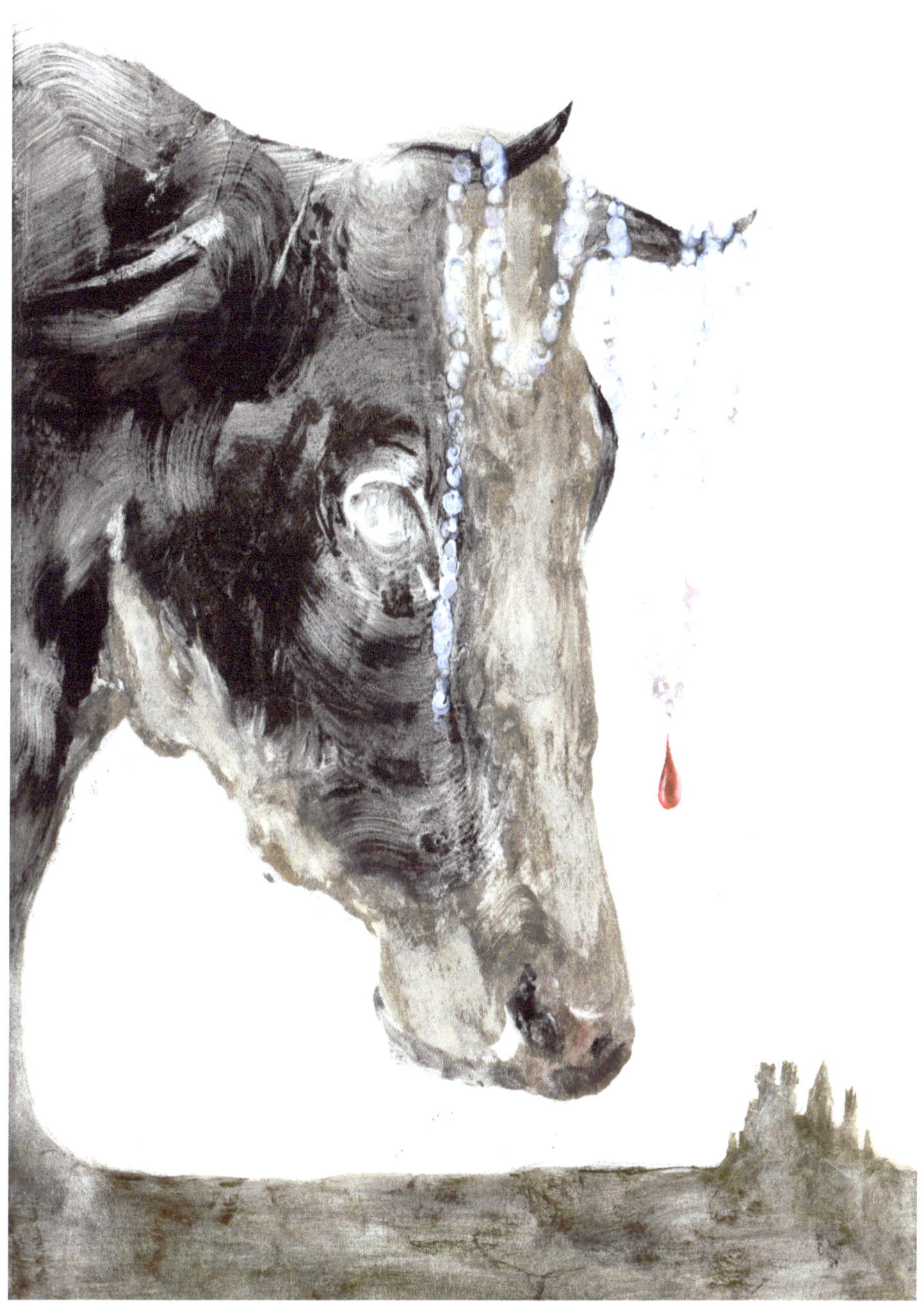

Laura Benson

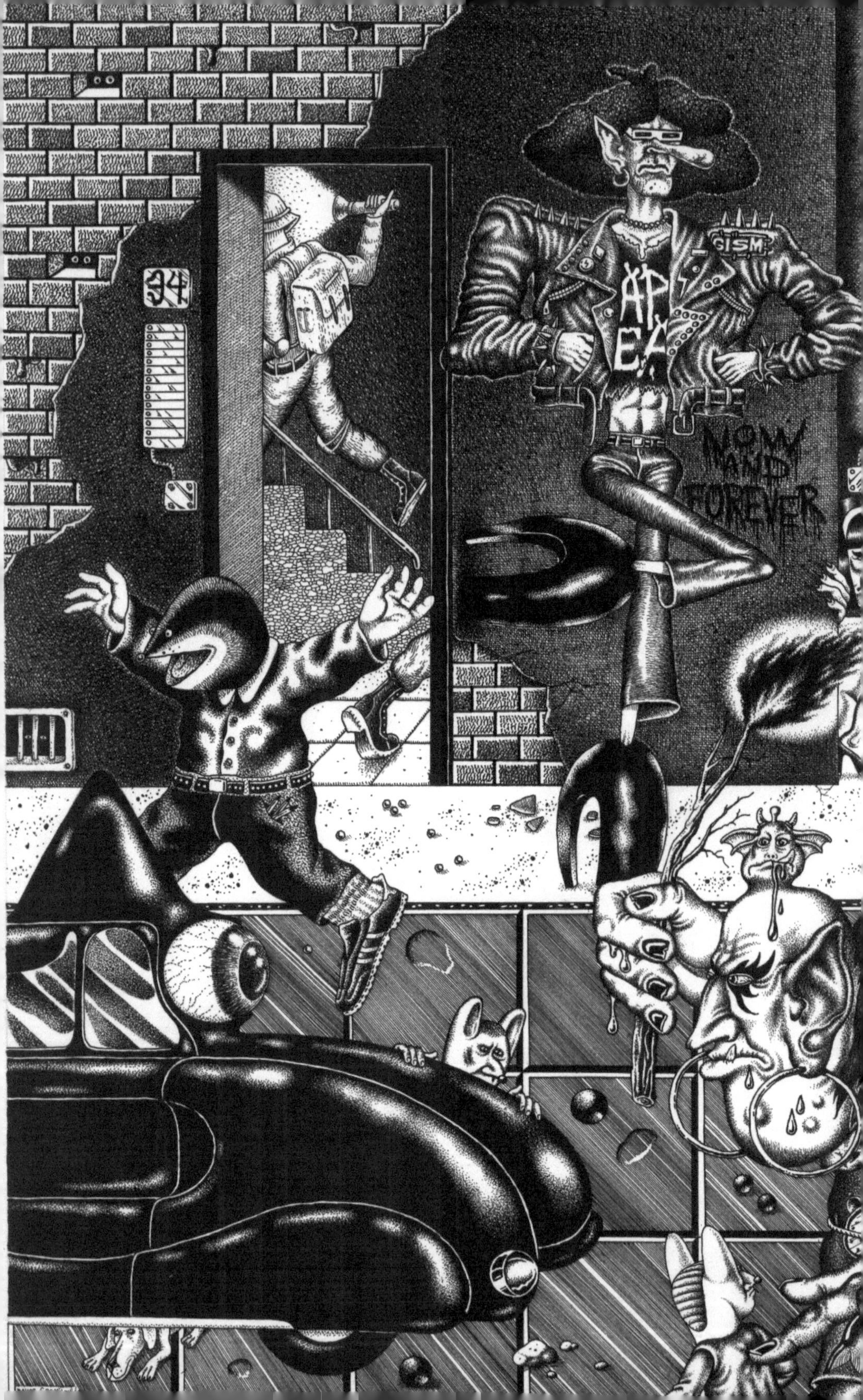
34
GISM
NOW AND FOREVER

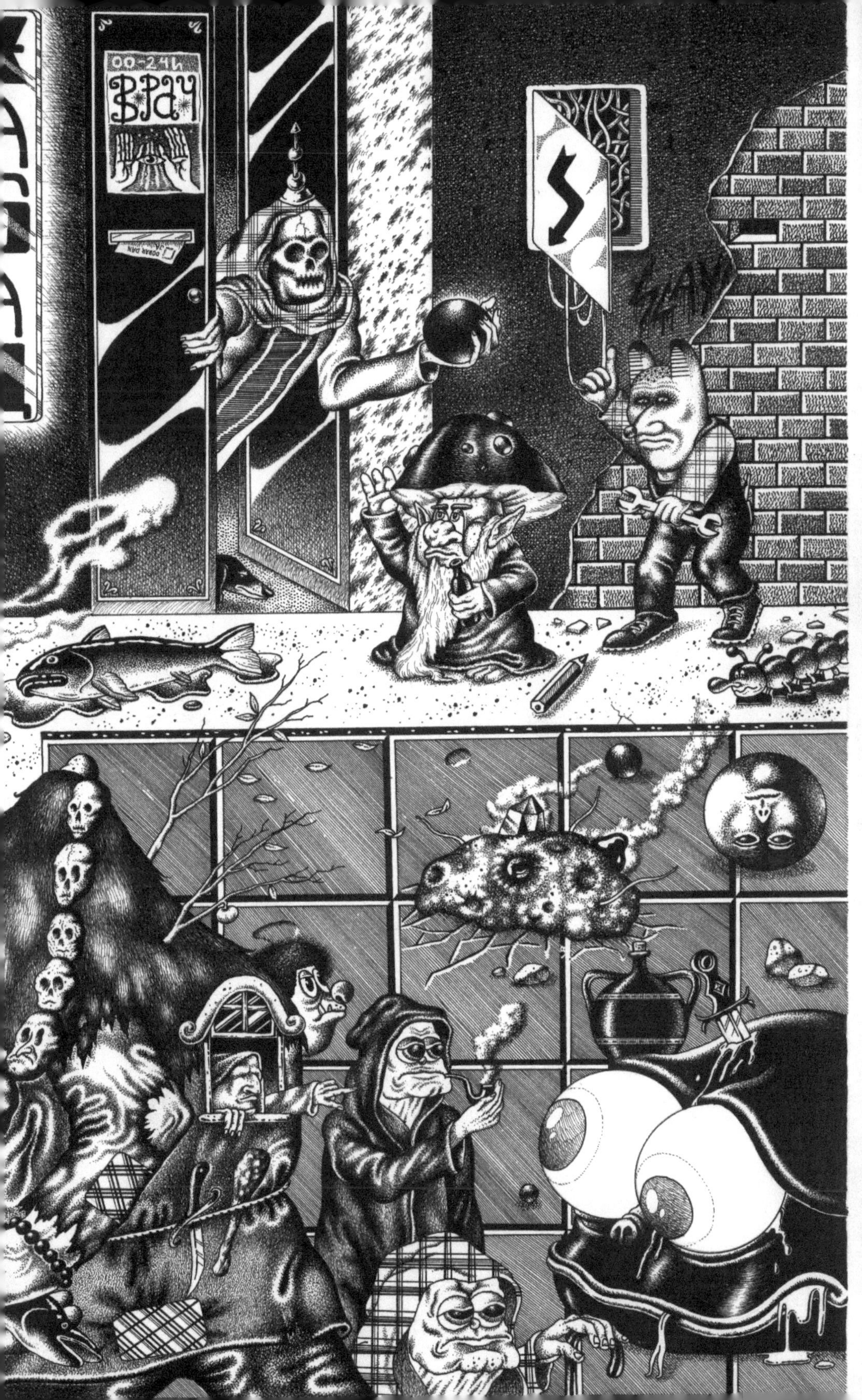

00-24h
$PAY
DEAR DAN
SLAY

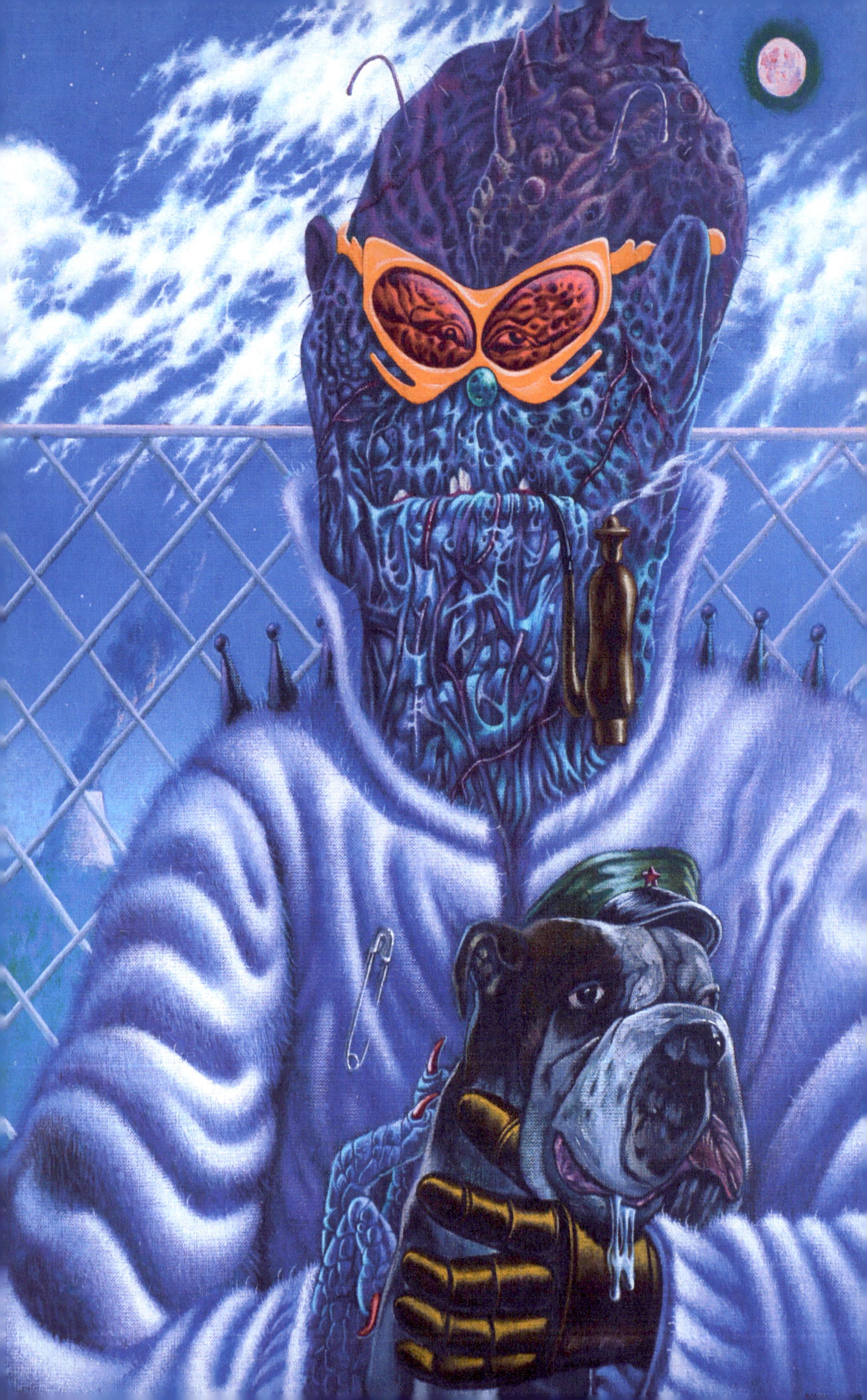

The Indulgent Confessionals Of Cyberpunk 2077

BY CHRISTOPHER MICHAEL

The world of *Cyberpunk 2077*, a video game set within Mike Pondsmith's larger *Cyberpunk* universe, is one where the promises of post-humanism have been fulfilled in an extreme late-capitalist form. Artificial intelligence can revivify the dead, brain-computer interfaces intervene between human nervous systems and machines, and cybernetic modification of the body has become massively popular thanks to the advent of "cyberware." In this setting, Katherine Hayle's idea of the "postmodern orthodoxy" where "the body is primarily, if not entirely, a linguistic and discursive construction" reigns supreme, as the "natural" body becomes less important when it can be modified and essentially remodeled.[1] This ethos is echoed within the actual gameplay, as the game features an extensive character builder where attributes like race, gender, and cybernetic intervention can all be modified. In this sense, a character's physical appearance becomes less important than their ideological and discursive construction within the world. These ideas

of post-humanism are also extended to the religions of the Cyberpunk universe, as seen prominently in the cybernetic confessional booths scattered across the game's main Night City setting.

The confessionals of *Cyberpunk 2077* bear little resemblance to those of their Catholic predecessors, the only signifiers to Christian tradition being the neon red cross at its top and the church kneeler at its bottom. Instead, they resemble an arcade game or ATM, and there is a simple interactive screen for confessing one's sins. The machines exist as an easter egg within the game, an interact-able device that does not advance or hinder the plot. Walking up to the confessional, players can choose whether to pay €6 to confess their sins. If they do, the screen will show that it is processing and then an animation of hands with chains breaking will play, followed by an animation of a devilish emoji gaining angel wings. Before confessing your sins, the machine features text that reads "Break the Chains of Your Sin!" Once your sins have been forgiven the machine's text reads "Your Sins

---

1. Hayles, Katherine, *How We Became Posthuman*, (The University of Chicago Press, 1999), 206.

Davor Gromilović (opposite/previous)

Are Forgiven. Remember Your Penance." The player does not actually have to take any action to confess their sins, just provide the proper amount of money. The game's lead Quest Designer, Pawel Sasko, has noted that the lack of action on the player's part was a purposeful move, done to present a criticism of commercialized religion.[2]

The idea of a transactional confession, based only on one's ability to pay the right price, recalls the commercialization of indulgences by the Catholic Church which led to the Protestant Reformation in the Middle Ages. During this period, indulgences were an alternative to normal confession, where one could pay for an indulgence from the church to absolve their sins. While Catholic dogma asserts there must be more action taken than paying for an indulgence for one to be absolved, this period of the Middle Ages saw much corruption of the practice.[3] The transactional form of sin absolution takes a new, cybernetic form within the space of *Cyberpunk 2077*. Like the abuse of indulgences in the Middle Ages, the confessionals of this game are completely commercialized, requiring no physical action other than one's ability to access the machine and pay the correct price. As Sasko points out, this confessional speculates on the future of religious practices, especially as they become further entangled with the capitalist means of the contemporary era. *Cyberpunk 2077* presents a particularly relevant take on this concept, explicitly gamifying the means of confession, as confessionals act like arcade machines rather than religious artifacts. In doing so, the game offers a longstanding criticism of such practices through a distinctly modern lens.

By presenting the confessional in this way, *Cyberpunk 2077* also makes a critique of the posthuman data-centric modes of contemporary power enforced throughout social media platforms and smart technologies. Through means like the cybernetic confessional, *Cyberpunk 2077* often embodies Byung Chul Han's idea that "Big Data has announced the end of the person who possesses free will."[4] In the current era, algorithms based on user generated data have come to impact everything from world economics to policing, with "predictive" technologies helping "experts" to determine new trends and shifts within the wider culture. In this vein, it could be implied that the confessionals of *Cyberpunk 2077* rely on algorithms which can predict one's sins simply based on who they are as a user. This would explain why no input of sins is needed from the users' end, as the machine's software could potentially predict their sins based on relevant data already encoded into the users' cyberware. After all, if predictive policing can be relied on for calculating crimes, who is to say algorithms cannot predict one's sins based on comparison of similar points of data? Considering the confessional as a predictive machine updates the idea of transactional confession, most prominently seen in the misuse of indulgences of the Middle Ages and brings it into a world reliant on algorithms and artificial intelligence.

Increasingly, these cyberpunk predictions are materializing in the real world. For example, the commercialization of Christianity in the US has led to the rise of Christian technologies and softwares like the application Hallow. Hallow, an app with celebrity sponsorships from the likes of Liam Neeson and Mark Wahlberg, has become the "#1 prayer app in the world."[5] The app operates like

2. See: u/KamilCesaro. "Quest Director Mr. Pawel Sasko talks about confession in Cyberpunk 2077." *Reddit*, 2021.
3. For more on the Catholic history of indulgences see: O'Malley, John W. "The Complex History of Indulgences ." *America: The Jesuit Review*, 30 Mar. 2009.
4. Han, Byung-Chul, *Psychopolitics: Neoliberalism and New Technologies of Power*, (Verso, 2017), 15.
5. This title is self-proclaimed

popular wellness apps, tracking the amount of time users spend praying, helps them create daily routines, and even allows them to connect with friends and family like other forms of social media. As such, the app is reliant on user generated data creating an algorithmic form of digital prayer largely inspired by Silicon Valley "solutioneering" methods. This app is being used by religious Christians across the globe and is one of the most prominent examples of the datafication of religious experience. While posthuman confessionals may only exist within fictional spaces for now, real world counterparts like the Hallow app bring to life many of their predictions.

The confessionals are also symbolic of a larger trend in the world of Cyberpunk, where once-spiritual ideas like the afterlife or concepts of prayer are absorbed into the logic of capitalist posthumanism. Erik Davis, writing on contemporary spiritual media practices, notes that "like the Holy Ghost, an invisible medium which allows us to plug into the spirit of God, the virtualizing machineries of media and information offer to port our data-souls into a digital otherworld."[6] In *Cyberpunk 2077*, this digital otherworld plays a prominent role in the space of the game. This is seen both in the main storyline, where a dead rockstar/terrorist is kept alive via artificial intelligence and neural link technology, as well as in tangential features like the cybernetic confessionals. This is accomplished not only through "virtualizing machineries" but also in the reconceptualization of humans as data-centric cybernetic beings. In focusing on humans as raw data, the game can reimagine immaterial spiritual concepts as having a new sense of tangibility through cybernetic achievements. As such, many of the religious practices of the game, like the confessionals, reveal a world where post-human forms of religion have gained dominance, and where our data-souls can only be saved through algorithmic means.

Christopher Michael is an anti-disciplinary artist and writer interested the spiritual and the virtual. You can find him at christophermichael.online, or on instagram (@c11111hris_)

6. Davis, Erik. *TechGnosis: Myth, Magic & Mysticism in the Age of Information*, (North Atlantic Books, 2015), 119.

FROM NEW MEDIA TO ABSOLUTE MEDIATION:

THE SELF-DEFEATING DIALECTIC OF PURE AGENCY IN REZA NEGARESTANI'S PHILOSOPHY OF ARTIFICIAL INTELLIGENCE

BY FRANCIS K.
& ANNA K. WINTERS

The importance of Reza Negarestani's philosophical work is not just in the technical rigor that he brings to bear on his subject matter (especially in *Intelligence and Spirit*, in which theoretical computer science is wedded to speculative philosophy in highly creative and disciplined fashion, opening up lines of flight to tackle the problem of "artificial general intelligence" anew) but also in the singular polemical position he takes up within contemporary debates on artificial intelligence. This is evident in his later texts, such as "Galatea Reloaded," which are very much activist interventions meant to fundamentally reshape the terms in which AI is conceived, in the aftermath of the rise of machine-learning technologies like DALL-E, which were still in embryonic form when *Intelligence and Spirit* was written.

There is a common (and essentially un-Hegelian) understanding of the philosophical concept known as "dialectic" that echos Aristotle's Golden Mean: we begin from two opposing positions, and the right answer is to be discovered in the middle that is given between those two extremes. In the context of artificial intelligence, there are two perspectives: the *deflationary*, which downplays the capabilities and potential impact of AI, and the *inflationary*, which excessively elevates expectations and fosters hype around AI's possibilities. The "obvious," seemingly "dialectical" stance would be to choose the position that sits between the inflationary "hype" and its deflationary opposite; the "true" position would then be that which is rationally equipped to mediate both forms of hysteria from within the field given by their own premises. Negarestani, however, argues that the problem with both positions is that *they are ultimately identical*.

It is through his cheeky discernment of this speculative identity of opposites that he attempts to establish a qualitatively distinct position, indicating that which this identity (according to Negarestani's argument, proceeding along both poles of the opposition from naive naturalist premises) excludes, or fails to raise itself to, in order to constitute the existing terms of its discursive legibility. This *excluded* middle, the endorsement of which represents a speculative risk on Negarestani's part, would be a properly

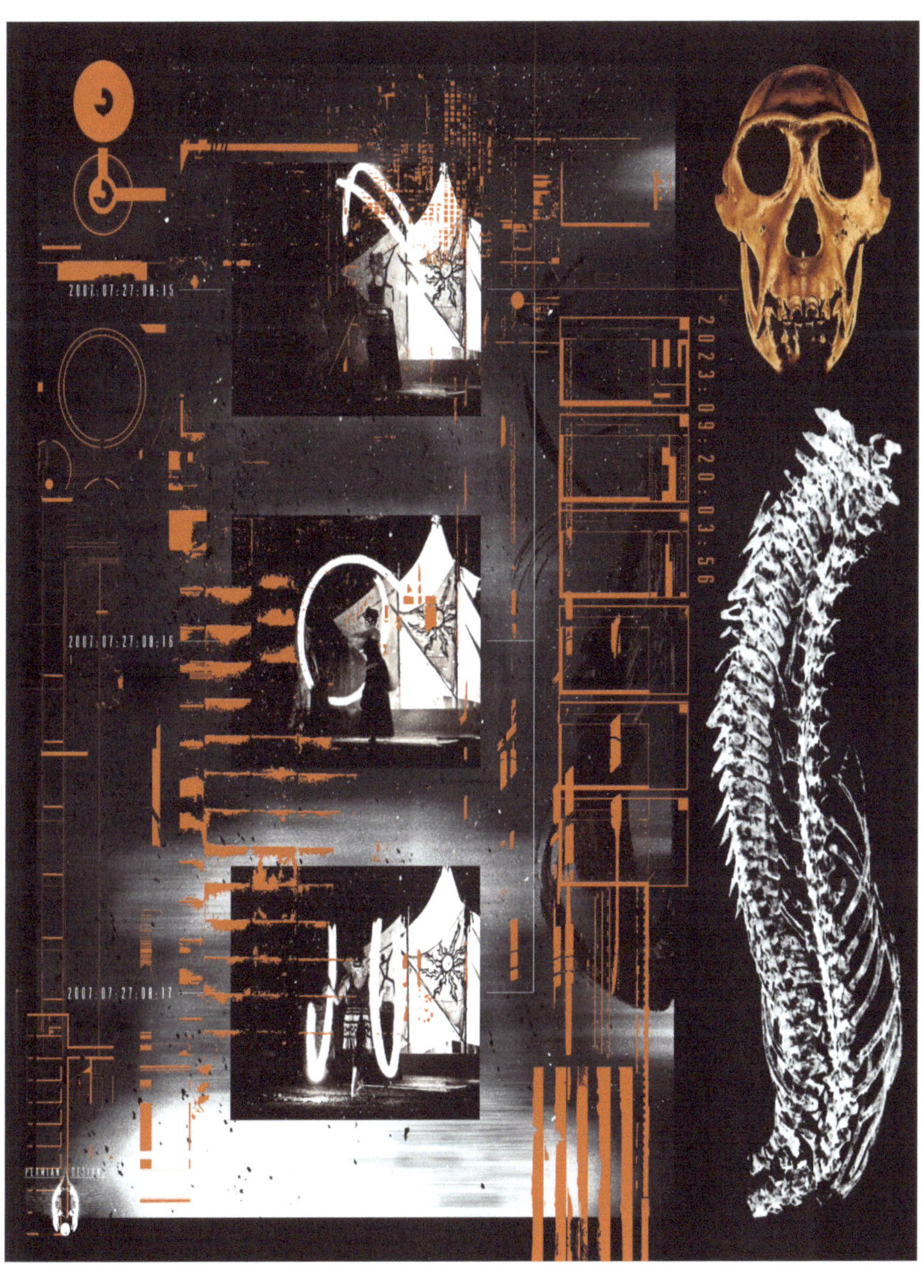

John T Allen

phenomenological position on AI—one that resists the temptation of a naturalist reduction. We applaud the boldness of this move while also recognizing that it is beset by fatal flaws which undercut its true speculative potential.

Negarestani begins by exposing the shared fallacious premises that he proceeds to reverse: while the inflationary position on AI is that it "can be realized by entirely bottom-up processes that have no use for the concept of rational agency as an account of agency operating under inter-subjective configurations and bound to constraints of objectivity in theory and praxis," if freed from the last anthropocentric constraints holding it back, we can expect it to apotheosize into a super-intelligence—a position itself split ethically between AI safety groups and "effective accelerationists," the deflationary position, by contrast, argues that "AI can be said to be just an efficacious bundle of so-called blind practices that has dropped any pretense to rationality or agency, and thus, notions of accountability and responsibility,"[1] dovetailing with a more left-wing critique that may, for example, consider generative AI models to be *just* plagiarism machines.

In Negarestani's view, the place of rational agency is missing from the discourse surrounding the capabilities of AI; phenomenology then becomes a way of reactivating the ability to make proper distinctions between concepts, harkening back to the rhetoric of Husserl's *Crisis of the European Sciences*. The issue with the field's current approach to organizing a conceptual toolkit for AI, according to this phenomenological critique, is in the suspicion that existing assessments are merely anthropomorphic judgments assigned to artificial agents by means of overextended surface analogies. To preserve the coherence of a (perhaps future) rational science in this area, Negarestani would like to allow for the construction of measured and determinate analogies between our activities and those of our AI programs. This measured approach is particularly important because these programs are *sentient*, not *sapient*, so how can we attribute to them features that are "after-the-fact models of sapience reformatting its own sentience"?[2] This is a reiteration of Chapter 3 of *Intelligence and Spirit*, which discusses the attribution (in an as-if analogical fashion) of judgments and perceptions to sentient agents lacking discursive apperceptive awareness. The danger lies not only in attributing over-inflated capabilities to AI programs but also in adopting an overly "objective" naturalist stance which denies even measured attributions.

Negarestani explains the bipolar attitude toward AI as the tendency to either "lavishly furnish artificial intelligence with such concepts without any restraints, or from the start, cynically doubt or entirely deprive it from the prospects of operating under such concepts."[3] This is a symptom of a naive science that operates purely on the order of explanation. Such a science can explain a range of imaginative acts by operationalizing them, but, without phenomenology as a propaedeutic that would give proper descriptions of these acts, such a science "reinforces the commonsense dogmas about imagination and creates an aura wherein imagination is just this x or y blind operationalized process." It is this posture that Negarestani associates with Dennett's naturalism. For Negarestani, the Husserlian discovery is that the "description of the phenomenon to be explained precedes explanation in epistemological and phenomenological orders."[4] It is not sufficient to assert that

---

1. Negarestani, R. (2024). Galatea Reloaded. In R. A. Trillo & M. Poliks (Eds.), Choreomata: Performance and Performativity after AI (p. 190). essay, CRC Press
2. Ibid., pg 196
3. Ibid., pg 197
4. Ibid., pg 198

the imagination has a Darwinian or neurological origin; there is also a properly anti-psychologistic dimension that such an explanation effaces.

Here, the purpose of phenomenology is not to ground the sciences in a phenomenology that would establish itself as the "first science"–a foundational science on which all others depend; consequently, it is not the Husserl of transcendental idealism that interests Negarestani. Phenomenology plays a polemical role against the rise of a "new conduct of science," according to which "science's power to explain precedes a phenomenon, not only in an ontological order but also in the orders of epistemology and phenomenology." Here, a skeptical movement does not stall in hyperbolic doubt or sophistry; rather, it serves as the starting point for a positive labour of science. Negarestani situates Husserl as a contemporary of Boltzmann, who would begin with skepticism as an "enabling way-in" regarding "an established perception or observation of a phenomenon."

By being systematically skeptical of a phenomenon whose entrenched description is taken for granted, we perform two tasks at once: we open new avenues of explanations for phenomena which were once bunched together under vague terms and habitual viewpoints, and we challenge the unexamined dogmas of descriptions of phenomena yet to be explained from within and equally from without of sciences.[5]

This enabling skepticism is linked to Husserl in "Galatea Reloaded," but it is given a Hegelian cast in *Intelligence and Spirit*. "Hegelian suspension can be linked back to the Pyrrhonian sceptical epoché or suspension of judgment regarding non-evident propositions," he writes. While the epoché stems from the Pyrrhonic idea that "for any proposition or property, its contradicting opposite or incompatible property can be put forward with equal justification," Negarestani presents a reading in which "Hegel's aufhebung seeks to break from the stasis and practical untenability of Pyrrhonian scepticism by directly assimilating it into reason in such a way that scepticism is no longer idly opposed to reason but becomes a dynamic and productive vector of it."[6]

This move is linked to his rejection of the unconscious as characterized by psychoanalysis, which one might consider the main plank of his discursive intervention. He points out in the interview "Re-engineering Philosophy" that the only unconscious that he would countenance is "what neuroscience calls the mechanisms and computational processes that act beneath the threshold of an attentional system or global workspace." The Freudian view he rejects he characterizes as: "a kind of reality that works against consciousness."[7] In his view, this perspective is self-defeating, as the very faculty that would allow us to talk about the unconscious–consciousness–has already been compromised by the unconscious.

The same line of argument is then repeated in "Galatea Reloaded," a text that is striking for the paranoid position that Negarestani takes vis-a-vis the unconscious.

The unconscious is akin to a Thing-like cosmological parasite adept at mimicking its host down to its nitty-gritty details. Then ultimately what appears as the conscious agency is merely the unconscious in the state of its eternal dissimulation, deceptive imitation, and hypercamouflage.[8]

Negarestani refers to a metaphor of Freud's from the *Introductory Lectures to*

5. Ibid., pg 198
6. Negarestani, R. (2020). In Intelligence and Spirit (p. 9), Urbanomic.
7. Negarestani, R., & Mackay, R. (2018). Reengineering Philosophy. Urbanomic.
8. Negarestani, R. (2024). Galatea Reloaded. In R. A. Trillo & M. Poliks (Eds.), Choreomata: Performance and Performativity after AI (p. 190). essay, CRC Press.

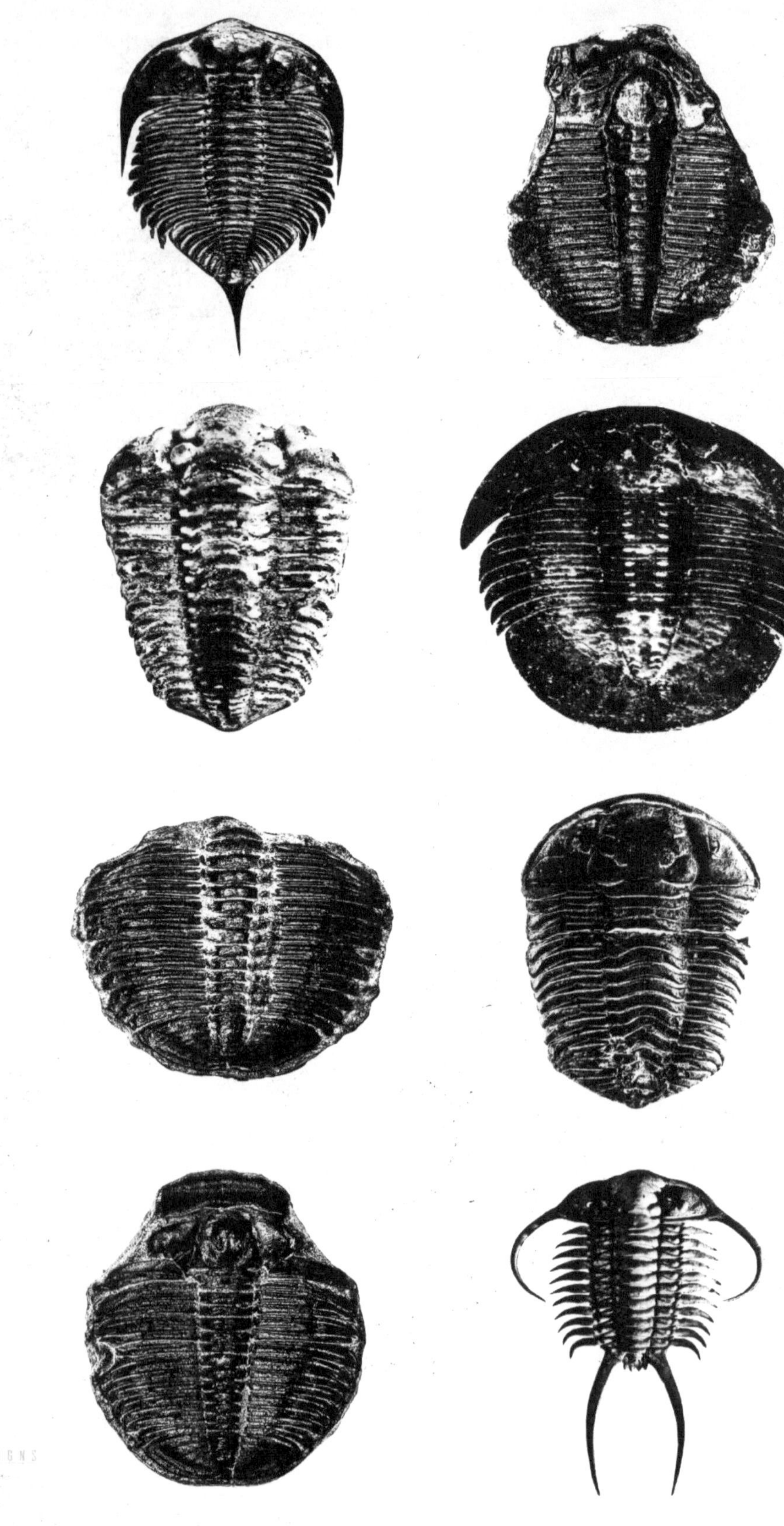

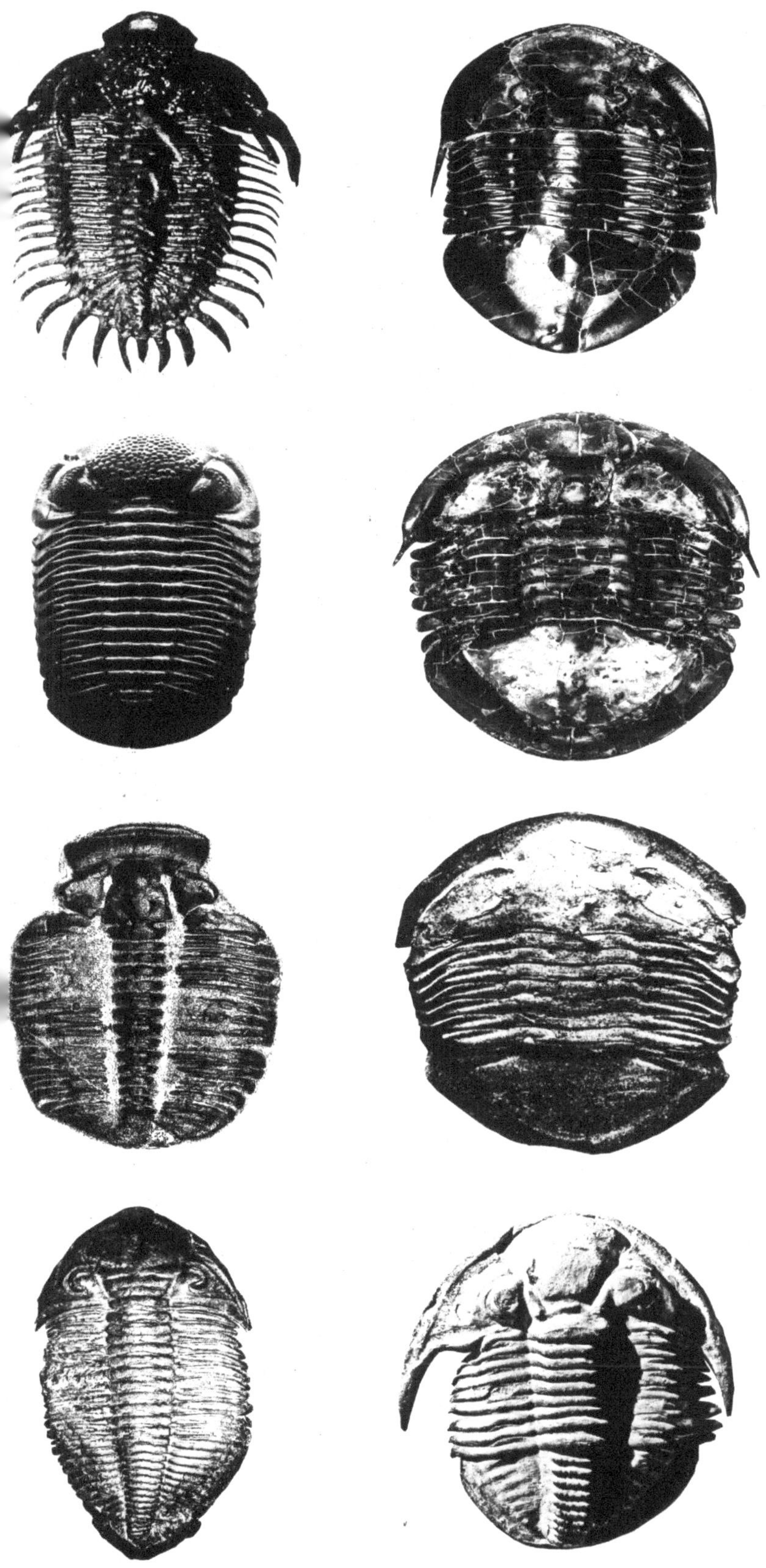

Psychoanalysis, that of the "two chambers" of the unconscious and the conscious, with a "door-keeper" between them situated as the agency of repression (a metaphor which Freud himself describes as "crude"). Negarestani does not take into account any of the more rigorous, non-metaphorical and "conscious agency"-sensitive developments in the elaboration of the concept of repression as the process of constituting the unconscious since Freud–in particular, Lacan's development of a theory of "denegation" involving various structural reactions to traumatic content, including repression, foreclosure, and disavowal, premised explicitly on a sort of materialist inversion of the function of the Cartesian *cogito.*

Following Bouveresse and emphasizing the Freudian metaphor of repression as a "door-keeper," reframed by Negarestani as a sort of "agent within an agent," he argues that the notion of the Freudian unconscious is an extreme example of the homunculus fallacy. As part of a strategy to immunize rational agency from the threat of the unconscious, Negarestani claims that the unconscious lays claim to rational agency while existing in a milieu where this is absent. To support his "homunculus fallacy" argument, Negarestani radically distorts the terms of Freud's own text, claiming–falsely–that Freud identifies the unconscious directly with the metaphorical door-keeper used to illustrate the function of repression, rather than the ante-room wherein repressed thoughts are kept by the repressive door-keeper. But Freud explicitly states the opposite:

The unconscious may therefore be compared to a large ante-room in which the various mental excitations are crowding one another, like individual beings...The excitations in the unconscious, in the ante-chamber, are not visible to consciousness, which is of course in the other room, so to begin with they remain unconscious.[9]

The door-keeper is not the unconscious itself, but rather the repressive function that maintains the coherence of the contents of the unconscious.

The purpose of this excursion into a critique of Freud is not to truly tarry with psychoanalysis, but to expel the fallacy that Negarestani sees underlying the rejection of rational agency in both the left and right: "the doctrine of social practices and performances as the unconscious milieu of the rational agency actively undermining the latter" and "the extremist forms of discourse on the primacy of practice over theory."[10] This attitude is omnipresent, and drives both left and right perspectives toward AI, with the left focusing on the blind practices of capitalism and the right emphasizing the blind naturalist processes that function in both natural and artificial neural networks.

At the one side of the aisle, this sketchy critical analysis appears as the enforcing muscle of the reinvigorated left's critique, and at the other side is, by all accounts, what has always been the thesis of the right-inclined AI discourse, from LessWrong forums' cascading threads to the Musk-Thiel-Zuckerberg libertarian-conservativism-liberal null politics connection mob.

But is it not the case that this "extremist" rendition of the "primacy of practice" reappears in Negarestani's own discourse

9. Freud, S. (1922). Introductory Lectures on Psycho-analysis: A Course of Twenty Eight Lectures Delivered at the University of Vienna. United Kingdom: G. Allen & Unwin. pp 249
10. Negarestani, R. (2024). Galatea Reloaded. In R. A. Trillo & M. Poliks (Eds.), Choreomata: Performance and Performativity after AI (p. 192). essay, CRC Press

John T Allen (previous)

at a higher level, in terms of an effective "doubling" of agency between, on the one hand, the phenomenological consciousness of the agent developed by reference to Husserl and, on the other, the "objective inter-subjectivity" which he articulates by referencing Boltzmann's mechanical conception of discourse, rooted fundamentally not just in the sort of statistical framework favored in its Bayesian variant by LessWrong forums, but also operating as the Freudian daemonic gate-keeper ensuring the effective repression of excess "fantasy" material not to be raised to the level of objectified perception?

In the opposition between Husserlian and Boltzmannian poles of his own framework, Negarestani re-inscribes the Freudian metaphorology of the two chambers onto a more technically and philosophically sophisticated level. In making this move, Negarestani was fully anticipated by Jacques Lacan. Effectively, we have graduated from the simple Freudian opposition between the conscious and the unconscious to the Lacanian opposition between the imaginary order and the symbolic order, both of which consist of both conscious and unconscious components. Even if the maintenance of the distinction is still fundamentally a privilege of the symbolic, Lacan refers to this as "the instance of the letter in the unconscious," sometimes translated into English as "the agency of the letter in the unconscious."

This is the point where Lacan offers us a *psychoanalytic materialist* theory of "objective inter-subjectivity." He demonstrates how repression operates through what he calls "the field of the Other," which is constituted by discourse as a social link rather than solely through the internal struggles of bodily excitations

confined to distinct individuals. Lacan discusses an explicitly mechanical discursive function not fundamentally distinct from that of Boltzmann's, and premised, to an extent, on his studies in cybernetics and information theory.

However, something is clearly missing in this conjugation of the imaginary and symbolic orders in Negarestani's text: the *third* Lacanian order, the real. Before we introduce the Lacanian concept of the *encounter with the real* into Negarestani's discourse, let us first take a detour through the problem of scientific epistemology to clarify its specific relevance to this element of his work.

Any epistemology that is to demarcate science from non-science begins with a decision (more or less "ethical" in character) on how to define "good" science, or, in other words, what mixture of naivete and sophistication is acceptable in the development and framing of scientific hypotheses. For instance, Karl Popper has taken a more "deflationary" stance, adopting Einstein's interventions in physics as exemplary, while rejecting the "unfalsifiable" frameworks for social analysis developed by Freud and Marx. In contrast, Louis Althusser has taken an "inflationary" position, such that these "unfalsifiable" frameworks are still to be interrogated for the precise sense of their possible claims to scientificity (even if this scientific status involves a "subjective" or "militant" investment at the outset, a particular perspective for posing problems, from within which one then seeks to evaluate those problems "scientifically").

This "ethical" decision regarding the "good" in science itself tends to dialectically transform the sciences under its purview, providing a means to better contextualize a proper interpretation of their own work within this ethical register (the register of "good" science). None of this is to advocate for a relativization of all epistemology, such that everyone might have their own "equally valid" preferences for various crackpot models of the real–with one person's epistemology founded on the premises given by self-proclaimed psychic Uri Geller, and another's based on Lysenkoism, without a legitimate means to adjudicate success and failure. While one might make an (un)ethical decision in the realm of epistemology that affirms a "science" where Uri Geller's paranormal claims are pre-eminent, it is by the *fruits of such a program* (a metaphysical research program, as in Lakatos) that we can judge this epistemological decision ("truth is consequences").

This understanding of "ethical decision" as a necessary guiding principle for scientific practice follows from what we might call a meta-epistemology of the *encounter with the real*, as developed by Jacques Lacan in *The Four Fundamental Concepts of Psychoanalysis,* articulated through a reinterpretation of Aristotle's concept of τύχη (*tuchē*), sometimes translated as "luck," a form of "chance": "an appointment to which we are always called with a real that eludes us."[11] Just consider the "eureka" (or even "that's funny...") moment associated with scientific discoveries, often arising from accidental revelations of unexpected or exciting results following from experimental procedures.

This encounter consists in the discovery, at once always new and each time the same, with an order of the real irreducible to any pre-given sense-making system or bounded perspective; this encounter is, furthermore, irreducible to any *single* scientific meta-language, but indicates an "elusive" point of contact at the limit of sense, possibly amenable to multiple distinct or competing interpretations, each of which can only prove their worth as an interpretation according to two basic conditions: a) an ethical decision as to the "good" in science, and b) an evaluation of the consequences generated by pursuing this interpretation in further conceptual detail, applying the orienting possibilities it opens up to one's experimental practice. The rejection of any full sufficiency on the order of a bounded metalanguage is one of the most important points of post-Lacanian philosophy; therefore, interpretive decisions on an ethical level are foregrounded as effects of this epistemology of the encounter.

Neo-rationalists like Negarestani err in accusing post-Lacanian philosophers, such as Gilles Deleuze, of thinking from an unmediated "direct" perception of reality, or an intellectual intuition capable of direct "metaphysical" apprehension. They do so because they lack a robust concept of the *real* as a limit of sense that demands an *interpretive act* (Lacan), a *philosophical decision* (Badiou, Laruelle), or a *conceptual creation* (Deleuze and Guattari). Even Hegel's concept of *speculation* illustrates his sensitivity to how the real operates as a limit of sense. Proper philosophical speculation, in his sense, begins with a commitment to a rational discernment of "being," conceived in its identity as immanent to its own thought of itself, rather than being carved up arbitrarily at its "objective" joints by the agency of the understanding. This effort to think beyond the understanding is a *decision* made at the point of Absolute Knowing, conceived as a *limit* on thought–an encounter with the failure of the "experiment" of thinking from a transcendental subjectivity whose cognition is divorced from any identity with the being it thinks of, as pro-

11. Lacan, J. (1977). The Four Fundamental Concepts of Psychoanalysis (J.-A. Miller, Ed.). Hogarth Press. (pg. 53-54)

filed in the *Phenomenology of Spirit*. Hegel is here, like Deleuze (though in a different register), not claiming any direct or "immediate" apprehension of being in itself, but rather an apprehension of being as a form of *absolute mediation* itself, as the point at which a philosophical decision is demanded and taken up as a response to the need to conceive of identity as mediated rather than immediate (in Lacanian terms: mediated by the encounter with the real).

In fact it is here that Negarestani is not Hegelian enough, and falls back into a naive form of Platonism, because, far more than a thinker like Deleuze, he preserves a conceit of scientific immediacy apprehended through a rational consciousness of its mental objects as situated "objectively" on a plane of reference, which Hegel's whole project was devoted to overcoming; this is precisely why he must return to the phenomenology of Husserl, a man who infamously claimed that he could not understand Hegel. Husserl's project is, nevertheless, of exemplary interest precisely because of how his theory of the transcendental ego immanently unravels its own foundations exactly as Hegel demonstrated in the *Phenomenology of Spirit*.

Part of Negarestani's failure to fully grasp this Hegelian insight stems from his inability to adequately thematize what we might call the dialectics of enchantment and disenchantment. Instead, he reduces the former to the latter. It may be instructive here to recall the thesis of Adorno and Horkheimer's *Dialectic of Enlightenment*, which argues that any effort towards pure Enlightenment ultimately dooms itself to effectively cutting off the ethical feet upon which it stands. From a Deleuzian perspective, not only is Negarestani only able to think in terms of

the "functions" treated by science as situated on a plane of reference,[12] but he also fails to contribute directly to this scientific project. Instead, he engages in an abortive philosophical endeavor of concept creation that does not situate its ideas in a way meaningfully distinguishable from the scientific functions provided by the model of natural science.

In effect, this reduces his thinking to a *popularizing exhibition* of *existing scientific functions*, embellished with some philosophical flair and erudition (which ultimately amounts to little more than a tautological insistence on the necessity of a *cogito*, an irreducible pure consciousness thinking of itself thinking itself; perhaps, if we're lucky, it may also think itself into a more or less arbitrary, if not occasionally interesting, language-game). This is why Deleuze and Guattari critique both phenomenology and logical positivism in *What is Philosophy?*; they argue that classical phenomenology is not able to create genuine concepts, merely meditating on the functions of the lived.[13] It's unsurprising, then, that Negarestani shifts from drawing on Carnap's logical positivist philosophy in *Intelligence and Spirit* to taking inspiration from Husserl's phenomenology when addressing the subject of imagination.

While Negarestani employs the concept of the "encounter" to advocate for "Brentano-Husserl's idea of the unconscious" as "a concrete encounter with a foreign object encapsulating what the conscious life has always been and will be,"[14] this is not an encounter with the *real* in Lacan's sense. Instead, it is merely a noetic encounter with an object-cause of desire (or "intentionality") in the shimmering mirror of what Lacan termed the *imaginary order*. The phenomenological theory of the encounter can only extend

12. Deleuze, G., & Guattari, F. (1994). In What is Philosophy? (pp. 112-133). Columbia University Press.
13. Ibid., pp. 136-162
14. Negarestani, R. (2024). Galatea Reloaded. In R. A. Trillo & M. Poliks (Eds.), Choreomata: Performance and Performativity after AI (p. 199). essay, CRC Press.

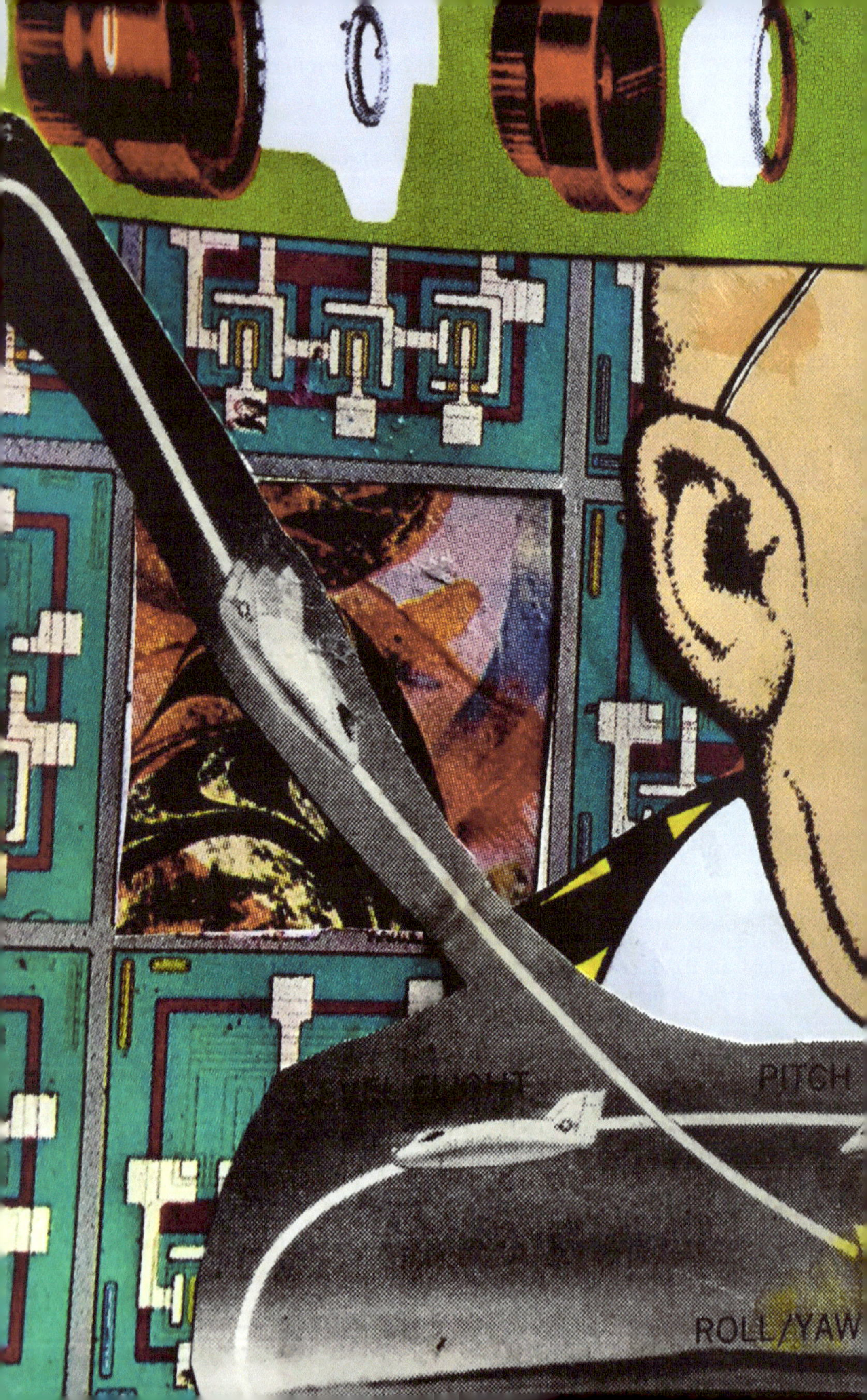

PITCH
ROLL/YAW

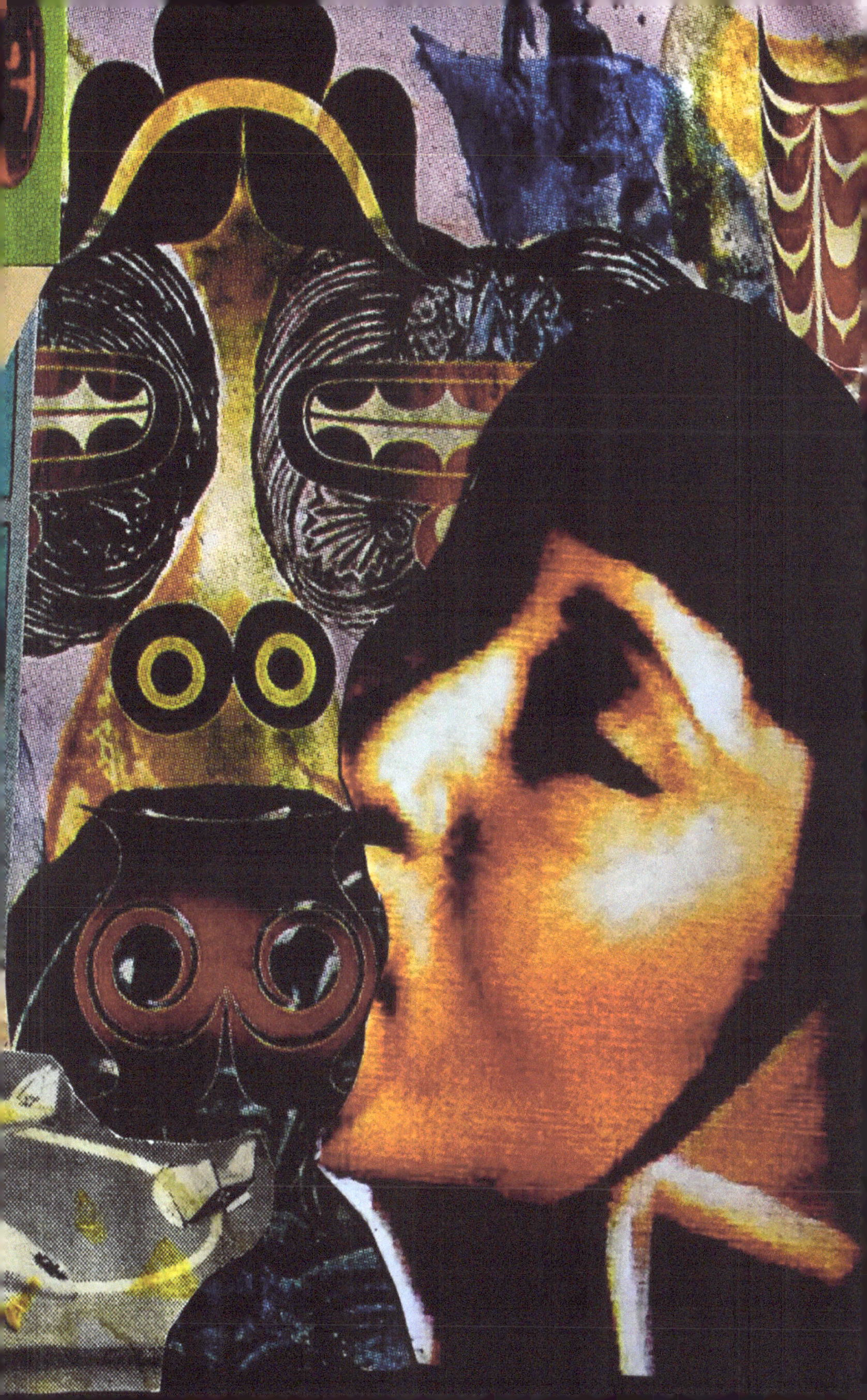

as far as what Heidegger called *disclosure,* while Lacan's theory of the encounter with the real adopts a radical stance similar to Emmanuel Levinas' critique of all hitherto existing phenomenology; this position demands that we contemplate the encounter from the standpoint of the *revelation* of something fully Other than the subjective consciousness of the transcendental ego. It seems that Negarestani can only conceive of such an Other as a naturalistic or deterministic hindrance to the free play of the cogito's imagination; that such an Other may be the absolute mediation which is itself required to enable the dialectical articulation of a legitimately creative imagination in the first place–one capable of sensitivity to the real–goes fully unconsidered.

The problem here is that, effectively, there is no *jouissance* (enjoyment) of the Other in Negarestani's discourse, in Lacan's sense of the term; the field of the Other is presented entirely as a means of repression or denegation of fantasy, assumed always to be more or less autotelic, rather than as a means of *enabling* it. This limitation leads him to a naive split between the imaginary and the symbolic, absent the real. The real, in this context, is precisely what represents the impossibility of reducing social fantasy to a particular autotelic imaginary closure. Negarestani cannot account for the *objectivity* of fantasy itself; while he seems to allow this in the guise of his theory of imagination, it must nevertheless be obsessively checked by an inter-subjective process of linguistic repression, *reducing* imagination to something conceived as more accurately reflective of the plane of reference rather than *transforming* it for the purpose of producing more desirable social effects within an ethical register.

It is at this point that we would like to introduce a pair of concepts inspired by, but differing from, the distinction between concepts and functions in Deleuze and Guattari's *What is Philosophy?*. While Deleuze and Guattari argue that this distinction corresponds to the divide between philosophy and science, our distinction is meant to allow for a double inscription of this conceptual difference within both philosophy and science themselves. For Deleuze and Guattari, both science and philosophy are oriented toward chaos, which they must confront and respond to, but do so in radically different fashions. Philosophy selects a particular set of infinite movements, functioning like a sieve for the "infinite speed" on a plane of *immanence.* In contrast, science relinquishes the infinite by effecting a fantastic slowing down, enabling objects to be located and constructed on a plane of reference.

Instead of "concepts," we propose the term *high definition*s, and instead of "functions," we propose *low definitions*. A high definition is not simply an idea at "infinite speed," but it is rather an idea founded on the persistence of a *jouissance*–an enjoyment. Rather than sacrificing its animating ethical fantasy, it re-articulates the inscription of this fantasy all the more as it passes through the processes of its repressive reduction, producing a dialectic of subl(im)ation (Hegel's concept of Geist can be fully interpreted along these lines, and the same can be said, in a more limited register, for Husserl's phenomenological imagination). In the philosophy of science, it is perhaps Feyerabend who demonstrates the greatest sensitivity to this register when he declares that instead of the humbleness the Popperian falsificationist assumes when her theory has been falsified, she should stubbornly stick to her research program. After all, we can never tell if a particular line of questioning might not

Amanda Yskamp (previous)

bear fruit (and it is here, we may add, that a stage is set for an ethical decision regarding the meaning of the "fruit"). This is why Feyerabend combines a shocking *épater les bourgeois* toward the sciences, indulging the orienting passions of pseudosciences like astrology and homeopathy, while also affirming the "great scientists" such as Bohr and Einstein. What is involved in this gesture is not only a rational assessment on the future of a theory, but also the persistence of a *jouissance* that is enacted through a "failed" science. Galileo exemplifies a figure who pushed through precisely this sort of scientific research program, one widely considered to have "failed" (heliocentrism), so it could be developed to the level of overturning fully its supposedly "falsifying" premises (the geocentric intuition). This disputation transcends empirical facts, addressing the very distinctions underlying the facts themselves; the avowal and revision of which were required to introduce the notion of relative motion on a non-empirical level.

A low definition, while it involves a certain sort of "slowing down," is more profoundly that which suspends the persistence of any singular or partial enjoyment or imaginative content for the sake of an "empty" formal mediation–principally between enjoyments which may be maximally irreconcilable. It is through low definitions that "objectivity" is produced. We observe low definitions of this type in the establishment of procedures of scientific formalization, and at the limit we can conceive of the formulation of *entropy* in both thermal and informational terms as an index within the space of low definitions themselves for the collapse of the high into the low; Boltzmann's procedural approach to mechanical deliberation is effectively a means for securing more effectively an inter-

subjective passage into a state capable of grappling with the entropic reduction of the ethical fantasies of living beings, which tend instead towards a negentropic counter-movement within this very reduction.

Statistics, therefore, especially in its Bayesian form, becomes the *preeminent science of low definitions*, insofar as it promises to make thought itself calculable under the regime of probability theory. It draws and classifies a proliferating series of low definitions generic enough to be applicable from astrophysics to the social sciences, including the functioning of minds–both human and artificial–as a science focused on extracting as much usable information as possible from messy and incomplete data. The limit of statistics therefore becomes the limit of what can be operationalized, which leads to the aporia of the social sciences–the reproducibility and the generalizability crises. Insofar as the modern emergence of machine learning is predicated on the neural network as a statistical predictor, modern artificial intelligence stands as the fulfillment of this program. However, the question raised by an encounter between the project of artificial intelligence and the phenomenological thinking of a Hegel or a Husserl is something entirely different: *is it possible for artificial intelligence to be more than a statistical engine, that is, is it possible for it to enjoy?* This is the question that Isabel Millar asks in *The Psychoanalysis of Artificial Intelligence*, as an analogue to the Kantian question "What can I know?"

Here, Negarestani's philosophy of AI encounters a self-defeating dead end. While it raises what are effectively psychoanalytic questions about the nature or possibility of enjoyment for an artificial mind, treated in terms of "Geist" or "imagination," it can never, in the end, treat these questions on their own terms. The irony is that it is precisely his fixation on the concept of "rational agency" which *undoes* any possible subjectivity within the constitution of an artificial intelligence itself, effectively substituting a Cartesian *res cogitans* (a thinking substance) for agent-free materialist premises. This substitution subjects the thinking substance to the same entropic reduction through low definitions as any other statistical inquiry. This move cannot ultimately yield new philosophical frontiers for the study of artificial intelligence because it misses the fundamental Hegelian dialectical insight: the subject is not identical to the agent itself, but rather stands for the *immanent self-differentiation* of agency constituted only as a function of the encounter with the real. This understanding voids any possible absolute separation between a thinking substance and its material conditions. What is at issue, instead, is not absolute separation, but *absolute mediation*.

Francis K. lives in Singapore where he is an engineering student. He tweets at @pachabelcanon and has a scratchpad blog at https://listed.to/@pachabelcanon.

Anna K. Winters is a former "Hegelian egirl" and independent scholar based in Philadelphia. She can be found on X (@tenshi_anna).

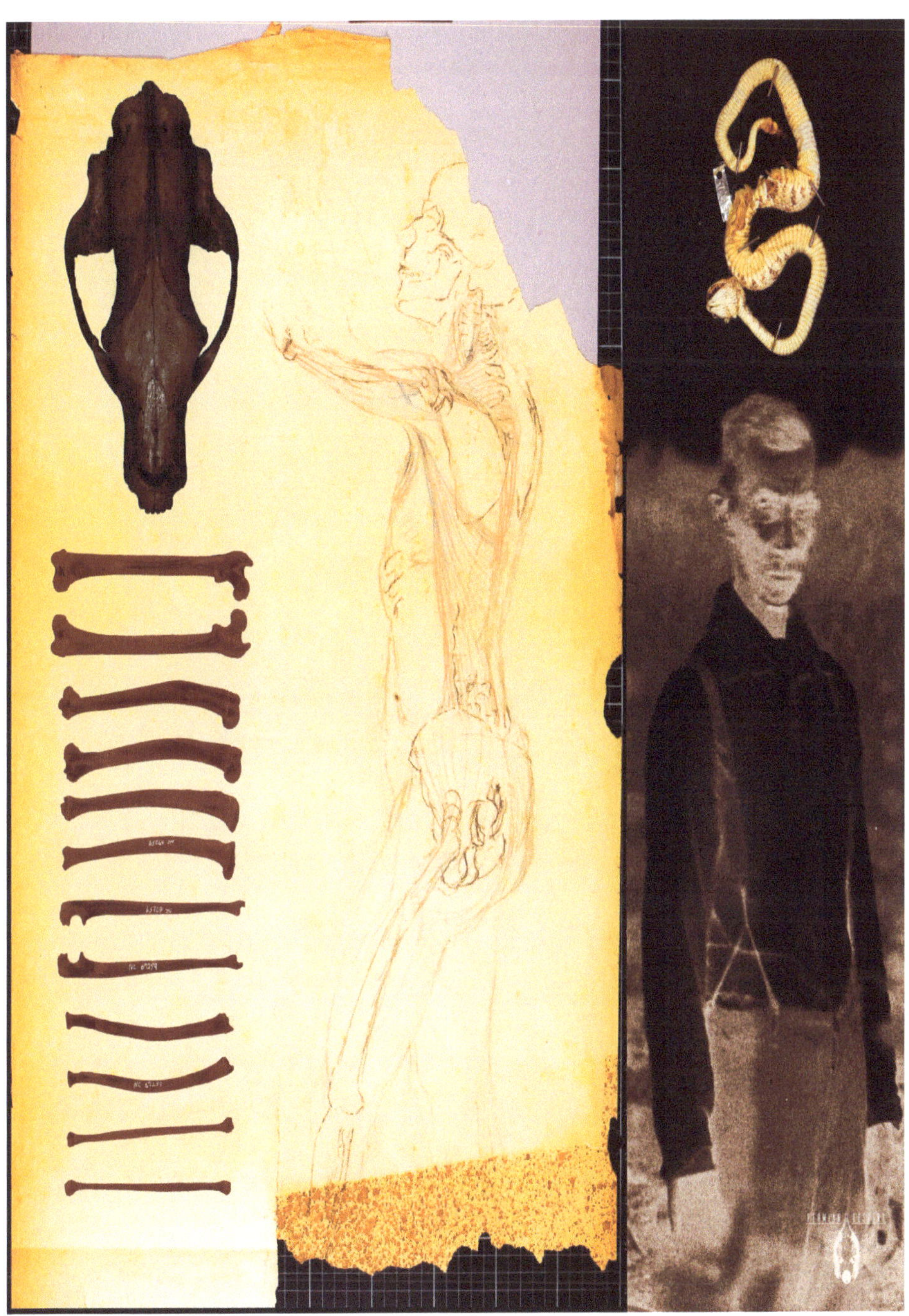

John T Allen

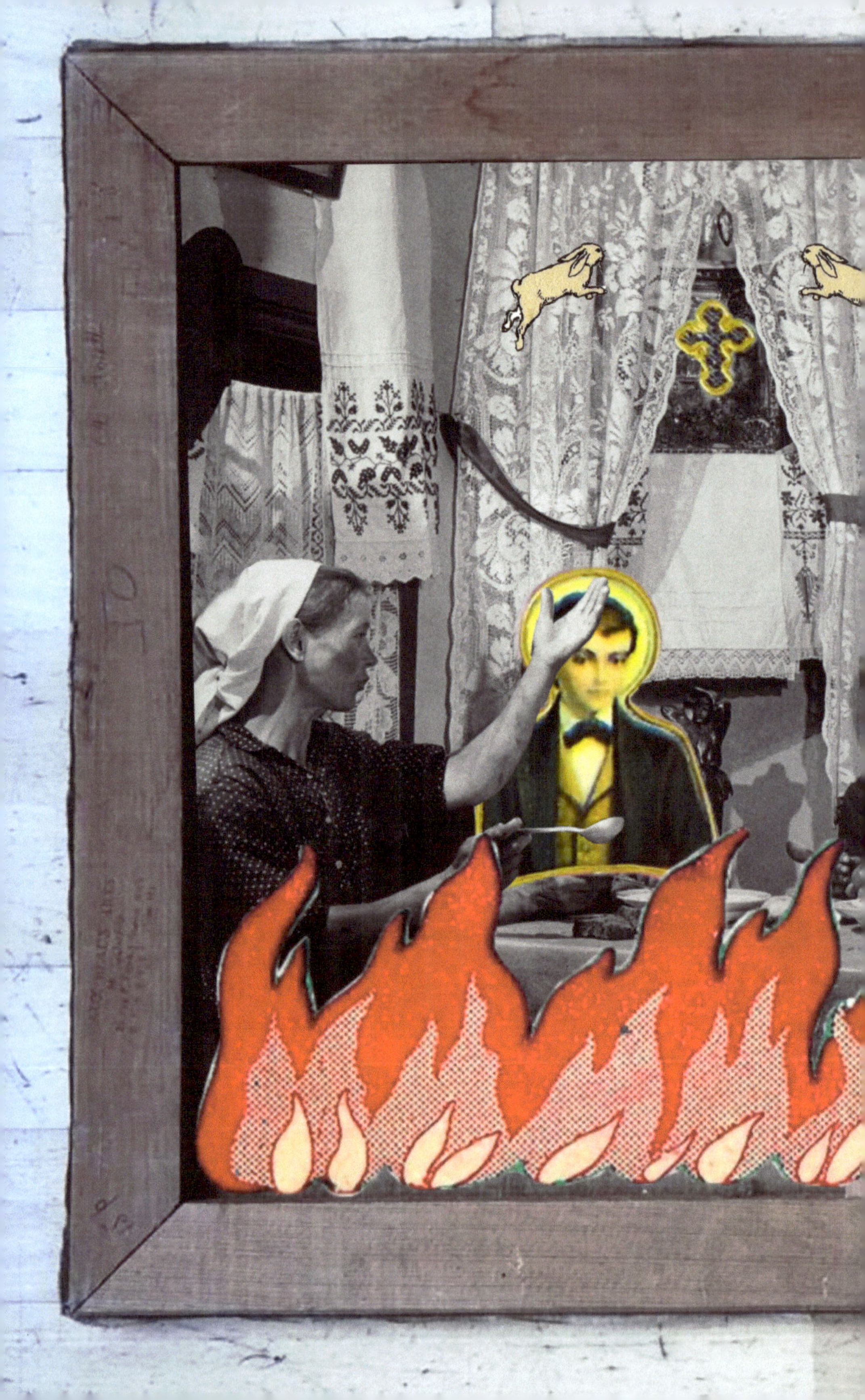

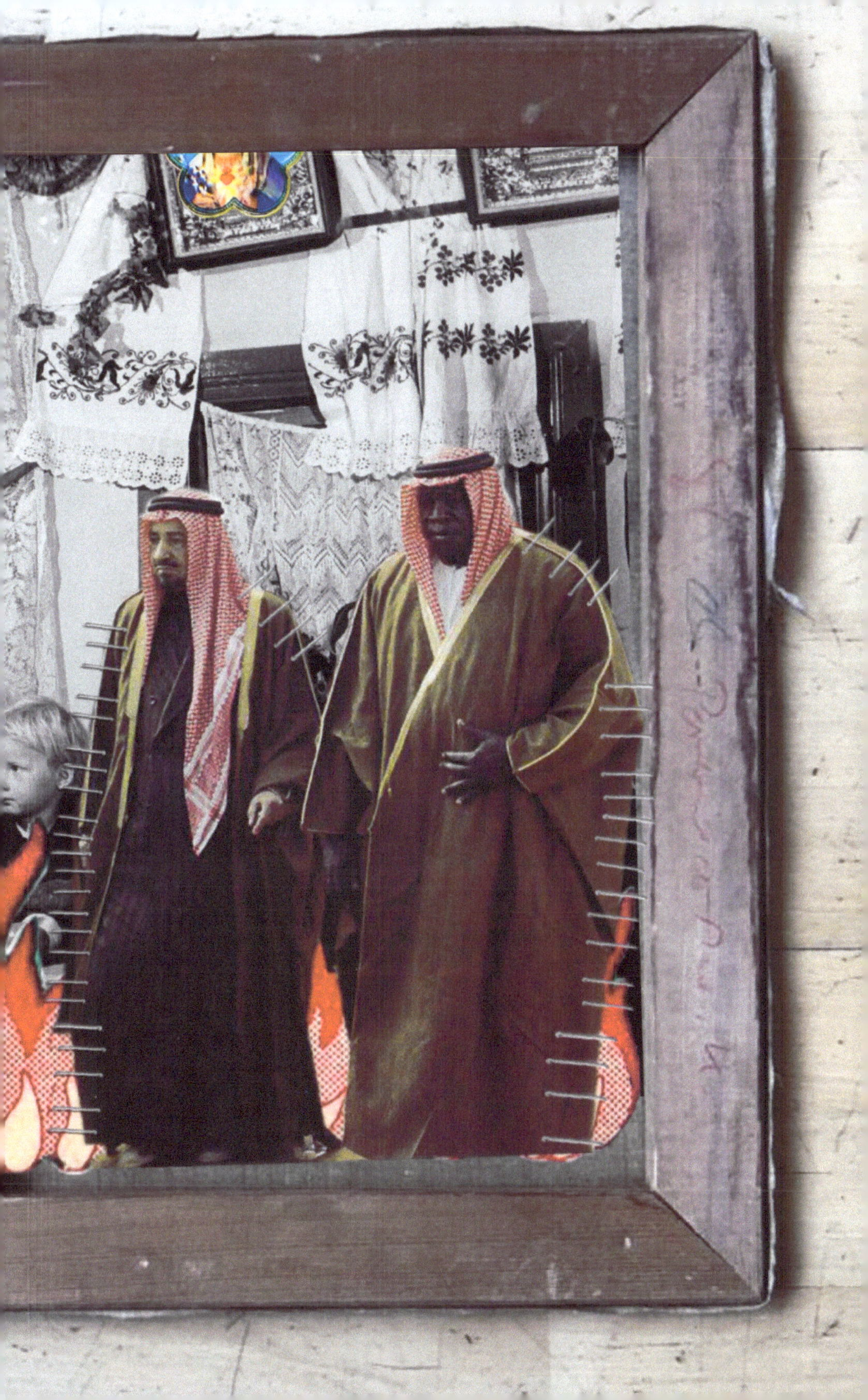

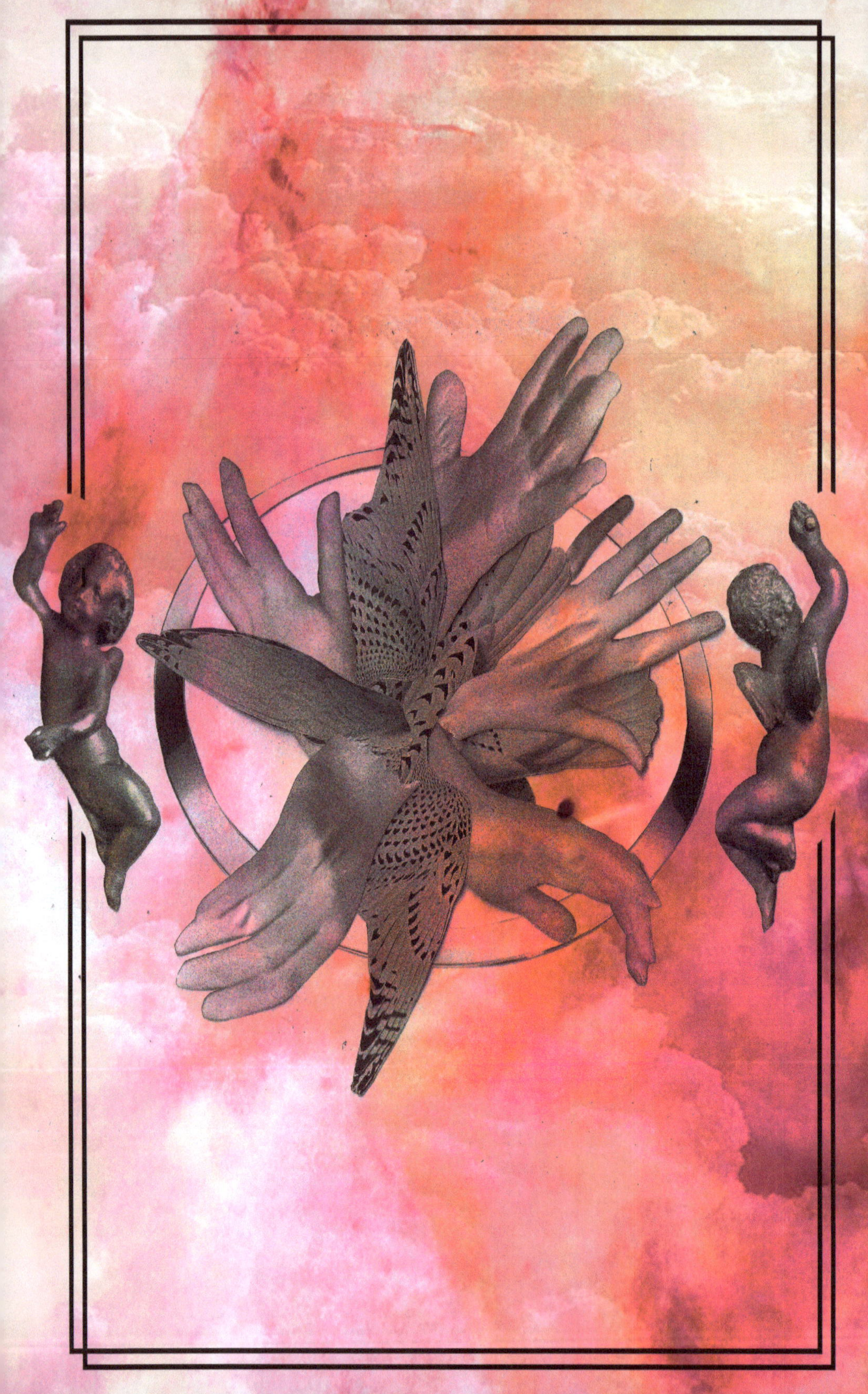

Haelegenic Visions

AN INTERVIEW WITH HAELA HUNT-HENDRIX
OF LITURGY

Haela Ravenna Hunt-Hendrix–a polymath straddling the realms of philosophy, theology, art, drama, and music–is perhaps best recognized as the the creator, composer, lead guitarist, and singer of the transcendental black metal band Liturgy.[1] Marked by critical acclaim and controversy, Liturgy, in their departure from traditional black-metal conventions, inflamed the metal and avant-garde music worlds. Haela's infusion of Christian theology and affirmational philosophy into black metal simultaneously transgressed upon and breathed new life into a music culture historically encoded with a dark and nihilistic vision.[2]

Haela's controversial manifesto, *The Transcendental Black Metal Manifesto: A Vision of Apocalyptic Humanism,*[3] had positioned black metal within a Hegelian framework. Here, classical "hyperborean" black metal represented the pinnacle of nihilistic expression, echoing Nietzsche's affirmation that "God is dead." By contrast, "transcendental" black metal sought to transcend the "haptic void" of despair and entropy by creating new musical techniques such as the life-affirming "burst-beat" to bring about a novel musical tradition of uniquely American origin–one which allows for the rays of divinity to shine brilliantly through a sonic dynamism of increasing intensity and beauty.

Liturgy, ever-evolving, incorporated symphony, opera, glitch electronics, trap, and more into their music.[4] This blending of disciplines mirrors Haela's broader pursuit: weaving together her philosophical systems, fine art, and music to achieve a form of *Gesamtkunstwerk,* the construction of a total artwork as envisioned by Wagner. Beyond this, Haela envisions a broader renaissance–a religious healing of culture and a resolution to secular humanist decay. Her vision proposes a heavenly futurist society where the void between discord and harmony is bridged, ideologies are transcended, and the disparate realms of politics, art, science, philosophy, and religion unite in a heavenly union.

In this interview, we discuss the philosophy of Transcendental Qabala and Apocalyptic Humanism, the need for a "total artwork," the satanic dimensions of accelerationism, the relationships between Marxism and Christianity, the TradCath phenomenon, the transcendental nature of The Ark, transgenderness, the cycles of counterculture, and the construction of a true vision of Heaven.
–Cori Hart

Jonah Campos (previous)

C.H.–Let's just dive right into the deep end. From what I have been able to glean, there seems to be two major philosophical projects you have been developing: Apocalyptic Humanism and Transcendental Qabala. When did you begin formulating these systems and what compelled you to take on such an ambitious project?

Haela–So, Transcendental Qabala is an ongoing syncretic system of philosophy with many interrelated concepts which span theology, axiology, metaphysics, eschatology, philosophy of history, political philosophy, philosophy of science, and aesthetics. The main intent behind it is to expand the horizons of Christianity to our current world to make sense of it. It's something like what you would see in German Idealism–a total philosophical system. Each of its thirty-six concepts correspond to a decan of the zodiac,[5] and so every year, I devote a particular ten-day period to presenting my current understanding of a concept online.

Apocalyptic Humanism, however, is more of an attitude or orientation than a true philosophy. It lacks a metaphysical foundation but is grounded in ten antinomies that mark the current limits of reason.[6] It should be understood rather as the ethical, spiritual, and social consequence of Transcendental Qabala, while still also reciprocally informing the ideas within that system. The ability for Transcendental Qabala to evolve within its own self-imposed structure is essential.

These terms first began crystallizing around 2016 when I became really interested in producing philosophy online after having been active with Liturgy for some time. I had used the term Apocalyptic Humanism in the first philosophy text I ever wrote back in 2009, which accompanied early Liturgy music. It was called *"Transcendental Black Metal: A Vision of Apocalyptic Humanism."* I think I got the term from Northrop Frye's commentary on William Blake,[7] who at the time, I had sought to emulate. Much of the vision in that early text was a premonition that foreshadowed what the system would eventually become. At that point, I was reading a lot of Nietzsche and Deleuze, and I really wanted to create this sort of life-affirming black metal that put their ideas into practice–especially involving futurist vitalism and the divinity of extremity and matter. I was also inspired by the idea of Wagnerian total artwork (Gesamtkunstwerk),[8] so I knew it had to have this philosophy component.

These ideas had formed while I was studying philosophy and fine art in a more high-culture context. However, my primary focus began shifting to music–DIY touring and those kinds of things. While doing that, and precisely because of the experience of executing those ideas, I gradually turned away from their more pagan aspects and found myself drawn closer and closer to Christianity and Rationalism between 2009 and 2016. It was after the release of Liturgy's third album, *The Ark Work*, that I began putting more effort into articulating the system.

C.H.–You mentioned the album, but *Ark Work* is also an important concept in your philosophy.[9] From what I think I understand, Ark Work is sort of a method for synthesizing various domains of human endeavor such as religion, science, politics, and art to bring about a new vision of the future. Did this come to you as a discovery while working across some of these different domains?

Haela–I think in some ways, it was a discovery, but these things are also always an invention on some level. One aspect of Ark Work involves transmitting the energy–so to speak–of the Christian church beyond an ecclesiastical context. Rather than being an actual church or cult, it harnesses contemporary cultural machinery, such as the music industry and the art world (which are churches in their own right), and pushes them beyond their self-imposed or assumed limits. The goal is to allow something new and better to blossom forth. I am very dispositionally blind to those social and institutional conventions we often take for granted. I'm more attuned to future possibilities within what we traditionally consider art.

Try to imagine a decentralized infrastructure for creation–one that taps into and hijacks existing cultural machinery without being beholden to their logic, interfacing with them as a multimodal structure operating with its own logic of development, independent from the established matrix. For instance, we can disseminate philosophical ideas through the reach created by music, bypassing traditional academic channels. Simultaneously, we can avoid dependence on the music industry by promoting music through Substack posts and video essays.[10]

But at the same time, I'm passionate about traditionalism and the eternal–ideas about asceticism and discipline that don't square with a punk or avantgarde ethos. My approach to Christianity is very orthodox; I believe in the dogmas and the sanctity of scripture. While I draw inspiration from other religions–for instance, Sufi approaches to music–I don't like the idea of perennialism or creating new religions at all. Faith always involves making a conscious decision, and my decision is Christianity.

So, there are two sides: the religious aspect and the pursuit of total art. A lot of my recent philosophical work is just an attempt to articulate precisely what this project is and how it distinguishes itself from perennialism, kitchen sink Fluxus, rock music occultism, and so on.

C.H.–Right. So, it seems that you have three major concepts that are central to Transcendental Qabala: The Ark, Metaperichoresis, and Haelegen. I get those are big concepts which will take a lot to fully unpack, but if you could just briefly discuss them and their interrelation, I think that will help us get a grip on this.

Haela–Yeah, that's a great idea! Those are great concepts to choose because they cover various dimensions. The Ark, for example, explores the potential of expanding the Body of Christ concept from Christianity into the broader, seemingly secular world. It's a matter of employing the abilities affirmed by humanism–like artistic creativity, scientific inquiry, and political acumen–as conduits for divine revelation aimed towards the kingdom of Heaven. People often associate Christianity with the repression of these abilities–which has happened and still occurs–but that is a misapplication of Christianity. We shouldn't throw the baby out with the bath water. The goal isn't to supplant religion with humanism or to adopt some brain-dead anti-humanism, but rather to incorporate the fruits of humanism into an eschatological framework that further amplifies human potential, especially in the domains of love, compassion, and self-esteem–possibly with the assistance of technology.

The critique of ideology is a key component of this, a task that's become more challenging than ever since many of its concepts from the previous generation have been co-opted to lure people into these faux-political infotainment communities. The current cultural horizon is deceptively oppressive in unbelievably nuanced ways, manipulating not just ideas but also habits and emotions. Philosophical work is needed to tackle this, which I discuss in the concept of The Armistice. The idea of Sacred Labor synthesizes ideas of the Christian faith with psychoanalysis, proposing a new creative process which evades capture by the Armistice.[11]

C.H.—Let's stay on The Ark. I'm just trying to get my head around this... it sounds like The Ark isn't necessarily a material object, but rather like a thought form or an egregore existing in an un-manifest state, or perhaps it's akin to a Platonic form, having a sort of pre-ontological nature. It also seems to posses a teleological quality in that we are guided by it, or at least once orientated towards it, there's a magnetism that pulls humanity and history in its direction. Am I on track with any of that at all?

Haela—Yeah, absolutely! So, the hope is that The Ark *isn't* an egregore, as Christianity cautions against creating those. But yes, it's pre-ontological, possessing a flickering quality where it seems to both exist and to not exist. This alteration between presence and absence acts as a lure, beckoning creative work in its name because of its indiscernibility. You know, a lot of French psychoanalysis is good at describing this logic, albeit abstractly. Lacan calls it "insistence."[12]

But yeah, I'm very interested in embracing Christianity over Gnosticism or Paganism. The idea of crafting a hyperstition or an egregore as a creative force that influences the universe through cultural mimesis is tantamount to black magick, which is evil. Ideally, The Ark should emanate from God. I imagine that as the generations progress, what exactly The Ark *is* becomes clearer specifically due to the work being carried out in its name. But it must originate from God, with its only purpose being to connect people to their innate compassion and creative potential.

C.H.—Hmm. I know we should move on to the other two concepts, but I have what I suppose is a somewhat critical observation of your work: I noticed that while your philosophy is very much couched in Christianity, you rarely seem to touch on the idea of Satan, or the "Adversary." So my question is, if we have The Ark, an object from God which pulls man towards Him, would there not also be the possibility of an Anti-Ark, a false object or adversary which pulls us away from the fulfillment of Heaven?

Haela—Hm, yeah. Well, there might not be just one adversary; I see two primary ones. First, there's ordinary secular humanism, which just aims to maintain the current cultural status quo, hindering the expansion of intelligibility and preserving outdated power structures by libidinally boxing people into matrix-like controversies that have no effect on the world. But the second is accelerationism, which is also a deception because, while it presents a lot of ideas similar to what I'm saying, it discourages the blossoming of the human spirit and endorses coldness instead, making it an Anti-Ark.

What accelerationism does is co-opts

Haela Hunt-Hendrix (opposite)

II — METAPHYSICS

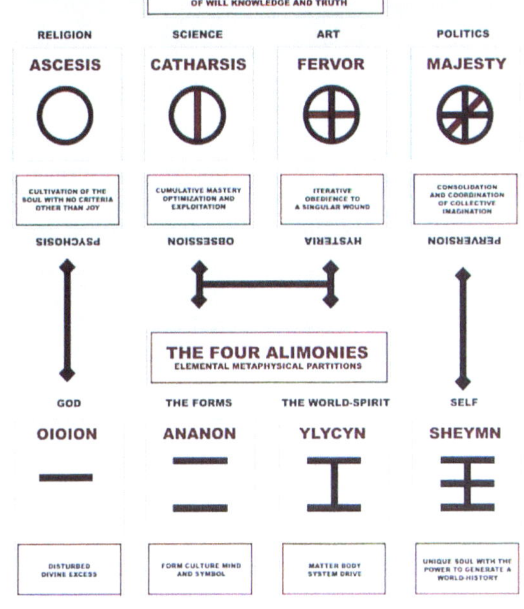

revolutionary ideas, making reactionary gesturing feel fashionable, but in truth, it's just consolidating more power. Unfortunately, many poets, artists, and writers who lack the cognitive ability to reason syllogistically–and also lack a knowledge of world history and the history of philosophy–end up being preyed on and tricked into supporting these people. My main interest in having any relationship with dissident right communities is to demonstrate that there's another way to reject the overtly oppressive mainstream horizon without falling into the sphere of the more shadowy one.

C.H–It's interesting because, in the *Transcendental Black Metal Manifesto*, you situate black metal within a sort of theory of history, designating it as the musical apex of nihilism and the "death of God." Similarly, I view Nick Land and many different branches of accelerationism as the philosophical and political apex of nihilism. They adopt this incredibly fatalistic stance, dismissing the human subject and embracing submission to AI, a complete surrender to demiurgic forces.

Haela–Absolutely! The term *demiurgic* is apt because accelerationism–and Nick Land's work in particular–leans into what is essentially Gnosticism.[13]Though it may not be overtly stated, it can be translated into the revival of an ancient heresy which Christianity had denounced and triumphed over thousands of years ago; it's just rearing its ugly head again with modern terminology. This resurgence is why I advocate for orthodoxy. From a Christian standpoint, there are other forms of spirituality out in the world that are heresies. Continental philosophers like to give currency to styling oneself as heretical; they have this attitude of "this is so fun, people think we are these wild heretics," but in my view, no, those are just actual heresies.

The idea of the Demiurge is that there's this evil divine spirit which created and governs the world, and that therefore the world is evil, and we must escape from it or destroy it, or whatever, and that the way to do it is to basically just become a creepy gooner with secret knowledge. I would hope it's possible to conceive of a really radical post-humanist futurism that embraces technology's annihilation of certain social (and even biological) horizons convention considers better left alone, but to have it be in commune with the true Christian God, fostering things like egalitarian flourishing, ever more sensitivity to individual uniqueness, and true maturity.

Even though the context is very different between now, in this era of AI, and the world of 300AD, the spiritual choices still remain fundamentally unchanged. There's this kind of Hegelian Paganism and a kind of Landian Gnosticism, and then the Christian option. I'm looking to connect the dots for people to show them that the Christian option is the only desirable one, and that it's also perfectly realistic once the various veils of ideology are pierced.

C.H.–This might be a slight detour, but I'm curious about your feelings on the TradCath movement–all these young, reactionary, chronically online people returning to conservative religious values and aesthetics.[14] We also have the Angelicism trend that's happening within Theorygram and New Net Art circles,[15] which basically appropriates Christian and angelic imagery for aesthetic purposes.

While both can seem somewhat superficial, I can't help but feel sympathy for the reactionary impulse to reject the more soul-destroying and degenerate elements of modernity. It feels to me like an honest reaction to the same sort of nihilistic secularism you've been reacting to with Liturgy, albeit with less sophistication.

Haela–I guess to summarize, here's the way I see it: In recent years, some of the most interesting culture has either been in the TradCath direction or, conversely, in the nihilist futurist vein we discussed. The people on these two ends often get along together in this sort of absurd way that seems to make no sense. They seem like opposites, but what they share is a critical attitude towards the dominant horizon of modernity (and they're also just all friends). However, both groups also seem to oppose civil rights, which I don't think is a great thing. That opposition is only possible if you're failing to understand that the world is real, how it works, and how human affordances depend on the contingencies of state power.

But resolving the glaring contradiction of this sphere is exactly the path to the correct vision for the future. It requires having the traditionalist element in the Christianity, and blending it with a futurist, techno-optimistic outlook–and I'd consider myself a techno-optimist, basically. This is a combination yielding the best of both worlds: something good and, most importantly, something filled with love. I just feel there's a lack of love in both of those trajectories currently, and we all know that love is essential; being human is all about love. Christianity should be a path towards that, and technology should be a path towards that. So yeah, it seems like there's a sort of space opened by those trajectories that will allow a combination that transcends both.

C.H.–**I feel like there's still a line of dialogue that can't be opened up yet until we get to the other two major concepts fundamental to Transcendental Qabala: Metaperichoresis and Haelegen.[16] Could you speak on those two concepts?**

Haela–Yeah, I'm not too sure where to start. I've been enjoying flipping coins recently.

Haela flips a coin.

Haela–Okay, so I'll do Haelegen first. Haelegen is the name I give to Heaven. The thought here is that the kingdom of Heaven is something that can realistically be created on earth; it's something that civilization can achieve. To do so, there are two aspects to consider: first, we must not take any limitations for granted; we need to excavate or uncover the ideals inherent in the civilization of Heaven, which we can find in Abrahamic theology. Second, we must identify the concrete affordances available to construct this ideal civilization and determine how we can appropriate them.

Specifically, if we are exiting modernity and entering something new, what are our new axioms? Currently, we have freedom, equality, and fraternity as the ideals of modern humanism. For Heaven (or Haelegen), the ideals I've outlined are: sovereignty, hierarchy, emancipation, and individuation. No matter how much the fabric of society or reality changes, these would be the moral absolutes for that era. Maybe we could talk more about what exactly those mean at length, but those are their names, and they're derived

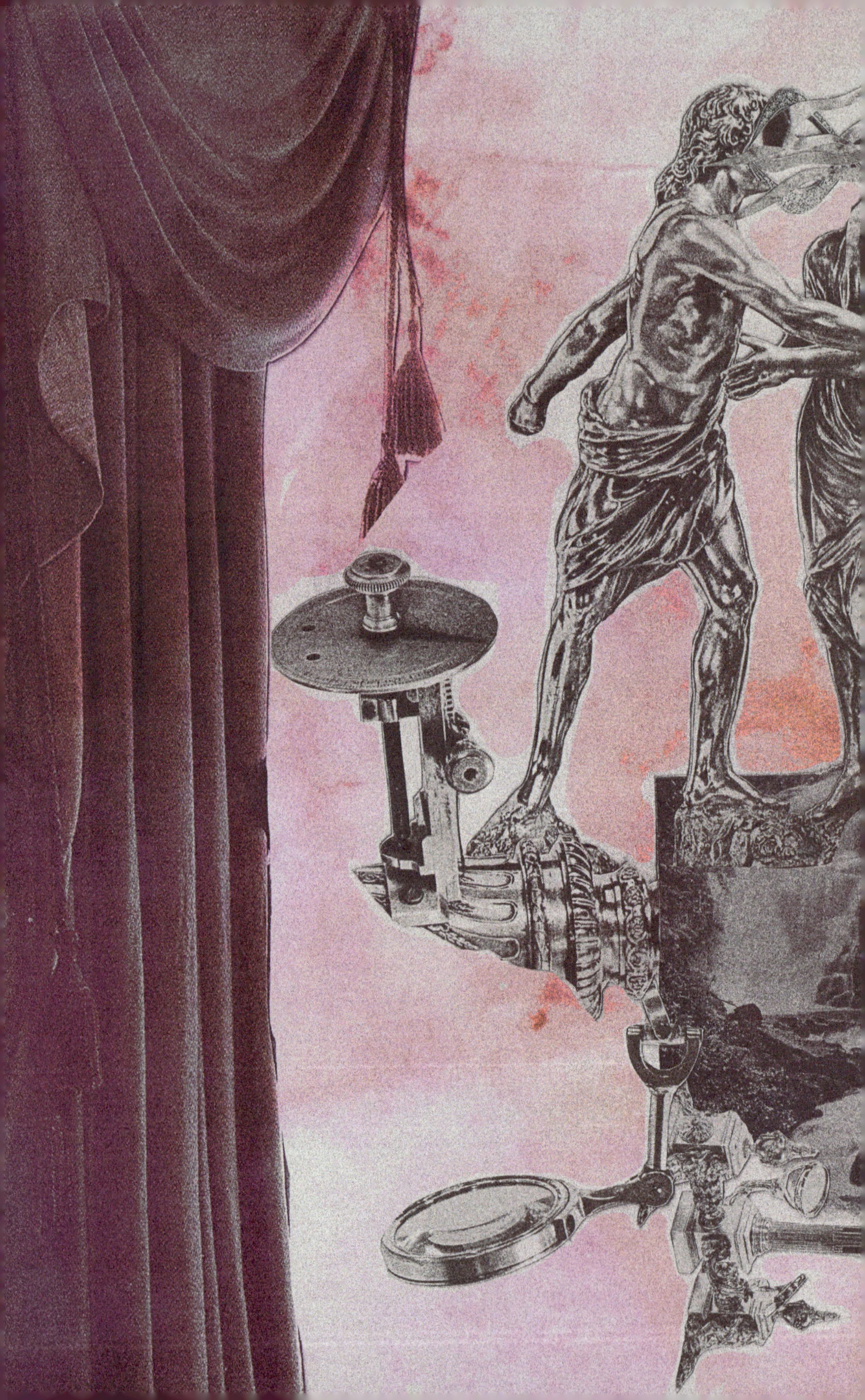

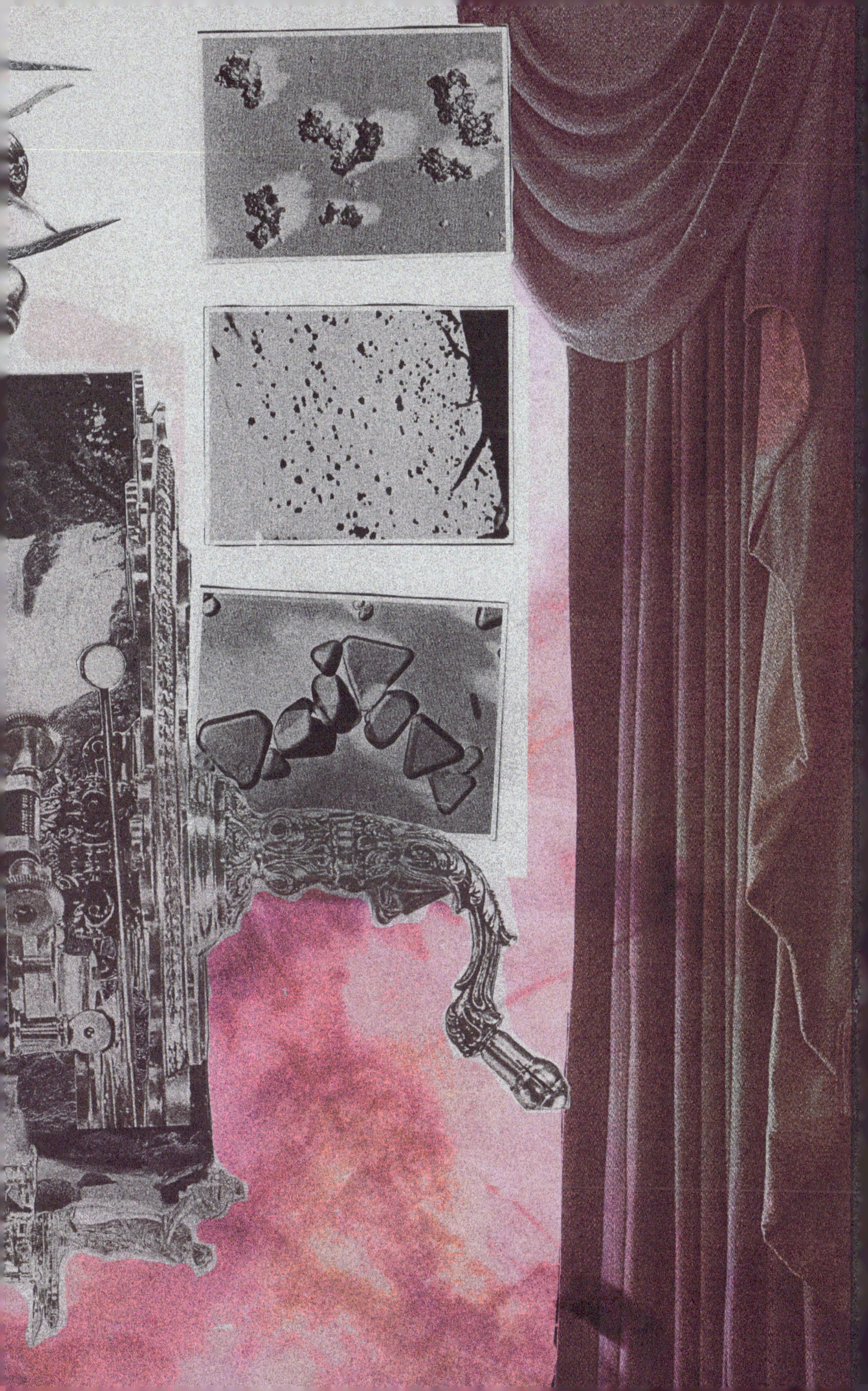

from theology and psychoanalysis. Essentially, they are meant to inspire increased creativity, compassion, and heightened subjectivity. Guided by these ideals, civilization should increasingly break free from the constraints of matter, better assess and coordinate the needs and abilities of its citizens, adaptively revise its legal structure to account for new subjectivities, and, crowning it all, foster the infinite unearthing of talents and the sharing of reciprocally inspiring works amongst us.

As for how to achieve this Heaven, I remain somewhat agnostic. From an Abrahamic theological perspective, we can imagine a purely Messianic scenario where Christ simply returns and transforms the world into Heaven. On the other hand, techno-optimists envision constructing an AGI (artificial general intelligence) that will design a heavenly world for us. I don't really trust the latter option. I don't know precisely how it's supposed to unfold, but I hope to be generating a cultural field that makes the most of technological change, which is underway whether we like it or not.

Now, let's discuss Metaperichoresis. It's a proposal for a way to transition from our current world to Heaven using total art. Perichoresis is a technical term in Christianity, not widely known, referring to the life of the Trinity; with God, Christ, and the Holy Spirit, their mutual interpenetrating love of one another causes them to sort of circulate. So, the life of the living God is perichoresis. In Orthodox Christianity, it's affirmed that there's another kind of life of the Trinity that takes place in the world—one that we have access to and can participate in; sometimes called the economic Trinity, or God's energies.[17] In Orthodox Lent, at the time we are having this conversation, the theologian associated with this idea is Saint Gregory Palamas, and his Sunday in Lent was just yesterday.

Anyway, to get to the point—with Metaperichoresis, I map the three persons of the Trinity onto music, art, and philosophy. I propose that we can create music, art, and philosophy because these three activities mirror the three persons of God, and perhaps there's a way to merge these three realms continuously, eventually generating a heavenly world. Their braided histories will ultimately yield God's body. This thesis represents what is my single most unique thought: music is God, philosophy is Christ, and art is the Holy Spirit. My art, music, and philosophy aim to correlate them, encompassing the histories of each discipline, and making God come alive. But the theory is detachable from the rest of my work. My way of doing it is my own, and we are all different. So, the idea is that, on a higher level, anybody could create Metaperichoresis; I'm just doing it in my own way.

C.H.—So, Metaperichoresis is a praxis that combines different domains of creativity to bring about Haelegen—Heaven on earth. When I look at the ways in which you interrelate your work with fine art, film, music, and philosophy, I don't really know if I can think of anyone else performing Metaperichoresis along those lines.

Do you feel like there might be unexplored opportunities to inspire others to engage in this total artwork, perhaps through the creation of new collective projects or institutions that could generate think-tanks and workshops, maybe funding and promoting creatives and thinkers working along these lines? Do you have any ambitions in that direction?

Haela–Yeah, I've thought a lot about it. I would love this to be more widespread. It would make sense for it to be a sort of institution, or a kind of religion–some sort of structure that could get more people involved. I could probably be doing a better job at turning it all into something that extends beyond my own practice. But now, I'm very accustomed to this all seeming completely insane.

We both laugh

Back in 2016 or whenever, people did think it was totally crazy. But these days, I think there is more similarity between what I am doing and things I'm seeing other people I kind of know doing. So, I guess I imagine that the world will be tending in this direction more and more, and it will just be a matter of articulating how my vision is different from other competing ones. But yes, that more structural aspect of it is still very much a work in progress, and I'm not great at that kind of thing.

That being said, there's something important about the marginal–truly staying on the outside. I think it was in a podcast with Justin Murphy that Nick Land said something like, "The thing is, once anything starts to grow, it becomes capital."[18] That phrase has resonated in my mind for years. He meant it as a defense of anarcho-capitalism against idealism, but to me, the point is the Christian one made by Michel Henry: true Christianity must stay outside of the world, intrinsically. My choice to know a lot of Dimes Square people but not participate in it is partly inspired by his choice to not live in Paris but engage the post-structuralism scene from a slight distance where he could preserve his heart.

C.H.–Right. Well, I wanted to ask you about contradictions. They appear to proliferate your work–in art, music, and philosophy–and there seems to be an intentional synthesis of them. For instance, by making black metal something affirmational with Liturgy to the point where it seems to share more in common with the essence of Beethoven than Burzum. Not to mention weaving in everything from IDM and trap rap to opera. Even in your own beliefs and values, you blend the extremely orthodox and dogmatic tenets of religion with Marxism and other highly progressivist politics.

Are you consciously attempting to blend these contradictory elements within yourself and your work? Is that something vital to Metaperichoresis?

Haela–The way I see it, those contradictions are there to be exploited. They are only contradictions in the Hegelian since of determinant negation or something. In the past, critics have accused me of randomly combining elements in my work, but I don't view the contradictions in my work as random at all. Instead, they're like little knots waiting to be untied. By doing so, we can open a wider cultural field that is vital and beneficial to everyone. Consider the relationship between black metal and real 19th century classical music–it's genuinely there to be exploited. These things appear contradictory on the surface, but deep down, there's real material to try and integrate. Another example of this, which is becoming more widespread, is the intersection of Marxism and religion. Marxism and Christianity really go together. To assume that Marxism is inherently anti-Christian or that Christianity is anti-Marxist fails to fully respect either of those tendencies.[19]

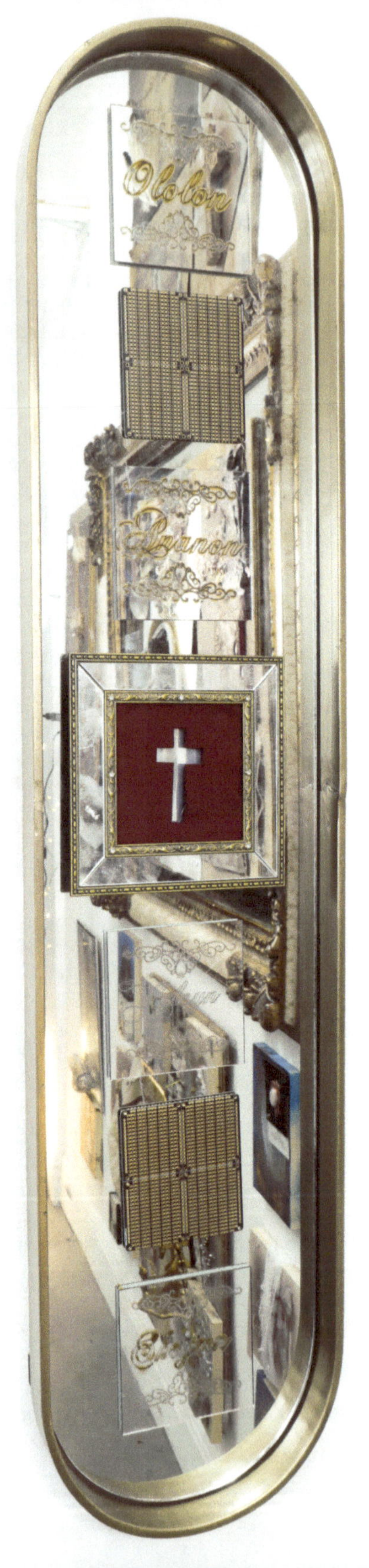
Ololón
Pranam

C.H.–That sheds light on some of the vitriol you faced when Liturgy was first exploding. This time we live in can feel very fragmented, dualistic, and black-and-white. People can get confused and angry when they're confronted with things that don't fit neatly into prepackaged boxes. Do you think this lack of appreciation for synthesis contributed to the fury directed at you? Also, what was it like to endure such intense hatred during that time? I can't imagine it was easy to ignore, even when logged off.

Haela–Yeah, it was not fun. I'm not totally sure why it was, and I don't feel like it's totally over either. Liturgy remains controversial. This is bleeding-edge stuff even now, a decade or more after my initial emergence.[20] I mean, I've always been interested in the future, and you could say that I was expressing ideas that just didn't make sense to people at the time. But that's not quite the whole story; the last decade felt like quite an anti-intellectual era, and perhaps there were earlier cultural periods where Liturgy would have been more welcome. The 2010s were a very weird time; there appeared to be a lot more freedom, yet the internet's strong dominance over counter-culture spaces paradoxically made them a lot more closed-minded than maybe even the '90s. Maybe it's not entirely linear. Gender stuff might have played a role too. Maybe there are other reasons that I'm not aware of. Funny how things unfold.

C.H.–Speaking of gender, when you initially came out, my mind instantly drew parallels to Genesis P. Orridge. I suppose I've always noticed a lot of similarities between you two. Both of you were radical countercultural fig-

Haela Hunt-Hendrix (opposite)

ures who interwove extreme music, art, film, philosophy, and spiritual practice to dissolve the boundaries between them.[21] Now, I don't pretend to fully understand anyone's subjective experience with gender, but it did seem that with Genesis, their gender identity and transition was, in some ways, tethered to the spiritual work and the art they were engaged in.

Have you ever felt any affinity for Genesis?

Haela–I share a kind of love-hate thing with Genesis. I do feel they were a little bit evil, or like, literally extremely evil–like maybe they could have killed people or something.

We both laugh.

Haela–But I also don't really love any music they made.

C.H.–Really? That's surprising.

Haela–I mean, I've listened to a lot of it, and I certainly love the concept of it, but it's not as musical as the music that I especially love. However, in terms of them creating a religious movement within an avant-garde context–existing in a space in-between DIY punk and the art world–while also infusing it with a spiritual message, the way they achieved that during that time was amazing. Spiritual ideas of any kind were totally anathema during the punk era. Although, in some ways, it seems like having a genuine counterculture was easier back then.

The 2010s brought a shift, partially because of music journalists posting interviews to ad-driven cultural organs at a way more finger-on-the-pulse, out-there level, and partly because the micro-niche internet landscape created an awkward phase before social media fully matured, where everything was online but heavily mediated by journalists. Even without realizing it, music journalists serve more conservative ideologies in a way, that and they're wordsmiths, so they want to be the smart one, but don't know anything about theory or classical music, so they feel threatened by references going over their heads. It was very hard to be off the grid in the 2010s in a way that was easier before and is easier now. Well, nowadays, there's practically no grid.

Anyway, my criticism of Genesis is that there was too much evil energy in their work–too much sex magick and not enough love. It seems like there was a lot of abuse in that whole situation. However, it's clear they were a genius too, similar to Lacan. I've been a big follower of Lacanian psychoanalysis, and Lacan holds a very similar fascination for me–it seems like he was pretty evil and abusive in a lot of ways, but there's still a lot of genius that he produced. But as far as gender, I don't know that Genesis's gender issues have anything to do with my gender stuff particularly.

C.H.–You can just speak for yourself then. I think the question I was trying to get at was if you look at your gender identity and the path that took you to transition as having any correspondence to the philosophical work and the art you've been doing. Are they intertwined in any way?

Haela–There must be some connection, although I'm not particularly interested in gender. (I mean, I'm glad that being trans is more accepted now compared to about a decade ago). I guess to the extent that femininity is linked to love or a cer-

tain type of softness, there's certainly an underlying feminineness that's charged everything I create–a quality that I know once bothered the metalheads who encountered my music. But what precisely defines femininity? What defines things like love and softness? It's not that I want to divorce my gender from my art; I'm not saying it's just a coincidence that I happen to be a trans woman and it has nothing to do with my art. I think there is a resonance between trans-anything and a kind of emancipatory futurism, so there is some connection there, sure. And then introducing the subjective feminine experience into metal, where it has traditionally been either totally ignored or objectified, surely carries significance.

C.H.–Speaking of an emancipatory futurism, I've noticed that you tend to reference and utilize Marx quite frequently. What is the relationship between your Haelegenic vision and Marxism?

Haela–As far as I know, Marx was the first person to combine a vision of a kind of Heaven (Communism is a kind of heavenly vision of society) with a theory of history following Hegelian lines. In this framework, there are horizons of intelligibility, or horizons of culture and technology, which cascade from one to the next. An earlier horizon cannot fully conceive of the next one, but it gives birth to it through contradictions immanent within it. Those who care about this process are tasked with identifying these contradictions and, by devoting attention to them, help to propel us from one age to the next. Alister Crowley also embodied some of this,[22] although it might sound like a crazy comparison to make.

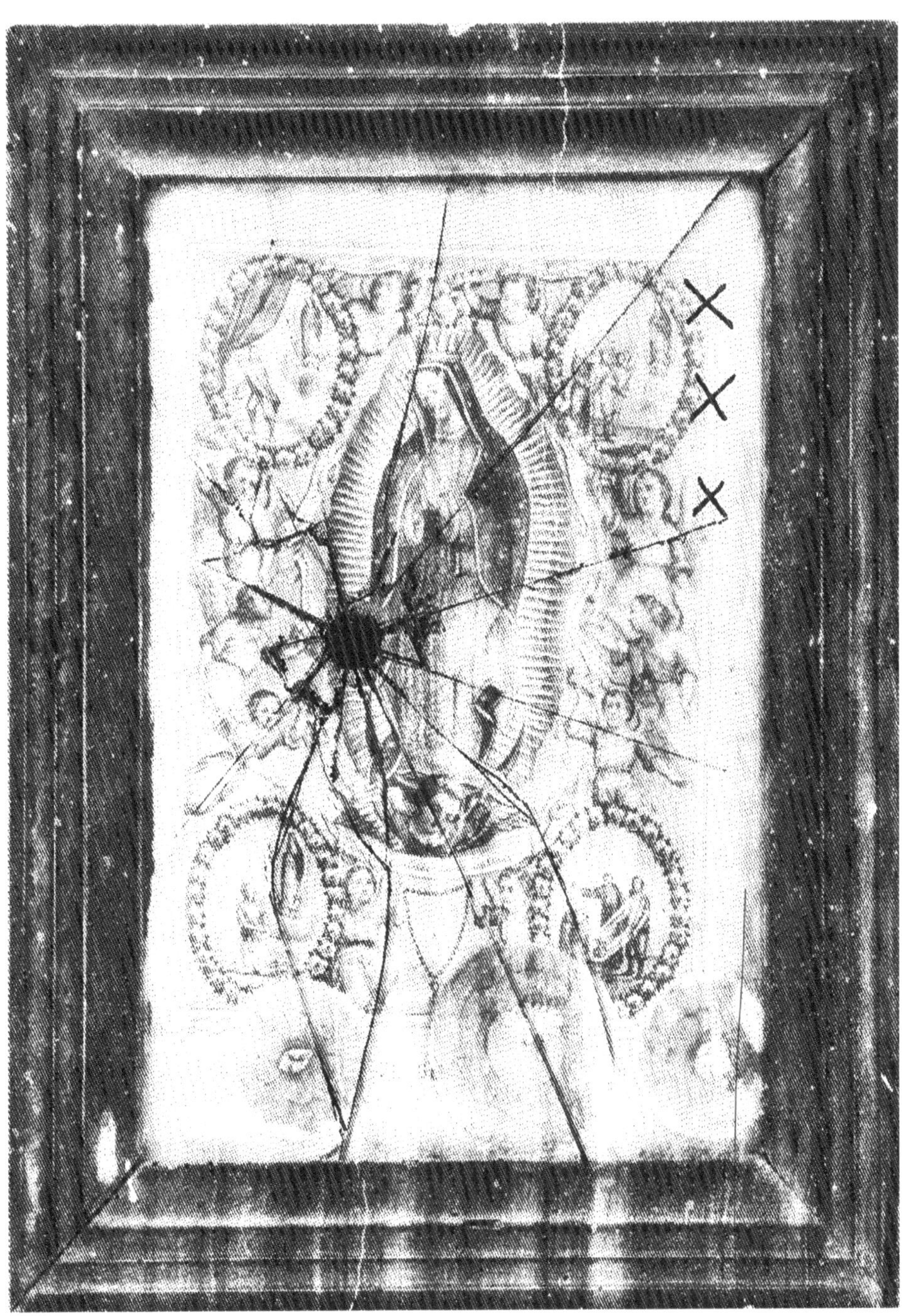

Jonah Campos

C.H.–No, that makes sense.

Haela–But then, on top of that, and what Crowley fails to provide, an explicit critique of contemporary ideology should always be a part of it. You're trying to make sense of the world, describe what the contradictions are, and then put all that together to arrive at a world characterized by justice. Probably one where a market is no longer needed–a planned economy where people can pursue the realization of their dreams, where those dreams become the fabric of their reality, effectively becoming the economy itself. If there's a market, it's one that is made of love. This concept is explored in Klossowski's *"Living Currency."*[23]

While I believe you can find elements of this vision in Marx, it's certainly not the most common interpretation of his work. There are many interpretations of Marx, and what I'm describing is somewhat closer to the vulgar Marxism of Russian Communism than the more France-mediated Althusserian forms. Perhaps it's a synthesis of those perspectives. Regardless, Marx was undoubtedly a kind of prophet. His work was internally contradictory, lacking the super-coherent system found in the works of Aquinas or Hegel, but he channeled a lot of powerful ideas.

C.H.–A common critique of Marx and his dream of a Communist Utopia, as we get in Dostoyevsky's writings, is that Communism is just antithetical to human nature. The argument that humans will always strive for more individual success and material gain than what a planned economy offers. With regards to this Haelegenic vision, what do you believe are the political and spiritual preconditions necessary for humanity to acquire before reaching a place where a planned economy is both desirable and possible?

Haela–Two things: religion and technology. The technology must truly be there. I don't particularly endorse versions of Marxism that don't want to let Capitalism finish the job of achieving abundant energy–finding a way to eliminate scarcity. We need a post-scarcity, post-work context, but it must unfold in a manner to where it preserves the human spirit and freedom. First and foremost, it should benefit everyone, avoiding any totalitarian regime. People have an odd way of forgetting that Lenin (etc.) desired the latter outcome. Additionally, the work being undertaken–whether it be in art, science, or other pursuits–must be spiritually nourishing. Individuals should be realizing their potential, experiencing joy, and sharing the fruits of their labor.

But the thing is, there is so much danger in technology too! There are people who say things that are similar to this whom I don't like at all; there's a version of this that's very cringe and not sensitive to aesthetics or history, and they just want to make tech-worshipping cults.

C.H.–We would really need to thread the technological needle.

Haela–Exactly. But that's not a reason to deny the importance of technology.

C.H.–Right. Well, if it's okay with you, I'll leave you with one last extremely difficult question.

Haela–Sounds good.

C.H.–So you are, in many ways, a true futurist whose work reflects ideals set far beyond our current horizons.

So, my final question is: where are we headed next? What might the next cultural horizon look like? I suppose there's probably multiple possibilities.

Haela—Yeah, I think there are multiple possibilities. That's the first part of the answer. I view the continued, very rapid development of technology as inevitable, it won't be stopped. I believe it will transform the world in ways that, even though everyone is expecting them now, will still be utterly surprising. But just because something is inevitable doesn't mean it's good. Probabilistically, I the most likely outcome for civilization is unfortunate; but strictly speaking, it doesn't make sense to think probabilistically about the future. Given everything happening with technology, there's at least a possibility of having certain communities where technology is harnessed through things like virtual spaces and cryptocurrencies to help realize the potential of human nature and the human condition.

So, the short answer is that the age of Haelegen, were it to manifest, would happen quite soon. This is not merely an abstract ideal anymore due to how fast things are changing. My hope is that we actually can have a post-human world—one that is even more than human—and one that is ultimately ruled by Christ, reigning forever.

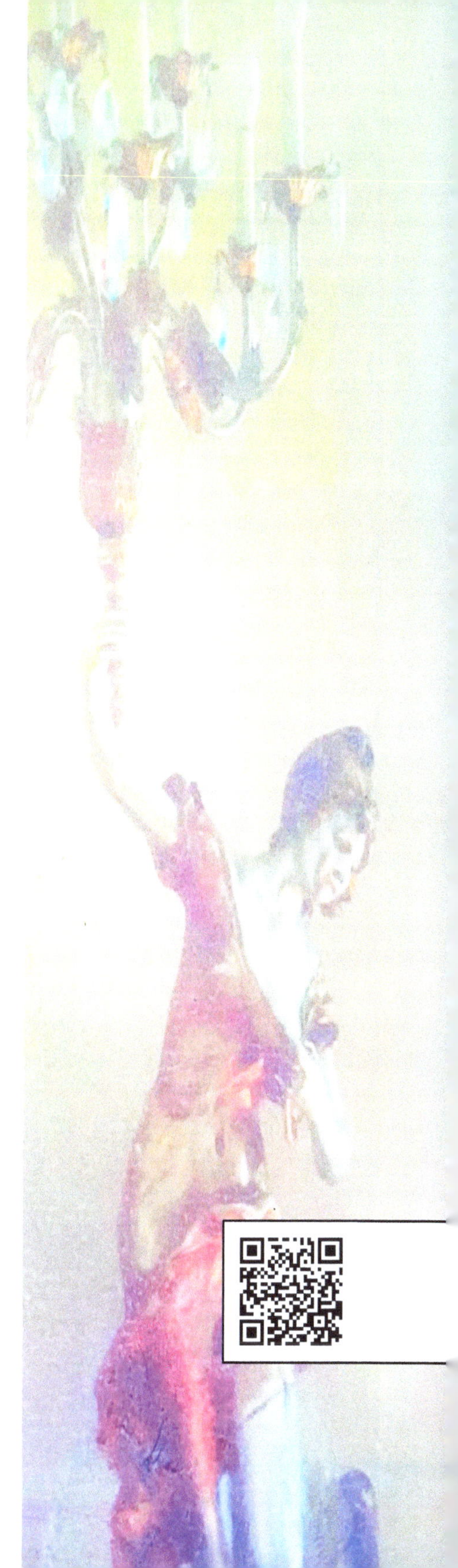

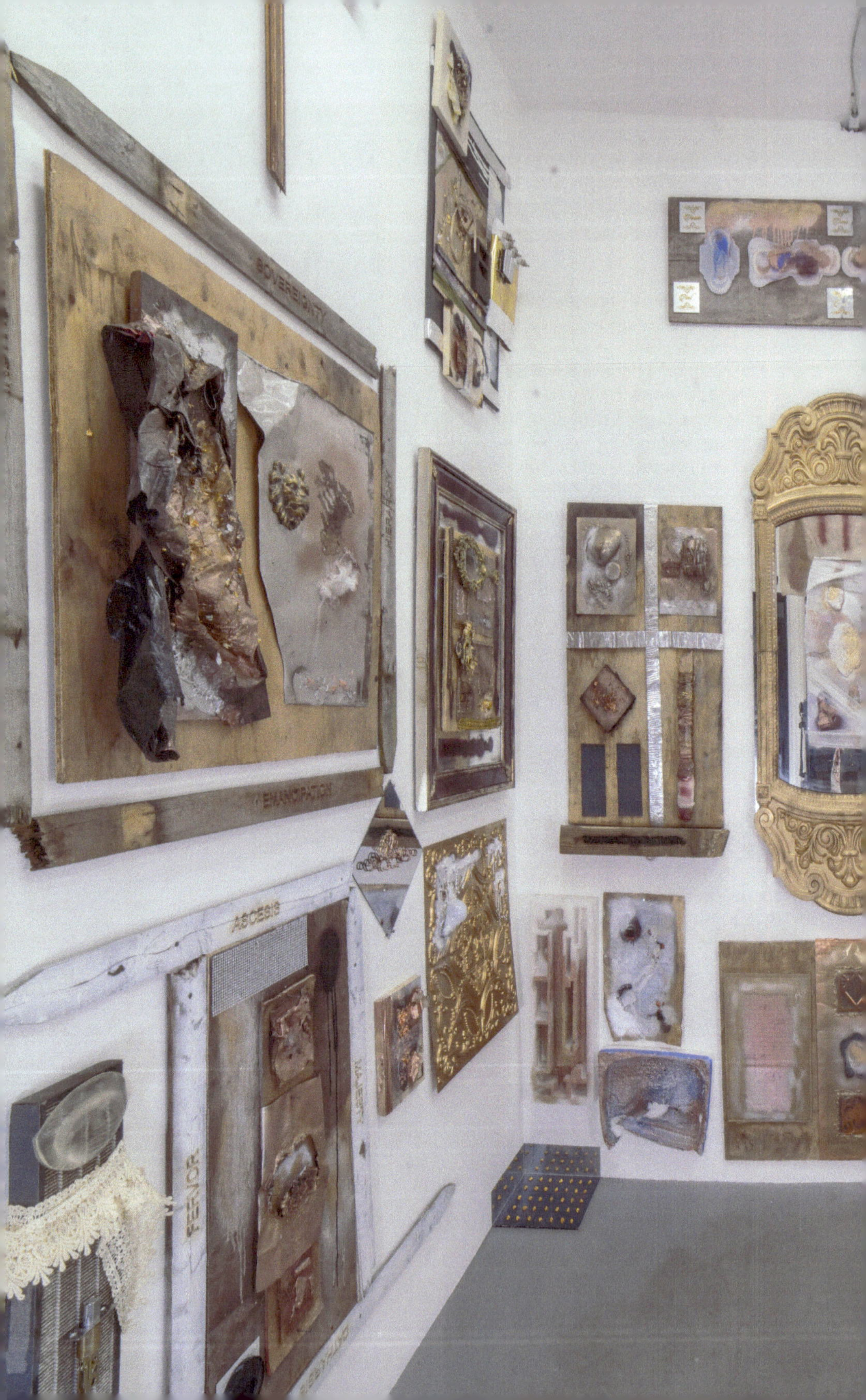

SOVEREIGNTY
EMANCIPATION
ASCESIS
FERVOR
MAJESTY

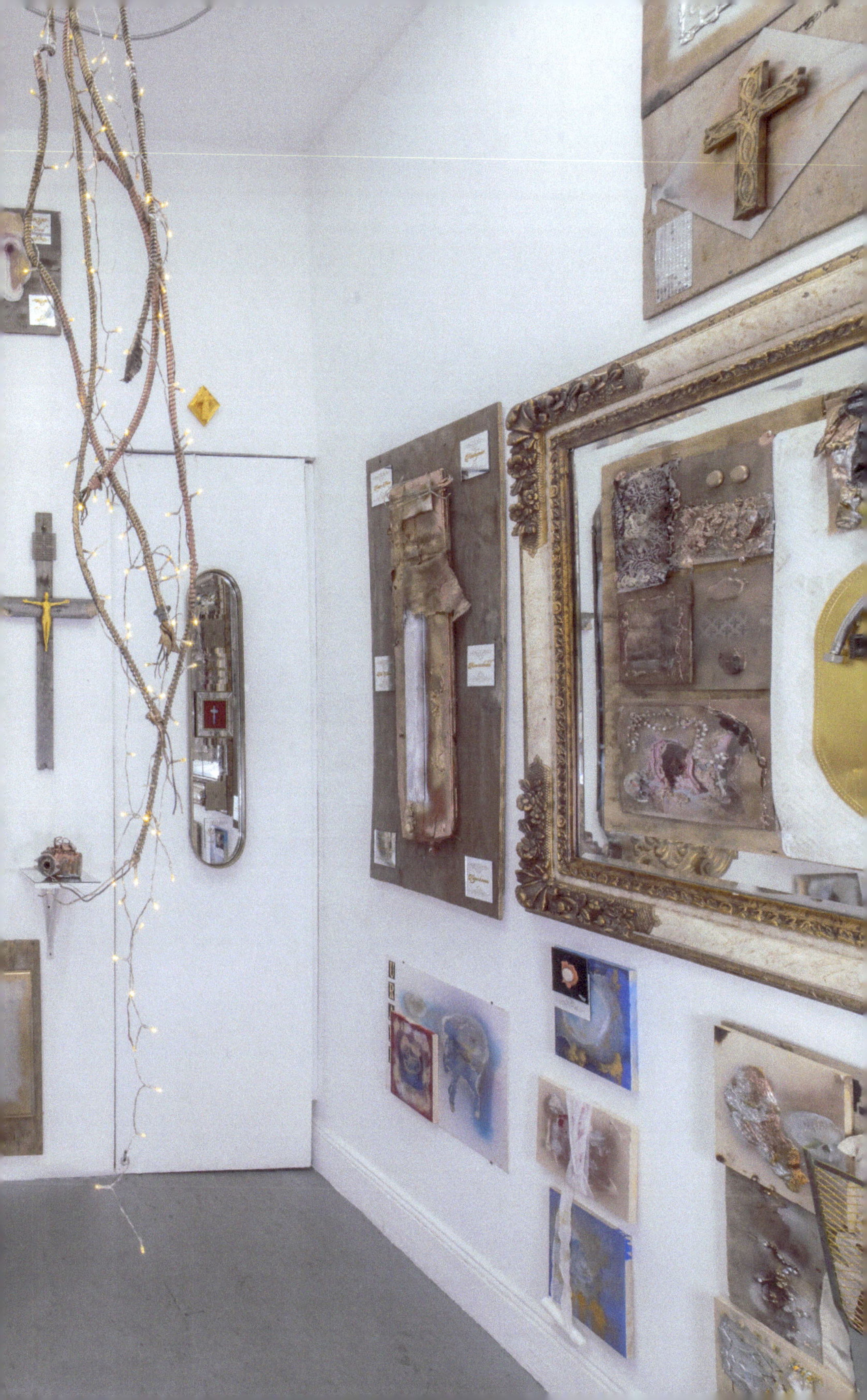

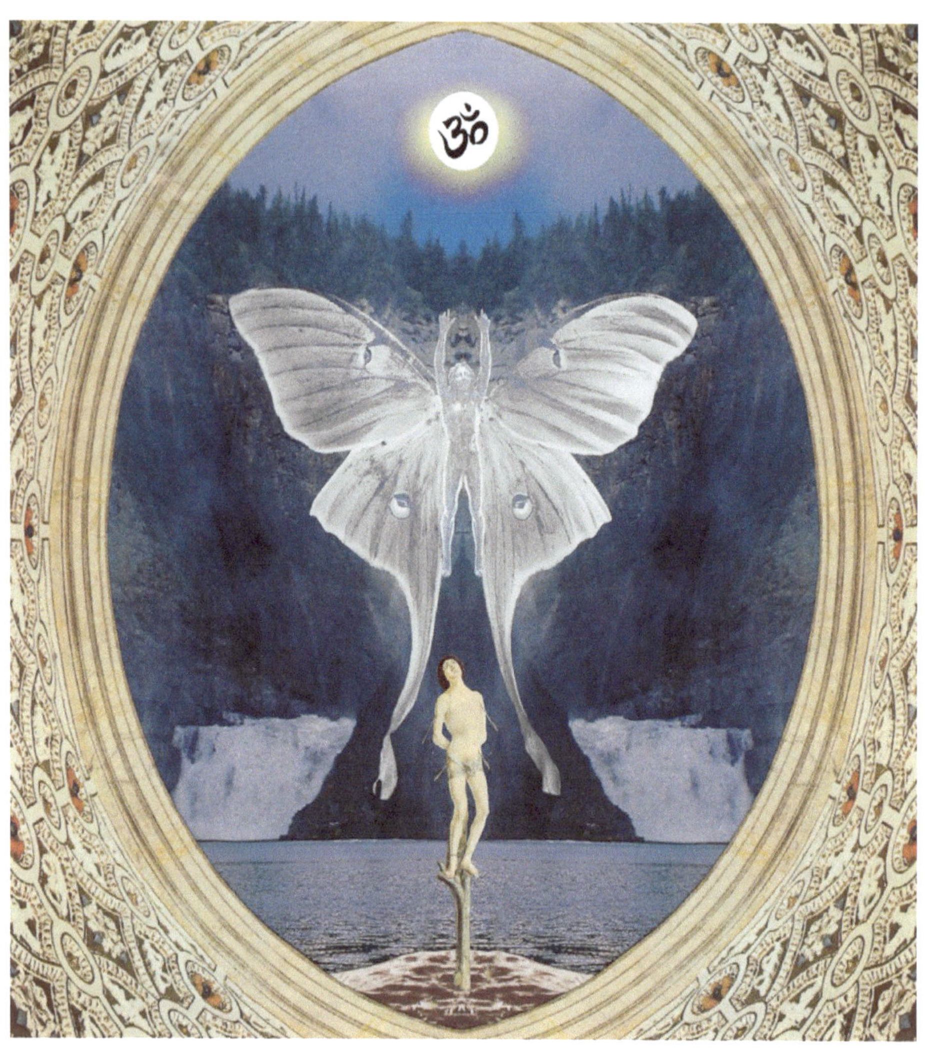

Ed Capos
Haela Hunt-Hendrix (previous)

Spirit Level

BY LORRAINE SCHEIN

flinging the shifting time crystals into malleable dusk
I open the dream portal to the oneirosphere
enter the silver light sector though the blurred void
white hole spewing schizoid intensity.

invisible, the beings existent on this plane–
quark-entities, thought-forms, quantum thread-ghosts
(evident only through tenth-dimensional psi)
possibility-witches, dark matteroids,
brane-bugs who stir and vibrate as I pass.

They thought-say to me,
"What is coming into being must be,
but lacks remotest viewers to see."

Though eyeless, they know
where matter likes to hide
how time, coiled in my childhood
a chrono-dragon awaiting flight
unfurls at sunlight's unseen last ray,
soars into the instaton of my death.

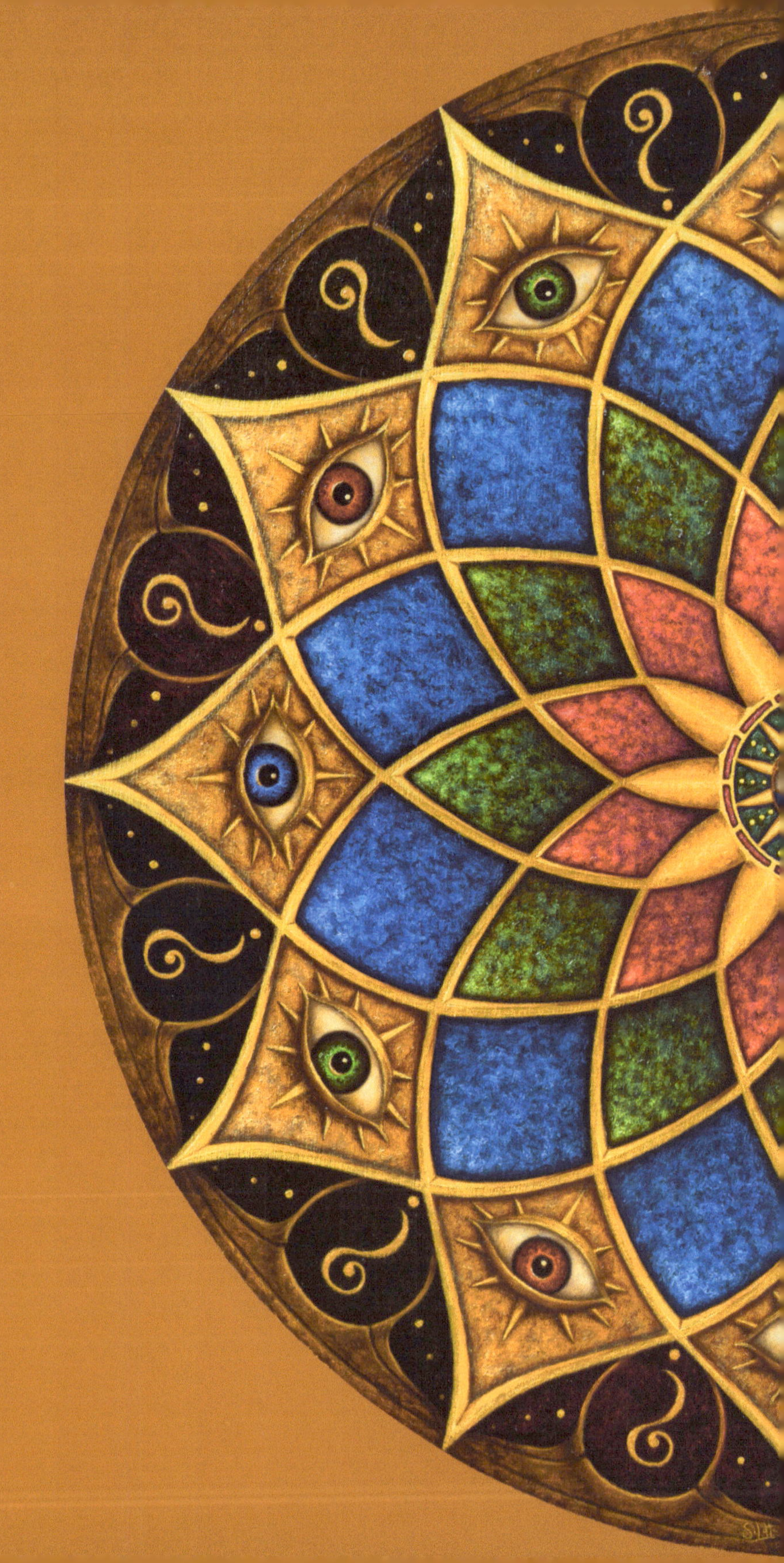

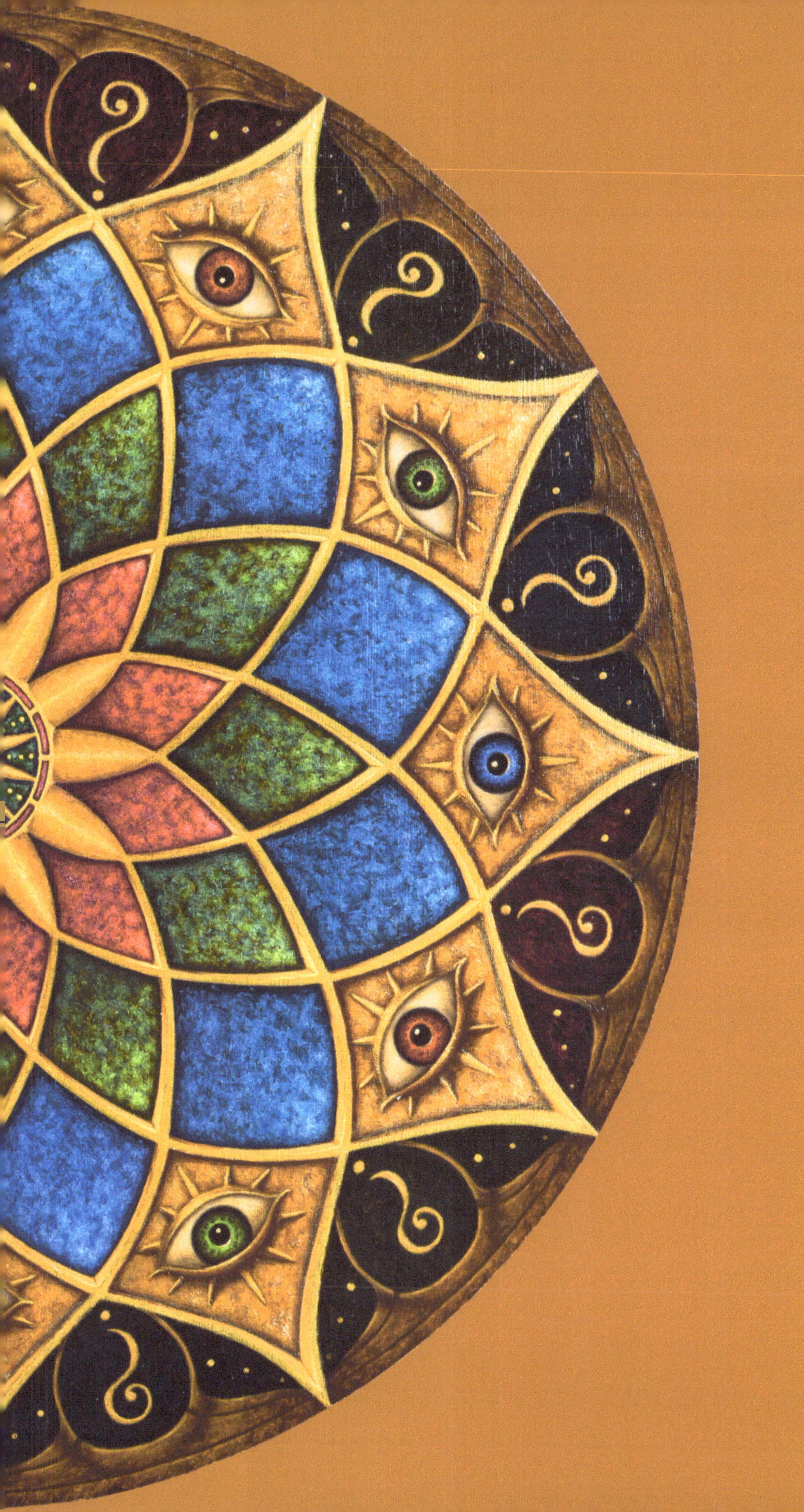

Editors:
Cori Hart
Cliff Hensley

Design/Layout:
Cori Hart

Illustrator
Caleb Butcher

Cover Art:
Ed Capos

Contributing Artists:
John T Allen
Laura Benson
Caleb Butcher
Jonah Campos
Ed Capos
Davor Gromilović
Haela Hunt-Hendrix
Cam Jennings
Steve Latta
Sven Loven
Jake Robertson
Emma Stern
Paul van Trigt
Amanda Yskamp

Contributing Writers:
Cori Hart
C.N. Jaimes
Francis K.
Henry Luzzatto
Catherine McGuire
Christopher Michael
Matthew Pettefer
Kristen Phillips
Lorraine Schein
Sasha Serge
Anna K. Winters

Interviews:
Jasun Horsley
Georgina Rose (Da'at Darling)
Haela Hunt-Hendrix (Liturgy)

Conceptualized by:
Cori Hart

Steve Latta (previous)

Artist & Poet Biographies:

John T Allen:
Based in the Washington, D.C. area with a background in Sacred Space/Cultural Studies in Architecture and Sustainable Design, John T Allen focuses on questions of temporality as explored through a body of work spanning over fifteen years in a wide range of mediums from mixed media to collage, digital art, photography, and music with a specific focus on prehistory, the built environment, and the natural world. Permian Designs is the visual arm of this ethos while its offshoot, A Virtual Memory (which John has been operating under the pseudonym "S. Taillifer" since 2017), explores these notions through sound in the form of a continuous, ever-evolving musical narrative. Website:permiandesigns.com, Ig:@permiandesigns

Laura Benson:
Laura Bensons work entangles the contrastingly mystifying and grounding allure of the natural world with the constant uncovering of a personal mythos. This process involves piecing together an internal landscape of sacred storytelling and the influence of her natural surroundings through often surreal and unsettling imagery using methods such as Gelli-plate printing, metal-work, collage, amongst others. Webite:laurabenson.com, Ig:@laurarbenson

Caleb Butcher:
Caleb Butcher is a visual artist born and based in Colorado. Working in collage / mixed media and sculpture, he's been making art for about ten years after getting his start making flyers for a DIY venue he helped run. He is most interested in art and culture from the outsiders perspective and how that shifts over time. Ig:@btchrd_

Jonah Campos:
Jonah Campos is a California based comedian and visual artist working primarily in collage/ mixed media. Ig:@pabstblueweenie

Ed Capos:
Ed Capos is a collage artist, hermit, and student of Christian Theosophy. Ig:@edcapos

Davor Gromilović:
Davor Gromilović, born in 1985 in Yugoslavia and currently residing in Sombor, Serbia, fo-

cuses on contemporary drawing and painting while also exploring art forms like books, sculpture, and clothing design. Inspired by fairy tales, pop surrealism, and Renaissance art, his symbolic work appears in collections such as the Solo Collection Museum Madrid and Luziah Hennessy collection. Gromilović has published solo books: *Bestiary*, *Wrong Time Wrong Place*, and *Melektenjal's Kingdom*, and his work features in global publications: *Nieves*, *Fukt Magazine*, *Hidden Champion Magazine*, *Hi-Fructose Magazine*, and *Le Monde Diplomatique*. Website:gromilovic.com, Ig:@davorgromilovic

Haela Hunt-Hendrix:
Haela Hunt-Hendrix (b. 1985, NYC) is a composer, musician, artist and philosopher who combines her practices in a religious synthetic unity. She wrote, directed, edited and stars in the operatic film *Origin of the Alimonies*, which premiered in 2022 at Roadburn Festival with a live score performed by her musical project, Liturgy. She has presented solo sculpture exhibitions at Gern en Regalia (NYC, 2022), Triest (NYC, 2023) and Centralbanken (Oslo, 2024), and her debut full-length philosophical treatise is forthcoming from Repeater in 2025. Twitter: @LITVRGY

Cam Jennings:
Cam is a multidisciplinary artist working primarily with paintings and tattoos. Inspired by surrealism, abstraction, anthropology and religion, Cams work attempts to amalgamate and question reality. He has work in multiple publications as well as shows inside and outside Canada. Based in Vancouver, Canada. Ig:@skinnycam

Steve Latta:
Steve Latta is a Brooklyn, New York based artist whose painting explores the mysterious place where altered states, mysticism, philosophy of mind, and the natural sciences converge. Website:stevelatta.com, Ig:steve.painting.perception

Sven Loven:
Sven Loven is an American artist from Manhattan who graduated from the Cooper Union School of Art in 2002. He is now involved in anti-materialist agitation. Website:svenloven.com

Catherine McGuire:
Catherine McGuire is a writer/artist with a deep concern for our planet's future, with five decades of published poetry, six poetry chapbooks, a full-length poetry book, *Elegy for the 21st Century*, a SF novel, *Lifeline* and book of short stories, *The Dream Hunt and Other Tales*.

Jake Robertson:
Jake Robertson is a photographer, illustrator and psychotherapist based in Sarasota, FL. His work creates an ongoing exploration of identity transformation and the formation of identity through change. Ig:@glowinggiant

Lorraine Schein:
Lorraine Schein is a New York writer and poet. Her work has appeared in *VICE Terraform*, *Strange Horizons*, *Scientific American*, *Witches & Pagans*, and *Michigan Quarterly*, and in the anthologies *Wild Women* and *Tragedy Queens: Stories Inspired by Lana del Rey & Sylvia Plath*. *The Futurist's Mistress*, her poetry book, is available from Mayapple Press. Her book, *The Lady Anarchist Cafe*, is out now from Autonomedia.

Emma Stern:
Emma Stern is a New York-based artist known for her vibrant, hyperreal oil paintings that blend traditional techniques with digital aesthetics. Using 3D modeling software, Stern creates fantastical "lava baby" avatar subjects which she then renders on canvas, exploring themes of subversion, femininity, and self-portraiture, while employing persistent motifs of perversion, fantasy, and an off-brand feminism. Ig:lava_baby

Paul van Trigt:
Paul van Trigt is a multidisciplinary artist who works in collage/mixed-media, photocopy manipulation and experimental sound based in Victoria, BC. Ig:p.vantrigt

Amanda Yyskamp:
Amanda Yskamp is a writer and a collagist. Her art has appeared in such magazines as *Black Rabbit*, *Riddled with Arrows*, and *Stoneboat*. She is the poetry editor and frequent cover artist for WordRunner chapbooks. She lives on the 10-year flood plain of the Russian River, teaching writing from her online classroom and serving as a librarian at the local elementary school. Website:amandayskamp.crevado.com

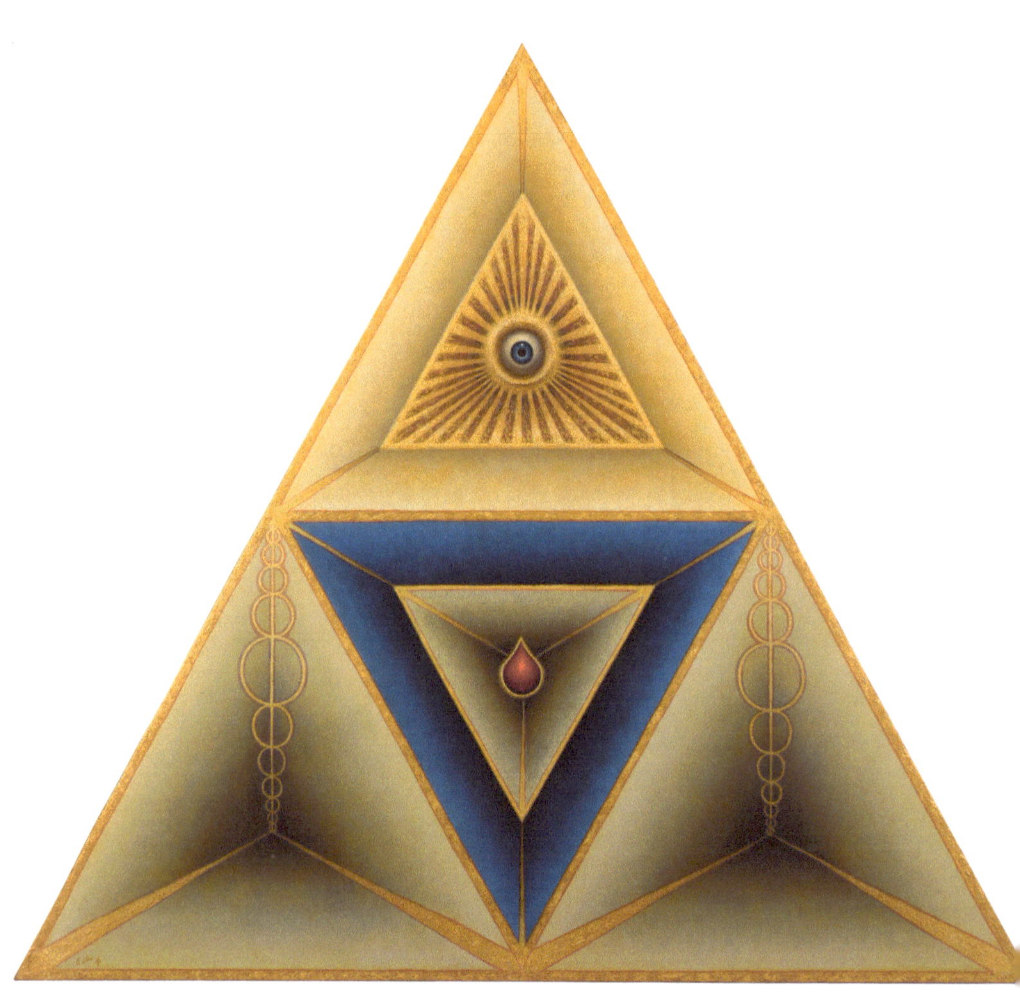

Steve Latta